MICROSOFT CERTIFIED SYSTEMS ENGINEER

TEST YOURSELF MCSE

Windows® 2000 Professional

(Exam 70-210)

Syngress Media, Inc.

Osborne/McGraw-Hill

Berkeley New York St. Louis San Francisco Auckland Bogotá
Hamburg London Madrid Mexico City Milan Montreal New Delhi
Panama City Paris São Paulo Singapore Sydney Tokyo Toronto

Osborne/**McGraw-Hill**
2600 Tenth Street
Berkeley, California 94710
U.S.A.

For information on translations or book distributors outside the U.S.A., or to arrange bulk purchase discounts for sales promotions, premiums, or fund-raisers, please contact Osborne/**McGraw-Hill** at the above address.

Test Yourself MCSE Windows 2000 Professional (Exam 70-210)

567890 CUS CUS 0198765432

ISBN 0-07-212769-4

KEY	SERIAL NUMBER
001	BHYRECXIO8
002	1WD5VBCVT8
003	Q2BFOIPB7C
004	QSILINC5EC
005	Q2CEBFTM9Z

Publisher
Brandon A. Nordin

Vice President and Associate Publisher
Scott Rogers

Editorial Director
Gareth Hancock

Associate Acquisitions Editor
Timothy Green

Editorial Management
Syngress Media, Inc.

Project Editor
Mark Listewnik

Project Manager
Laurie Stewart

Acquisitions Coordinator
Jessica Wilson

Technical Editor
James Truscott

Proofreaders
Dann McDorman,
Alison Moncrieff

Copy Editor
Ann Parkinson

Computer Designer
Maureen Forys,
Happenstance Type-O-Rama

Illustrator
Jeff Wilson

Series Design
Maureen Forys,
Happenstance Type-O-Rama

Cover Design
Greg Scott

This book was composed with QuarkXPress 4.11 on a Macintosh G4.

About Syngress Media

Syngress Media creates books and software for Information Technology professionals seeking skill enhancement and career advancement. Its products are designed to comply with vendor and industry standard course curricula, and are optimized for certification exam preparation. Visit the Syngress Web site at www.syngress.com.

Author

Joli Ballew (MCSE, MCT, and A+) is a technology trainer, writer, and network consultant in the Dallas area. Some of her previous employment positions have included technical writing, educational content consulting, working as a PC technician, a network administrator, a high school algebra teacher, and an MCSE instructor at Eastfield Community College. While teaching in the public school system, she achieved many acclamations for student achievement.

Joli attended high school at the Performing Arts Magnet in Dallas where she studied music and the arts and was a member of the National Honor Society. She attended college at the University of Texas at Arlington and graduated with a Bachelor's degree in Mathematics and a minor in English. The following year, she earned her Texas Teaching Certificate from the State of Texas. After teaching math and algebra for ten years, she decided to change careers and enter the world of computing. She earned all of her certifications in 14 months with the help of Dr. Tom Shinder at Eastfield Community College and entered the field of computer training and consulting soon thereafter. Joli spends her spare time golfing and surfing the Net and spending time with her wonderful family and friends.

Technical Editor

James Truscott (MCSE, MCP+I, and Network+) is an instructor in the MCSE program at Eastfield College and the Dallas County Community College District. He is also Senior Instructor for the Cowell Corporation and is teaching the Windows 2000 track for CLC Corporation in Dallas, Texas. He is also working with DigitalThink of California, developing online training courses for Windows 2000.

James is the Webmaster for Cowell Corporation in Richardson, Texas, and provides consulting services for several Dallas-based businesses. His passion for computers started back in the 1960s when he was a programmer for Bell Telephone. One of his current projects includes developing Web sites for his students.

Technical Reviewer

Stace Cunningham (CMISS, CCNA, MCSE, CLSE, COS/2E, CLSI, COS/2I, CLSA, MCPS, and A+) operates SDC Consulting in Biloxi, Mississippi. He has assisted several clients, including a casino, in the development and implementation of their networks, which range in size from 20 nodes to over 12,000 nodes. Stace has been heavily involved in technology for over 14 years. During that time he has participated as a Technical Contributor for the IIS 3.0 exam, SMS 1.2 exam, Proxy Server 1.0 exam, Exchange Server 5.0 and 5.5 exams, Proxy Server 2.0 exam, IIS 4.0 exam, IEAK exam, and the revised Windows 95 exam.

Stace was an active contributor to The SANS Institute booklet "Windows NT Security Step by Step." In addition, he has co-authored 20 books published by Osborne/McGraw-Hill, Microsoft Press, and Syngress Media. He has also served as technical editor for several other books published by Osborne/McGraw-Hill, Microsoft Press, and Syngress Media. Recently, an article written by Stace appeared in *Internet Security Advisor* magazine.

His wife Martha and daughter Marissa are very supportive of the time he spends with the computers, routers, and firewalls in his "lab." Without their love and support, he would not be able to accomplish the goals he has set for himself.

ACKNOWLEDGMENTS

We would like to thank the following people:

- All the incredibly hard-working folks at Osborne/McGraw-Hill: Brandon Nordin, Scott Rogers, Gareth Hancock, Tim Green, and Jessica Wilson for their help in launching a great series and being solid team players.

- Monica Kilwine at Microsoft Corp., for being patient and diligent in answering all our questions.

- Laurie Stewart and Maureen Forys for their help in fine-tuning the project.

CONTENTS

✗ 11 Implementing, Monitoring, and Troubleshooting Security and User Accounts **227**

Practice Exam **249**

Glossary **287**

PREFACE

This book's primary objective is to help you prepare for the MCSE Installing, Configuring, and Administering Windows 2000 Professional exam under the new Windows 2000 certification track. As the Microsoft program transitions from Windows NT 4.0, it will become increasingly important that current and aspiring IT professionals have multiple resources available to assist them in increasing their knowledge and building their skills.

At the time of publication, all the exam objectives have been posted on the Microsoft Web site and the beta exam process has been completed. Microsoft has announced its commitment to measuring real-world skills. This book is designed with that premise in mind; its authors have practical experience in the field, using the Windows 2000 operating systems in hands-on situations and have followed the development of the product since early beta versions.

In This Book

This book is organized in such a way as to serve as a review for the MCSE Installing, Configuring, and Administering Microsoft Windows 2000 Professional exam for both experienced Windows NT professionals and newcomers to Microsoft networking technologies. Each chapter covers a major aspect of the exam, with an emphasis on the "why" as well as the "how to" of working with and supporting Windows 2000 as a network administrator or engineer.

In Every Chapter

We've created a set of chapter components that call your attention to important items, reinforce important points, and provide helpful exam-taking hints. Take a look at what you'll find in every chapter.

Test Yourself Objectives

Every chapter begins with a list of Test Yourself Objectives—what you need to know in order to pass the section on the exam dealing with the chapter topic. Each objective in this list will be discussed in the chapter and can be easily identified by the clear headings that give the name and corresponding number of the objective, so you'll always know an objective when you see it! Objectives are drilled down to the most important details—essentially what you need to know about the objectives and what to expect from the exam in relation to them. Should you find you need further review on any particular objective, you will find that the objective headings correspond to the chapters of Osborne/McGraw-Hill's *MCSE Windows 2000 Professional Study Guide*.

Exam Watch Notes

Exam Watch notes call attention to information about, and potential pitfalls in, the exam. These helpful hints are written by authors who have taken the exams and received their certification; who better to tell you what to worry about? They know what you're about to go through!

Practice Questions and Answers

In each chapter you will find detailed practice questions for the exam, followed by a Quick Answer Key where you can quickly check your answers. The In-Depth Answers section contains full explanations of both the correct and incorrect choices.

The Practice Exam

If you have had your fill of explanations, review questions, and answers, the time has come to test your knowledge. Turn toward the end of this book to the Practice Exam where you'll find a simulation exam. Lock yourself in your office or clear the kitchen table, set a timer, and jump in.

About the Web Site

Syngress Media and Osborne/McGraw-Hill invite you to download one free practice exam for the MCSE Installing, Configuring, and Administering Microsoft Windows 2000 Professional exam. Please visit www.syngress.com or www.certificationpress.com for details.

MCSE CERTIFICATION

This book is designed to help you prepare for the MCSE Installing, Configuring, and Administering Microsoft Windows 2000 Professional exam. It was written to give you an opportunity to review all the important topics that are targeted for the exam.

The nature of the Information Technology industry is changing rapidly, and the requirements and specifications for certification can change just as quickly without notice. Table 1 shows you the different certification tracks you can take. Please note that they accurately reflect the requirements at the time of this book's publication. You should regularly visit Microsoft's Web site at http://www.microsoft.com/mcp/certstep/mcse.htm to get the most up to date information on the entire MCSE program.

TABLE 1	Core Exams

Windows 2000 Certification Track

Track 1: Candidates Who Have *Not* Already Passed Windows NT 4.0 Exams
All four of the following core exams are required:
Exam 70-210: Installing, Configuring, and Administering Microsoft Windows 2000 Professional
Exam 70-215: Installing, Configuring, and Administering Microsoft Windows 2000 Server
Exam 70-216: Implementing and Administering a Microsoft Windows 2000 Network Infrastructure
Exam 70-217: Implementing and Administering a Microsoft Windows 2000 Directory Services Infrastructure

Track 2: Candidates Who Have Passed Three Windows NT 4.0 Exams (Exams 70-067, 70-068, and 70-073)

Instead of the four core exams above, you may take the following:

Exam 70-240: Microsoft Windows 2000 Accelerated Exam for MCPs Certified on Microsoft Windows NT 4.0.

The accelerated exam will be available until December 31, 2001. It covers the core competencies of exams 70-210, 70-215, 70-216, and 70-217.

PLUS—All Candidates

One of the following core exams are required:

*Exam 70-219:** Designing a Microsoft Windows 2000 Directory Services Infrastructure

*Exam 70-220:** Designing Security for a Microsoft Windows 2000 Network

*Exam 70-221:** Designing a Microsoft Windows 2000 Network Infrastructure

Two elective exams are required:

Any current MCSE electives when the Windows 2000 exams listed above are released in their live versions. **Electives scheduled for retirement will not be considered current.** Selected third-party certifications that focus on interoperability will be accepted as an alternative to one elective exam.

*Exam 70-219:** Designing a Microsoft Windows 2000 Directory Services Infrastructure

*Exam 70-220:** Designing Security for a Microsoft Windows 2000 Network

*Exam 70-221:** Designing a Microsoft Windows 2000 Network Infrastructure

Exam 70-222: Upgrading from Microsoft Windows NT 4.0 to Microsoft Windows 2000

* Note that some of the Windows 2000 core exams can be used as elective exams as well. An exam that is used to meet the design requirement cannot also count as an elective. Each exam can only be counted once in the Windows 2000 Certification.

Let's look at the two scenarios in Table 1. The first applies to the person who has already taken the Windows NT 4.0 Server (70-067), Windows NT 4.0 Workstation (70-073), and Windows NT 4.0 Server in the Enterprise (70-068) exams. The second scenario covers the situation of the person who has not completed those Windows NT 4.0 exams and would like to concentrate ONLY on Windows 2000.

In the first scenario, you have the option of taking all four Windows 2000 core exams, or you can take the Windows 2000 Accelerated Exam for MCPs if you have already passed exams 70-067, 70-068, and 70-073. (Note that you must have passed those specific exams to qualify for the Accelerated Exam; if you have fulfilled your NT 4.0 MCSE requirements by passing the Windows 95 or Windows 98 exam as your client operating system option, and did not take the NT Workstation Exam, you don't qualify.)

After completing the core requirements, either by passing the four core exams or the one Accelerated exam, you must pass a "design" exam. The design exams include Designing a Microsoft Windows 2000 Directory Services Infrastructure (70-219), Designing Security for Microsoft Windows 2000 Network (70-220), and Designing a Microsoft Windows 2000 Network Infrastructure (70-221). One design exam is REQUIRED.

You also must pass two exams from the list of electives. However, you cannot use the design exam that you took as an elective. Each exam can only count once toward certification. This includes any of the MCSE electives that are current when the Windows 2000 exams are released. In summary, you would take a total of at least two more exams, the upgrade exam and the design exam. Any additional exams would be dependent on which electives the candidate may have already completed.

In the second scenario, if you have not completed, and do not plan to complete the Core Windows NT 4.0 exams, you must pass the four core Windows 2000 exams, one design exam, and two elective exams. Again, no exam can be counted twice. In this case, you must pass a total of seven exams to obtain the Windows 2000 MCSE certification.

HOW TO TAKE A MICROSOFT CERTIFICATION EXAM

If you have taken a Microsoft Certification exam before, we have some good news and some bad news. The good news is that the new testing formats will be a true measure of your ability and knowledge. Microsoft has "raised the bar" for its Windows 2000 certification exams. If you are an expert in the Windows 2000 operating system and can troubleshoot and engineer efficient, cost effective solutions using Windows 2000, you will have no difficulty with the new exams.

The bad news is that if you have used resources such as "brain-dumps," boot camps, or exam-specific practice tests as your only method of test preparation, you will undoubtedly fail your Windows 2000 exams. The new Windows 2000 MCSE exams will test your knowledge and your ability to apply that knowledge in more sophisticated and accurate ways than was expected for the MCSE exams for Windows NT 4.0.

In the Windows 2000 exams, Microsoft will use a variety of testing formats that include product simulations, adaptive testing, drag-and-drop matching, and possibly even "fill-in-the-blank" questions (also called "free response" questions). The test-taking process will measure the examinee's fundamental knowledge of the Windows 2000 operating system rather than the ability to memorize a few facts and then answer a few simple multiple-choice questions.

In addition, the "pool" of questions for each exam will significantly increase. The greater number of questions combined with the adaptive testing techniques will enhance the validity and security of the certification process.

We will begin by looking at the purpose, focus, and structure of Microsoft certification tests and examining the effect that these factors have on the kinds of questions you will face on your certification exams. We will define the structure of exam questions and investigate some common formats. Next, we will present a strategy for answering these questions. Finally, we will give some specific guidelines on what you should do on the day of your test.

Why Vendor Certification?

The Microsoft Certified Professional program, like the certification programs from Cisco, Novell, Oracle, and other software vendors, is maintained for the ultimate purpose of increasing the corporation's profits. A successful vendor certification program accomplishes this goal by helping to create a pool of experts in a company's software and by "branding" these experts so companies using the software can identify them.

We know that vendor certification has become increasingly popular in the last few years because it helps employers find qualified workers and because it helps software vendors like Microsoft sell their products. But why vendor certification rather than a more traditional approach like a college degree in computer science? A college education is a broadening and enriching experience, but a degree in computer science does not prepare students for most jobs in the IT industry.

A common truism in our business states, "If you are out of the IT industry for three years and want to return, you have to start over." The problem, of course, is *timeliness*; if a first-year student learns about a specific computer program, it probably will no longer be in wide use when he or she graduates. Although some colleges are trying to integrate Microsoft certification into their curriculum, the problem is not really a flaw in higher education, but a characteristic of the IT industry. Computer software is changing so rapidly that a four-year college just can't keep up.

A marked characteristic of the Microsoft certification program is an emphasis on performing specific job tasks rather than merely gathering knowledge. It may come as a shock, but most potential employers do not care how much you know about the theory of operating systems, networking, or database design. As one IT manager put it, "I don't really care what my employees know about the theory of our network. We don't need someone to sit at a desk and think about it. We need people who can actually do something to make it work better."

You should not think that this attitude is some kind of anti-intellectual revolt against "book learning." Knowledge is a necessary prerequisite, but it is not enough. More than one company has hired a computer science graduate as a network administrator, only to learn that the new employee has no idea how to add users, assign permissions, or perform the other day-to-day tasks necessary to maintain a network. This brings us to the second major characteristic of Microsoft certification that affects the questions you must be prepared to answer. In addition to timeliness, Microsoft certification is also job-task oriented.

The timeliness of Microsoft's certification program is obvious and is inherent in the fact that you will be tested on current versions of software in wide use today. The job-task orientation of Microsoft certification is almost as obvious, but testing real-world job skills using a computer-based test is not easy.

Computerized Testing

Considering the popularity of Microsoft certification, and the fact that certification candidates are spread around the world, the only practical way to administer tests for the certification program is through Sylvan Prometric or Vue testing centers, which operate internationally. Sylvan Prometric and Vue provide proctor testing services for Microsoft, Oracle, Novell, Lotus, and the A+ computer technician certification. Although the IT industry accounts for much of Sylvan's revenue, the company provides services for a number of other businesses and organizations, such as FAA pre-flight pilot tests. Historically, several hundred questions were developed for a new Microsoft certification exam. The Windows 2000 MCSE exam pool is expected to contain hundreds of new questions. Microsoft is aware that many new MCSE candidates have been able to access information on test questions via the Internet or other resources. The company is very concerned about maintaining the MCSE as a "premium" certification. The significant increase in the number of test questions, together with stronger enforcement of the NDA (Non-disclosure agreement) will ensure that a higher standard for certification is attained.

Microsoft treats the test-building process very seriously. Test questions are first reviewed by a number of subject matter experts for technical accuracy and then are presented in a beta test. Taking the beta test may require several hours, due to the large number of questions. After a few weeks, Microsoft Certification uses the statistical feedback from Sylvan to check the performance of the beta questions. The beta test group for the Windows 2000 certification series included MCTs, MCSEs, and members of Microsoft's rapid deployment partners groups. Because the exams will be normalized based on this population, you can be sure that the passing scores will be difficult to achieve without detailed product knowledge.

Questions are discarded if most test takers get them right (too easy) or wrong (too difficult), and a number of other statistical measures are taken of each question. Although the scope of our discussion precludes a rigorous treatment of question analysis, you should be aware that Microsoft and other vendors spend a great deal of time and effort making sure their exam questions are valid.

The questions that survive statistical analysis form the pool of questions for the final certification exam.

Test Structure

The questions in a Microsoft form test will not be equally weighted. From what we can tell at the present time, different questions are given a value based on the level of difficulty. You will get more credit for getting a difficult question correct than if you got an easy one correct. Because the questions are weighted differently, and because the exams will likely use the adapter method of testing, your score will not bear any relationship to how many questions you answered correctly.

Microsoft has implemented *adaptive* testing. When an adaptive test begins, the candidate is first given a level three question. If it is answered correctly, a question from the next higher level is presented, and an incorrect response results in a question from the next lower level. When 15 to 20 questions have been answered in this manner, the scoring algorithm is able to predict, with a high degree of statistical certainty, whether the candidate would pass or fail if all the questions in the form were answered. When the required degree of certainty is attained, the test ends and the candidate receives a pass/fail grade.

Adaptive testing has some definite advantages for everyone involved in the certification process. Adaptive tests allow Sylvan Prometric or Vue to deliver more tests with the same resources, as certification candidates often are in and out in 30 minutes or less. For candidates, the "fatigue factor" is reduced due to the shortened testing time. For Microsoft, adaptive testing means that fewer test questions are exposed to each candidate, and this can enhance the security, and therefore the overall validity, of certification tests.

One possible problem you may have with adaptive testing is that you are not allowed to mark and revisit questions. Since the adaptive algorithm is interactive, and all questions but the first are selected on the basis of your response to the previous question, it is not possible to skip a particular question or change an answer.

Question Types

Computerized test questions can be presented in a number of ways. Some of the possible formats are used on Microsoft certification exams and some are not.

True/False Questions

We are all familiar with True/False questions, but because of the inherent 50 percent chance of guessing the correct answer, you will not see questions of this type on Microsoft certification exams.

Multiple-Choice Questions

The majority of Microsoft certification questions are in the multiple-choice format, with either a single correct answer or multiple correct answers. One interesting variation on multiple-choice questions with multiple correct answers is whether or not the candidate is told how many answers are correct.

EXAMPLE:

Which two files can be altered to configure the MS-DOS environment? (Choose two.)

or

Which files can be altered to configure the MS-DOS environment? (Choose all that apply.)

You may see both variations on Microsoft certification exams, but the trend seems to be toward the first type, where candidates are told explicitly how many answers are correct. Questions of the "choose all that apply" variety are more difficult and can be merely confusing.

Graphical Questions

One or more graphical elements are sometimes used as exhibits to help present or clarify an exam question. These elements may take the form of a network diagram, pictures of networking components, or screen shots from the software on which you are being tested. It is often easier to present the concepts required for a complex performance-based scenario with a graphic than with words.

Test questions known as *hotspots* actually incorporate graphics as part of the answer. These questions ask the certification candidate to click on a location or graphical element to answer the question. For example, you might be shown the diagram of a network and asked to click on an appropriate location for a router. The answer is correct if the candidate clicks within the *hotspot* that defines the correct location.

Free Response Questions

Another kind of question you sometimes see on Microsoft certification exams requires a *free response* or type-in answer. An example of this type of question might present a TCP/IP network scenario and ask the candidate to calculate and enter the correct subnet mask in dotted decimal notation.

Simulation Questions

Simulation questions provide a method for Microsoft to test how familiar the test taker is with the actual product interface and the candidate's ability to quickly implement a task using the interface. These questions will present an actual Windows 2000 interface that you must work with to solve a problem or implement a solution. If you are familiar with the product, you will be able to answer these questions quickly, and they will be the easiest questions on the exam. However, if you are not accustomed to working with Windows 2000, these questions will be difficult for you to answer. This is why actual hands-on practice with Windows 2000 is so important!

Knowledge-Based and Performance-Based Questions

Microsoft Certification develops a blueprint for each Microsoft certification exam with input from subject matter experts. This blueprint defines the content areas and objectives for each test, and each test question is created to test a specific objective. The basic information from the examination blueprint can be found on Microsoft's Web site in the Exam Prep Guide for each test.

Psychometricians (psychologists who specialize in designing and analyzing tests) categorize test questions as knowledge-based or performance-based. As the names imply, knowledge-based questions are designed to test knowledge, while performance-based questions are designed to test performance.

Some objectives demand a knowledge-based question. For example, objectives that use verbs like *list* and *identify* tend to test only what you know, not what you can do.

EXAMPLE:

Objective: Identify the MS-DOS configuration files.

Which two files can be altered to configure the MS-DOS environment? (Choose two.)

A. COMMAND.COM

B. AUTOEXEC.BAT

C. IO.SYS

D. CONFIG.SYS

Correct answers: B, D

Other objectives use action verbs like *install, configure,* and *troubleshoot* to define job tasks. These objectives can often be tested with either a knowledge-based question or a performance-based question.

EXAMPLE:

Objective: Configure an MS-DOS installation appropriately using the PATH statement in AUTOEXEC.BAT.

Knowledge-based question:

What is the correct syntax to set a path to the D: directory in AUTOEXEC.BAT?

A. SET PATH EQUAL TO D:

B. PATH D:

C. SETPATH D:

D. D:EQUALS PATH

Correct answer: B

Performance-based question:

Your company uses several DOS accounting applications that access a group of common utility programs. What is the best strategy for configuring the computers in the accounting department so that the accounting applications will always be able to access the utility programs?

A. Store all the utilities on a single floppy disk and make a copy of the disk for each computer in the accounting department.

B. Copy all the utilities to a directory on the C drive of each computer in the accounting department and add a PATH statement pointing to this directory in the AUTOEXEC.BAT files.

C. Copy all the utilities to all application directories on each computer in the accounting department.

D. Place all the utilities in the C directory on each computer, because the C directory is automatically included in the PATH statement when AUTOEXEC.BAT is executed.

Correct answer: B

Even in this simple example, the superiority of the performance-based question is obvious. Whereas the knowledge-based question asks for a single fact, the performance-based question presents a real-life situation and requires that you make a decision based on this scenario. Thus, performance-based questions give more bang (validity) for the test author's buck (individual question).

Testing Job Performance

We have said that Microsoft certification focuses on timeliness and the ability to perform job tasks. We have also introduced the concept of performance-based questions, but even performance-based multiple-choice questions do not really measure performance. Another strategy is needed to test job skills.

Given unlimited resources, it is not difficult to test job skills. In an ideal world, Microsoft would fly MCP candidates to Redmond, place them in a controlled environment with a team of experts, and ask them to plan, install, maintain, and troubleshoot a Windows network. In a few days at most, the experts could reach a valid decision as to whether each candidate should or should not be granted MCDBA or MCSE status. Needless to say, this is not likely to happen.

Closer to reality, another way to test performance is by using the actual software and creating a testing program to present tasks and automatically grade a candidate's performance when the tasks are completed. This *cooperative* approach would be practical in some testing situations, but the same test that is presented to MCP candidates in Boston must also be available in Bahrain and Botswana. The most workable solution for measuring performance in today's testing environment is a *simulation* program. When the program is launched during a test, the candidate sees a simulation of the actual software that looks, and behaves, just like the real thing. When the testing software presents a task, the simulation program is launched and the candidate performs the required task. The testing software then grades the candidate's performance on the required task and moves to the next question. Microsoft has introduced simulation questions on the certification exam for Internet Information Server 4.0. Simulation questions provide many advantages over other testing methodologies, and simulations are expected to become increasingly important in the Microsoft certification program. For example, studies have shown that there is a very high correlation between the ability to perform simulated tasks on a computer-based test and the ability to perform the actual job tasks. Thus, simulations enhance the validity of the certification process.

Another truly wonderful benefit of simulations is in the area of test security. It is just not possible to cheat on a simulation question. In fact, you will be told exactly what tasks you are expected to perform on the test. How can a certification candidate cheat? By learning to perform the tasks? What a concept!

Study Strategies

There are appropriate ways to study for the different types of questions you will see on a Microsoft certification exam.

Knowledge-Based Questions

Knowledge-based questions require that you memorize facts. There are hundreds of facts inherent in every content area of every Microsoft certification exam. There are several keys to memorizing facts:

Repetition The more times your brain is exposed to a fact, the more likely you are to remember it.

Association Connecting facts within a logical framework makes them easier to remember.

Motor Association It is often easier to remember something if you write it down or perform some other physical act, like clicking on a practice test answer.

We have said that the emphasis of Microsoft certification is job performance and that there are very few knowledge-based questions on Microsoft certification exams. Why should you waste a lot of time learning filenames, IP address formulas, and other minutiae? Read on.

Performance-Based Questions

Most of the questions you will face on a Microsoft certification exam are performance-based scenario questions. We have discussed the superiority of these questions over simple knowledge-based questions, but you should remember that the job-task orientation of Microsoft certification extends the knowledge you need to pass the exams; it does not replace this knowledge. Therefore, the first step in preparing for scenario questions is to absorb as many facts relating to the exam content areas as you can. In other words, go back to the previous section and follow the steps to prepare for an exam composed of knowledge-based questions.

The second step is to familiarize yourself with the format of the questions you are likely to see on the exam. You can do this by answering the questions in this book, or by using Microsoft assessment tests. The day of your test is not the time to be surprised by the construction of Microsoft exam questions.

At best, performance-based scenario questions really do test certification candidates at a higher cognitive level than knowledge-based questions. At worst, these questions can test your reading comprehension and test-taking ability rather than your ability to use Microsoft products. Be sure to get in the habit of reading the question carefully to determine what is being asked.

The third step in preparing for Microsoft scenario questions is to adopt the following attitude: Multiple-choice questions aren't really performance-based. It is all a cruel lie.

These scenario questions are just knowledge-based questions with a story wrapped around them.

To answer a scenario question, you have to sift through the story to the underlying facts of the situation and apply your knowledge to determine the correct answer. This may sound silly at first, but the process we go through in solving real-life problems is quite similar. The key concept is that every scenario question (and every real-life problem) has a fact at its center, and if we can identify that fact, we can answer the question.

Simulations

Simulation questions really do measure your ability to perform job tasks. You must be able to perform the specified tasks. One of the ways to prepare for simulation questions is to get experience with the actual software. If you have the resources, this is a great way to prepare for simulation questions.

SIGNING UP

Signing up to take a Microsoft certification exam is easy. Sylvan Prometric or Vue operators in each country can schedule tests at any testing center. There are, however, a few things you should know:

- If you call Sylvan Prometric or Vue during a busy time, get a cup of coffee first because you may be in for a long wait. The exam providers do an excellent job, but everyone in the world seems to want to sign up for a test on Monday morning.

- You will need your social security number or some other unique identifier to sign up for a test, so have it at hand.

- Pay for your test by credit card if at all possible. This makes things easier, and you can even schedule tests for the same day you call, if space is available at your local testing center.

- Know the number and title of the test you want to take before you call. This is not essential, and the Sylvan operators will help you if they can. Having this information in advance, however, speeds up and improves the accuracy of the registration process.

TAKING THE TEST

Teachers have always told you not to try to cram for exams because it does no good. If you are faced with a knowledge-based test requiring only that you regurgitate facts, cramming can mean the difference between passing and failing. This is not the case, however, with Microsoft certification exams. If you don't know it the night before, don't bother to stay up and cram.

Instead, create a schedule and stick to it. Plan your study time carefully, and do not schedule your test until you think you are ready to succeed. Follow these guidelines on the day of your exam:

- Get a good night's sleep. The scenario questions you will face on a Microsoft certification exam require a clear head.

- Remember to take two forms of identification—at least one with a picture. A driver's license with your picture and social security or credit card is acceptable.

- Leave home in time to arrive at your testing center a few minutes early. It is not a good idea to feel rushed as you begin your exam.

- Do not spend too much time on any one question. You cannot mark and revisit questions on an adaptive test, so you must do your best on each question as you go.

- If you do not know the answer to a question, try to eliminate the obviously wrong answers and guess from the rest. If you can eliminate two out of four options, you have a 50 percent chance of guessing the correct answer.

- For scenario questions, follow the steps we outlined earlier. Read the question carefully and try to identify the facts at the center of the story.

Finally, we would advise anyone attempting to earn Microsoft MCDBA and MCSE certification to adopt a philosophical attitude. The Windows 2000 MCSE will be the most difficult MCSE ever to be offered. The questions will be at a higher cognitive level than seen on all previous MCSE exams. Therefore, even if you are the kind of person who never fails a test, you are likely to fail at least one Windows 2000 certification test somewhere along the way. Do not get discouraged. Microsoft wants to ensure the value of your certification. Moreover, it will attempt to so by keeping the standard as high as possible. If Microsoft certification were easy to obtain, more people would have it, and it would not be so respected and so valuable to your future in the IT industry.

1

Installing
Windows 2000
Professional

This chapter contains a concise summary of Windows 2000 Professional installation, and presents a number of self-test questions to assess your knowledge of the Windows 2000 installation process. It is divided into four parts: attended installations, upgrading, deploying service packs, and troubleshooting failed installations. The exam objectives in this area will test your knowledge of the installation process, hardware and software compatibility, file systems choices, and requirements for network installations. You will need to be extremely knowledgeable on these subjects before attempting Microsoft exam 70-210.

Some of the more important factors to consider when installing and deploying Windows 2000 Professional include: checking the HCL (Hardware Compatibility List); choosing a file system, FAT, FAT 32, and NTFS; if a dual-boot is needed, the type of installation required; and software compatibility. If you are installing over a network, a distribution server will be necessary.

TEST YOURSELF OBJECTIVE 1.01

Performing an Attended Installation of Windows 2000 Professional

An attended installation of Windows 2000 Professional is the most fundamental type of installation. Be familiar with the minimum system requirements, including a 133MHz or higher Pentium-compatible CPU; 64MB of RAM recommended minimum; at least 650MB of disk space (2GB recommended), additional free hard disk space is required if you are installing over a network; a network interface card (if you are connected to a network); video display adapter and monitor; CD-ROM (12X required, none for a network installation); and keyboard and mouse. Other points to remember include the following:

- You should check your existing hardware against the Hardware Compatibility List (HCL).

- Windows 2000 can be installed on a FAT, FAT32, or NTFS partition. NTFS is recommended for single-boot configurations. For dual-booting with Windows 95/98, you may choose the FAT or FAT32 file system.

- You can perform an attended installation of Windows 2000 Professional from a CD-ROM or across the network.

■ You can upgrade existing Windows 9*x* and NT 3.51 and higher operating systems (with the exception of Back Office Small Business Server) to Windows 2000, or install it separately for single or multi-boot configurations.

■ When a large number of installations are required, you may choose to install Windows 2000 Professional over the network.

■ You must have a valid product key in order to install Windows 2000 Professional.

■ To install Windows 2000 Professional over the network, you need to set up a distribution server.

exam
ⓦatch

Put in some extra study time understanding the file systems FAT, FAT32, and NTFS. Know that Microsoft suggests you ALWAYS use NTFS unless you will be dual-booting with another operating system like Windows 98. There is no file-level security with FAT or FAT32, as is available in NTFS. NTFS also has folder-level security, disk compression, disk quotas, and file and folder encryption. When choosing not to use NTFS, setup will determine whether the partition is formatted as FAT or FAT32, based on the size of the partition. A partition smaller than 2GB will be partitioned as FAT, while one larger will be set up as FAT32. If you choose a dual-boot scenario, only the system partition has to be FAT or FAT32, other drives can be NTFS. NT makes a 4GB FAT partition on which it can be installed. This can only be done in NT or Windows 2000, and not in DOS.

QUESTIONS

1.01: Performing an Attended Installation of Windows 2000 Professional

1. You are planning to install Windows 2000 Professional on the seven computers in your office. Before beginning the installation, which of the following tasks must be performed?

    A. Evaluate the hardware to ensure that it meets minimum system requirements.

    B. Determine whether you will upgrade or perform a fresh installation.

    C. Consider your options for partitioning your hard disk(s).

    D. Decide which file system(s) to deploy on each partition.

    E. All of the above.

2. Microsoft divides the installation process into four stages. Choose the stage number and description of the stage for the corresponding screen shot below.

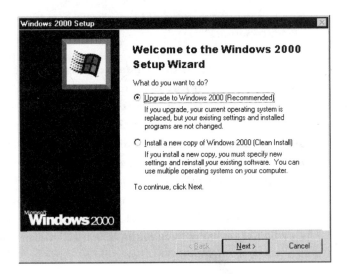

    A. Stage 1 (preparing hard disk and copies files)

    B. Stage 2 (graphical interface and information-gathering)

    C. Stage 3 (detecting NIC, installing networking software, and configuring protocols)

    D. Stage 4 (installing Start menu items, registering components, saving the configuration, and removing temporary files)

3. **Current Situation:** You wish to install Windows 2000 Professional on a computer currently running Windows NT 4.0 Workstation and connect to the present domain. The computer has a network interface card, is connected to the network, meets the hardware requirements on the HCL, and has a computer account created for it in the domain by a domain administrator.

Required Result: Install Windows 2000 Professional.

Optional Desired Results:

1. After installation, the user should be able to access the domain controller over the network.

2. The user's files and settings shall be preserved.

Proposed Solution: Install from the CD-ROM, choosing the option to install a new copy of Windows 2000 Professional (clean install). When prompted, choose to join a domain, and provide the name of the domain controller and the computer account name.

A. The proposed solution produces the required result and all of the optional results.

B. The proposed solution produces the required result and only one of the optional results.

C. The proposed solution produces the required result and only two of the optional results.

D. The proposed solution does not produce the required result.

4. Which one of the following statements is true concerning converting between FAT, FAT32, and NTFS?

A. Converting a FAT partition to NTFS causes all data to be lost.

B. You can convert from NTFS to FAT or FAT32 at any time, using the command line convert utility.

C. Data is preserved when you format the partition as NTFS.

D. You can convert a FAT or FAT32 partition to NTFS at any time, using the command line convert utility.

TEST YOURSELF OBJECTIVE 1.02

Upgrading to Windows 2000 Professional

Upgrading to Windows 2000 Professional is an option during Stage 2 of the installation process. Upgrading maintains most of the user's settings and preferences, and can be chosen if the computer is presently running one of the operating systems listed below. To upgrade Windows NT 3.5, upgrade to Windows NT 4.0 first, and then perform the Windows 2000 Professional upgrade. Windows 2000 can be used to print a report of the current status of your hardware and software using the Compatibility tool. This tool runs automatically when setup begins, but you can choose to run it before starting any upgrade to identify potential problems. Below are some other points to remember.

- Only Windows NT 3.51 and 4.0 Workstations, Windows 95, and Windows 98 can be upgraded to Windows 2000 Professional.

- You can upgrade using the CD-ROM, from a network distribution server or unattended.

- Make sure the computer meets the minimum hardware requirements.

- Make sure that all of the hardware and software is compatible with Windows 2000.

Make sure that you know the hardware is on the HCL before starting installation. The installation requirements are listed in the previous section. A hardware compatibility report can be generated in two ways: by running the Winnt32.exe /checkupgradeonly command, or by running the Chkupgrd.exe utility. The Winnt32.exe /checkupgradeonly command launches the Setup program and checks the hardware and software on your system, while the Chkupgrd.exe utility immediately generates a report. Both generate the same report as a text document.

QUESTIONS

1.02: Upgrading to Windows 2000 Professional

5. You are planning an installation of Windows 2000 Professional throughout your company. You are currently running 15 Windows NT 4.0 servers and 500 NT 4.0 workstations, and would like to do most of these installations over the network. You use TCP/IP as a network protocol. From the choices given

below, check all of the requirements necessary to install Windows 2000 from a network.

A. A distribution server that contains a shared folder with the installation files from the i386 folder on the Windows 2000 Professional CD-ROM

B. FAT partition on the target computer of at least 650MB

C. Network interface card on each computer and a connection to the network

D. All of the above

6. Your company is migrating to Windows 2000 products. You have been asked to install Windows 2000 Professional on a computer in your office that is currently running Windows NT Workstation. After placing the CD in the CD-ROM drive, which of the following commands could you use to begin the upgrade at this computer? (E is the drive letter for the CD-ROM.)

A. E:\i386\winnt32.exe

B. E:\i386\windows32.exe

C. E:\i386\setup.exe

D. E:\i386\install.exe

7. After running Winnt32.exe /checkupgradeonly, Mary Anne notices that her network interface card is not on the Hardware Compatibility List. What are her options?

A. Do not install Windows 2000 Professional; the upgrade will cause the system to crash.

B. Install Windows 2000 Professional and let the Setup program find the correct driver from its driver database.

C. Check with the manufacturer of the adapter and see if there is a newer version of the driver available.

D. Use the Windows 98 driver for the adapter.

Deploying Service Packs

Service packs are released by Microsoft to address issues concerning security and bugs in the software. These updates should be installed as they become available, tested for compatibility with other software and components on the system, and deployed throughout the enterprise.

Service packs no longer require that they be reinstalled after adding or deleting components, as with Windows NT. Windows 2000 automatically knows that a service pack has been applied and makes the appropriate changes to newly installed programs. Service-pack *slipstreaming* is a process in which you can install Windows 2000 with the service pack already applied to the installation files on a CD-ROM or distribution folder. You will not have to apply the service pack after installation of Windows 2000 Professional. Be aware of the items listed next.

- Microsoft periodically releases updates to Windows operating systems.

- These updates contain bug and security fixes called service packs.

- Service packs are installed using the Update.exe program.

- You don't have to reinstall service packs after adding or deleting components or services.

- You should test your service pack for software compatibility prior to deploying it.

- You can include a service pack in a distribution image.

- You can deploy service packs using group policies.

exam
ⓦatch

Be familiar with the idea of slipstreaming. Service packs can be included with installation files on a distribution server so that when the installation of Windows 2000 Professional is performed, the service packs are also installed. Know the Update.exe command and the /slip switch for applying a new service pack. Be familiar with the following files that are replaced when you apply a new service pack: Driver.cab, Layout.inf, Txtsetup.sif, and Dosnet.inf.

QUESTIONS

1.03: Deploying Service Packs

8. What utility program would you use to see the screen shot below and inform you of any service pack currently installed on the computer?

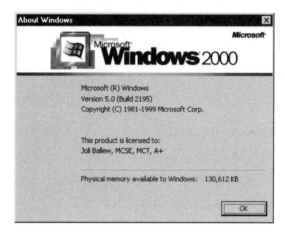

A. Winnt32.exe /v

B. Winnt32.exe /SP

C. Winver

D. Update.exe

9. Microsoft has just released a new service pack for Windows 2000 Professional, and you are planning to install it on a test machine before deploying it throughout your network. After installation, you would like to look over the changes made to the system. Which of the following files are replaced when a service pack is added to Windows 2000?

A. Driver.cab

B. Layout.inf

C. Txtsetup.sif

D. All of the above

E. A and C only

10. Which of the following statements are true regarding service packs?

   A. You can include service packs with a distribution image.

   B. When a service pack is applied, Windows 2000 tracks which service pack was installed, and which files were added and/or replaced which.

   C. You can see which service pack is currently installed on the computer by running the winver utility program.

   D. When a component or service is added or removed, if any of the required files were included in the service pack, the operating system will automatically retrieve those files from the service pack.

   E. All of the statements are true.

11. **Current Situation:** You are running Windows 2000 Professional on 50 network workstations. A service pack has been issued, tested by the company, and is now ready to be deployed to these computers.

   Required Result: Install the service pack on all the workstations on the network.

   Optional Desired Results:

   1. Alter the distribution's server installation files so the next network installation of Windows 2000 will include the service packs.

   2. The installation of the service pack at the workstations shall be unattended.

   Proposed Solution: Run Update.exe from the workstations. Run Update.exe /slip at the distribution server. Create an Unattend.txt file to correlate to the service pack installation and add the switch /u to the Update.exe command at the workstation.

   A. The proposed solution produces the required result and all of the optional results.

   B. The proposed solution produces the required result and only one of the optional results.

   C. The proposed solution produces the required result and only two of the optional results.

   D. The proposed solution does not produce the required result.

TEST YOURSELF OBJECTIVE 1.04

Troubleshooting Failed Installations

Occasionally, problems will arise when installing Windows 2000 Professional. It is imperative you are familiar with the troubleshooting tools available to you in Windows 2000. Setupact.log, Setuperr.log, Setupapi.log, and Setuplog.txt are all possible options. You can see these logs by exploring the C drive, opening the Winnt folder, and opening the appropriate file.

Additional problems may include a damaged CD-ROM, improper hardware, an installation partition that is too small, a bad network connection, not enough disk space, inability to find the domain controller and/or join a domain, and dependency service failures. Be prepared to address any or all of these issues on the Windows 2000 Professional exam. All points are listed below.

- If the installation CD-ROM is damaged, you will have to replace it.
- Ensure there is enough free disk space prior to installation.
- Make sure the domain controller is online and available.
- Verify that the DNS server is running.
- The Setupact.log contains details about the files that are copied during setup.
- The Setuperr.log contains details about errors that occurred during setup.
- The Setupapi.log contains details about the device driver files that were copied during setup.
- The Setuplog.txt contains additional information about the device driver files that were copied during setup.

exam
ⓦatch

Exam questions on troubleshooting installations may not involve problems during setup, such as being unable to find the server, join a domain, or even run the CD-ROM and begin installation. Some questions may address issues AFTER installation is complete. If Windows 2000 Professional fails to start, verify that all of the hardware is on the HCL, and that all of the hardware is being detected. Sometimes a dependency service will fail to start. Dependency service errors may occur because an incorrect adapter driver was loaded, or the adapter is not on the HCL. Also verify that you have installed the correct protocol and that the computer name is unique on the network.

QUESTIONS

1.04: Troubleshooting Failed Installations

12. Which of the following might cause the installation problem of being unable to connect to the domain controller?

    A. The domain name is typed incorrectly.

    B. The DNS service is not running on the domain controller.

    C. Network interface card is not on the HCL or is not working.

    D. All of the above.

    E. A and C only.

13. What is most likely the problem if, after installation and first boot of Windows 2000 Professional, a failure occurs involving a dependency service to start?

    A. Video card or video adapter

    B. Network card or network protocol

    C. Incorrect file system choice (FAT, FAT32, or NTFS)

    D. Insufficient disk space or RAM

14. Look at the following screen shot of the setuplog.txt file. Under what circumstances would you need to look at this file?

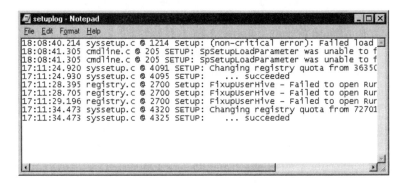

A. Disk space errors

B. Media errors

C. Domain controller errors

D. Device driver errors

Questions 15–17   This scenario should be used to answer questions 15, 16, and 17.

You currently have 25 workstations in your office and 5 domain controllers. 15 of the Workstations are Windows NT 3.5, and 10 are Windows 98. The domain controllers are running Windows NT 4.0 Server. None of the Windows NT 4.0 servers and Windows 98 computers have hardware conflicts with the HCL. The Windows NT 3.5 computers do not have CD-ROMs that are on the Windows 2000 HCL. You are part of a larger company and connect via a T1 line to the parent company in another state. You have been assigned the task of installing Windows 2000 Professional on all of the workstations.

15. Which of the existing computers would you upgrade to Windows 2000 Professional?

A. Windows 98 only

B. Windows 98 and Windows NT 3.5 workstations

C. All of the computers

D. Windows 98 and Windows NT 4.0 servers

16. It is necessary that the Windows 98 workstations be dual-boot configurations because some of the printers used in this department do not yet have Windows 2000 drivers written for them. They will be separated from the rest of the network and do not need any extra security measures set in place. Which file system would you use?

A. FAT or FAT 32.

B. NTFS.

C. CDFS.

D. Any of the above will work.

17. What would you do to upgrade the Windows NT 3.5 computers to Windows 2000?

    A. Run Winnt32.exe and choose to upgrade when prompted.

    B. Install from the four boot disks, choose to upgrade when prompted, and let Windows find a new driver for the CD-ROM in its driver database.

    C. Replace the CD-ROM with one on the HCL, install Windows 2000, and choose to upgrade when prompted.

    D. Replace the CD-ROM with one on the HCL, upgrade the systems to Windows NT 4.0, then install Windows 2000 and choose to upgrade when prompted.

LAB QUESTION

Objectives 1.01–1.04

Current Situation: You have a computer in your printing department running Windows 98. The entire company is migrating to Windows 2000, and all computers will either be upgraded or receive a clean install. After running the Winnt32.exe /checkupgradeonly command, you find this computer is running some custom graphics applications that are proprietary and may not work correctly with Windows 2000. There is also a problem with one printer/fax machine. This computer is presently in a workgroup and will need to join a domain during installation. Below are some of the steps involved in the installation process. Note anything that is incorrect or missing in this list.

1. Check that the computer meets the minimum level of requirements for the install. Since it is a computer in the graphics department, make sure that there is extra RAM.

2. Obtain device drivers for the printer/fax machine from the manufacturer prior to installation. Obtain any upgrade packs for other devices that are not listed in the HCL.

3. Ensure that you have sufficient rights to perform the installation. Create a computer account in the domain.

4. Insert the Windows 2000 Professional CD-ROM in the CD-ROM drive. When installation begins, choose to upgrade the current operating system.

5. Choose the file system FAT32.

6. When prompted, join the computer to domain using the administrative privileges. Leave the Administrator password blank since this is the first time the computer will join the domain.

7. Install any additional networking components that you require on this computer.

8. When the upgrade is complete, test the graphics applications to see if they are still running correctly.

QUICK ANSWER KEY

Objective 1.01	
1.	E
2.	B
3.	B
4.	D

Objective 1.02	
5.	D
6.	A
7.	C

Objective 1.03	
8.	C
9.	D
10.	E
11.	B

Objective 1.04	
12.	D
13.	B
14.	D
15.	A
16.	A
17.	D

IN-DEPTH ANSWERS

1.01: Performing an Attended Installation of Windows 2000 Professional

1. ☑ **E** is the correct answer because all of the answers listed are appropriate. Before installing Windows 2000 Professional, you must first evaluate the hardware on each computer and check it against the Hardware Compatibility List. You must also deal with certain issues, which will include deciding on an upgrade or fresh installation, formatting as FAT, FAT32, or NTFS, and what type of partitions you will have on your hard drive.

2. ☑ **B** is the correct answer. Stage 2 is aptly named "Running the Setup Wizard."

   ☒ **A** is incorrect because Stage 1 is a text-based Setup program and does not have a GUI (graphical user interface). **C** is incorrect because Stage 3 is installing networking components. **D** is incorrect because Stage 4 is completion of installation.

3. ☑ **B** is the correct answer. The required result of installation is met by choosing to install from the CD-ROM, and all of the hardware is on the HCL. The first optional result is achieved because a computer account is already on the domain controller, and the user is able to input the appropriate information during Stage 3 of the installation. The network interface card is also on the HCL. The second optional result is not met. In order for the user's files and settings to be preserved, the option to upgrade would have to have been chosen.

4. ☑ **D** is correct because you can convert from FAT or FAT32 to NTFS using the command line utility, *convert <drive letter>: /fs: NTFS*.

   ☒ **A** is incorrect because converting FAT to NTFS does not destroy the data. **B** is incorrect because conversion is a one-way process. FAT and FAT32 can be converted to NTFS, but not vice versa. **C** is incorrect because formatting a drive always results in lost data.

1.02: Upgrading to Windows 2000 Professional

5. ☑ **D** is the correct answer. All of these are necessary to install from a network.

6. ☑ **A** is the correct answer. Winnt32.exe is the only choice.

 ☒ **B, C,** and **D** are invalid commands.

7. ☑ **C** is the correct answer. The manufacturer may have a new driver, and this would be the best choice.

 ☒ **A** is incorrect because the unavailability of the adapter driver will not cause the system to crash. **B** is incorrect because if the driver were in the driver database, the product would be considered compatible. **D** is incorrect because the Windows 98 driver may not work.

1.03: Deploying Service Packs

8. ☑ **C** is the correct answer. Winver is the utility that is used from the command line to determine what version of Windows is running, the service packs installed, and the build.

 ☒ **A** and **B** are incorrect because Winnt32.exe is used to install Windows 2000, and the switches /v and /SP are invalid. **D** is incorrect because Update.exe is used to apply new service packs.

9. ☑ **D** is the correct answer. All of the files listed above are replaced when a new service pack is added.

10. ☑ **E** is the correct answer. Service packs can be included with a distribution image, and Windows tracks which service packs are installed and which files were changed, so **A** and **B** are correct. You can also see the currently installed service pack and build information by typing winver at the command prompt, making **C** correct. **D** is also true also. Once a service pack is installed, it will not have to be reinstalled simply because you add new applications. The operating system will automatically retrieve the necessary files from the service pack. This is not true in Windows NT.

11. ☑ **B** is the correct answer. By running Update.exe, the service pack is installed on the workstations, thus meeting the required result. Running

Update.exe /slip at the server will alter the installation files in the i386 folder for the next network installation of Windows 2000 Professional. The second optional result is not met because the unattend.txt file is not a correct choice for unattended installation (you would need an answer file), and is not applicable to service packs.

1.04: Troubleshooting Failed Installations

12. ☑ **D** is the correct answer. When troubleshooting errors during installation involving domain controllers, make sure the domain name is spelled correctly, that the DNS service is running, and that the NIC is working and on the HCL.

13. ☑ **B** is the correct answer. Once Windows 2000 is installed, the most likely reason a dependency failure would occur would be a problem with the NIC or protocol.

  ☒ **A** is incorrect because this would cause a POST error, or would be noticed as a video problem. **C** is incorrect because the file system choice would not affect a dependency service. **D** is incorrect because Windows would not install if there were insufficient disk space or RAM.

14. ☑ **D** is the correct answer. The setuplog.txt file is used to view details and additional information about the device driver files that were copied during setup.

  ☒ **A** is incorrect because disk space errors are addressed by creating a larger partition during installation. **B** is incorrect because media errors occur with CD-ROMs and are not dealt with in this log file. **C** is incorrect because domain controller errors have to do with network cards, controllers, and connections to the server, and do not have anything to do with driver installation errors.

15. ☑ **A** is the correct answer. The Windows 98 workstations are the only computers that can be upgraded.

  ☒ **B** is incorrect because Windows 3.5 cannot be directly upgraded to Windows 2000, it must be upgraded to 3.51 or 4.0 first, and the CD-ROM issue has not been addressed. This makes **C** incorrect, also. **D** is also incorrect.

The case study states that you want to upgrade the workstations ONLY. Be careful!

16. ☑   **A** is the correct answer. When a dual-boot is needed, the FAT or FAT32 file system must be used on the system partition.

☒   **B** and **C** are incorrect because they do not allow for dual-boot configurations.

17. ☑   **D** is the correct answer. You must first address the problem with the CD-ROMs not being on the HCL by replacing them with ones that are. The Windows NT 3.5 operating system cannot be directly upgraded to Windows 2000; the interim step of upgrading to NT 4.0 must be made. Finally, upgrading from Windows NT 4.0 to Windows 2000 is an option.

☒   **A**, **B**, and **C** are incorrect because they all leave out one or more of these necessities.

LAB ANSWER

Objectives 1.01–1.04

There are many errors in the solution provided in the Lab Question section.

1. After running the Winnt32.exe /checkupgradeonly command on this computer and discovering that it has applications running on it that have compatibility issues, installation should not be carried out until a new graphics program is chosen to replace the one presently being used. Back up all data before moving beyond this point.

2. Statements (1), (2), and (3) are correct. However, you will need to know the name of the new domain the computer will join.

3. Choosing to upgrade instead of installing a clean copy is a poor choice. Since a new graphics program will need to be used, and the computer will move from a workgroup to a domain, the best choice is to install clean.

4. Microsoft recommends that the only time you use FAT or FAT32 is for dual-booting. Since this computer will not be configured as dual-boot, NTFS should be used.

5. Leaving the password blank is incorrect for many reasons, but it is mainly a security issue.

6. Installing network components may include protocols or network adapter drivers.

7. Again (8) is incorrect because the computer will not be upgraded, and the incompatible graphics program will not be used.

8. Finally, ensure after installation that all programs, printers, and network connections are working properly.

MICROSOFT CERTIFIED SYSTEMS ENGINEER

2

Performing an Unattended Installation of Windows 2000

TEST YOURSELF OBJECTIVES

2.01 Understanding Disk Duplication Methods

2.02 Using the Scripted Method

2.03 Performing an Unattended Installation of Windows 2000 Professional

T his chapter focuses on issues encountered when installing Windows 2000 Professional on hundreds or thousands of computers in an enterprise. Because it would be implausible to try to install this many computers from a single CD-ROM, Microsoft 2000 includes various tools and methods that can be used to automate and customize the deployment of Windows 2000 Professional. Disk duplication methods are used when only clean installations are required. System Preparation (Sysprep) is used to prepare a complete installation and include applications, service packs, drivers, and many other options. Remote Installation Services (RIS) is used to install remotely.

Windows 2000 installation can also be automated using scripted files (answer files). The Setup Manager Wizard helps guide you through this process, and will provide assistance creating the various configuration parameters. This process can be completely automated; no input from the user is necessary. Unattended installations of Windows 2000 Professional are achieved by using the /u switch and adding the location of the installation and answer files when starting installation. Some of these deployment tools are included on the Windows 2000 Professional CD-ROM, while others can only be extracted from the Windows 2000 Server CD.

TEST YOURSELF OBJECTIVE 2.01

Understanding Disk Duplication Methods

Disk duplication methods allow an administrator to simplify installations of Windows 2000 Professional on multiple computers with identical hardware configurations. This is also referred to as "disk cloning" or "imaging," which represents the need for the computers to have identical hardware. In disk duplication, the entire partition is copied and replicated to another machine, thus reducing the time needed to deploy the operating system throughout the enterprise. The main aspects of disk duplication are listed below.

- Disk duplication methods can be used only for clean installs. These methods do not support upgrading from a previous operating system.

- System Preparation (Sysprep) is used to prepare an image of a computer fully configured with the operating system and the applications.

- Sysprep requires that the source master computer and all the destination computers have identical hardware, but Plug-and-Play devices are exempt from this condition. The image distribution job is handled by a third-party utility.

■ The Remote Installation Services is included with the Windows 2000 Server operating system for remote installation of Windows 2000 Professional. This service is dependent on Active Directory service, DHCP service, and the DNS service running on the network.

exam
ⓦatch

Although we've stated that the destination computers must have identical hardware, watch out for questions on the exam involving disk duplication on computers that are not exactly alike. There is an exception for Plug-and-Play devices. These Plug-and-Play devices need not necessarily be identical. Examples of such are video cards, network adapters, sound cards, and modems. The Sysprep master image automatically runs a full Plug-and-Play device detection on the destination computer.

QUESTIONS

2.01: Understanding Disk Duplication Methods

1. **Current Situation:** Jennifer's corporation has 250 computers running Windows 98, 150 running Windows NT 4.0 workstation, 175 brand-new computers with no operating system installed, and 15 servers running Windows NT 4.0 Server. The company is migrating to Windows 2000 products. Jennifer would like to use the disk duplication tools available with Windows 2000 to automate the deployment. The 175 brand-new computers have identical hardware, and Jennifer's company has a volume licensing agreement. Jennifer has a third-party image distribution utility.

   Required Result: Automate the installation of all of the 175 brand-new computers.

   Optional Desired Results:

   1. Automate the upgrades of the Windows 98 and NT Workstation computers.

   2. Install with no user interaction.

Proposed Solution: Using the Sysprep utility, create three different hardware configurations, creating three master images. Create one image for the Windows 98 machines, one image for the workstations, and one image for the 175 new machines. Use the third-party image distribution software to deploy the image. Use the switch /nouserinteraction with the Sysprep utility.

A. The proposed solution produces the required results and both of the optional results.

B. The proposed solution produces the required results and only one of the optional results.

C. The proposed solution produces the required results and none of the optional results.

D. The proposed solution does not produce the required result.

2. You are an administrator of a large network with multiple divisions. You need to use the Sysprep utility to create several images for disk duplication throughout these divisions. To simplify the process, you have chosen members of each department to help with this task. What group(s) should you make these employees members of?

A. Administrators group.

B. Account Operators global group.

C. Power Users local group.

D. All of the above allow Sysprep to be run on a computer.

3. Remote installation services are used to install Windows 2000 remotely on computers with similar or dissimilar hardware configurations. In order to use RIS, which of the following must be available?

A. Active Directory, DNS, and DHCP to be running on the network

B. Active Directory, DNS, and DHCP to be running on the network, and client computers need to have either one of the 25 supported network adapters or a PXE-based Boot ROM

C. DHCP, BINL, and TFTP

D. A previous version of Windows NT 4.0 installed on the client computer

4. Kimberly is trying to make remote boot disks for her clients whose computers do not meet Net PC specifications for remote installation and do not currently have an operating system installed. She inserted the Windows 2000 Professional CD-ROM in the E drive and typed the path in the screen shot below. The disks did not work for her clients. What did she do wrong?

```
E:\BOOTDISK\MAKEBOOT.EXE                                          _ □

*********************************************************
This program creates the Setup boot disks
for Microsoft Windows 2000.
To create these disks, you need to provide 4 blank,
formatted, high-density disks.

Please specify the floppy drive to copy the images to: a

Insert one of these disks into drive a:.  This disk
will become the Windows 2000 Setup Boot Disk.
Press any key when you are ready.
```

A. Makeboot.exe is used to make Windows 2000 setup disks for a new installation when there is no operating system installed.

B. By typing in the path to rbfg.exe, Kimberly could have made the boot disks that were required.

C. Kimberly cannot make the boot disks at her computer; they must be made at the client's computer.

D. Both A and B are correct.

Questions 5–6   This scenario should be used to answer questions 5 and 6.

Mary Anne is starting a new business and has purchased 15 new computers that do not currently have an operating system on them. She wants to create a network, making one computer a server and the other 14 computers clients. She plans to install Windows 2000 Server on the domain controller, and Windows 2000 Professional on the workstations. She only has one department and all of the computers will be configured exactly the same. She plans to install Microsoft Office 2000 Small Business Edition on each of the computers. Answer the following questions concerning Mary Anne's new network.

5. Since these computers will be joining a network and domain, how can Mary Anne run Sysprep without generating any security ID?

   A. Run sysprep.exe /nosecurityid

   B. Run sysprep.exe /quiet

   C. Run sysprep.exe /nosidgen

   D. Run sysprep32.exe /nosecid

6. How could Mary Anne choose to run Sysprep after she has logged on as administrator?

   A. Select Start | Run, and type **cmd**; at the command prompt change to the Deploy directory that the files were extracted to, and type **sysprep.exe**.

   B. From Windows Explorer, find the Deploy folder and double-click the Sysprep icon.

   C. Open Programs | Accessories | Command Prompt and type **sysprep.exe**.

   D. All of the above.

   E. Only A and B.

TEST YOURSELF OBJECTIVE 2.02

Using the Scripted Method

Scripting is a step up from disk duplication because it allows automated installations on computers that have varying configurations. The Setup Manager makes it simple to create answer files that are required for scripted installations. Since very few networks have hardware configurations where all of the computers are alike, this service is very useful. Answer files contain information such as username, computer name, domain or workgroup name, what type of computer it will be (server, workstation, member), password, time zones, etc. Some important points concerning scripted installations are listed below.

■ Windows 2000 Professional installation can be automated using scripted answer files that provide the answers to many or all of the setup questions.

■ The unattend.txt is the default answer file that comes with Windows 2000. This file can be modified to suit individual installation needs using Notepad.

■ The Setup Manager Wizard is used to create custom answer files that provide various configuration parameters.

■ The Setup Manager can create answer files for one or all of the computers that need unattended installations. The installation can be fully automated wherein the user is not prompted for any input.

exam
ⓦatch

You should know that the answer file, by default named unattend.txt, can be created in one of three ways: you can create the file yourself, use the Setup Manager, or use notepad to modify the generic unattend.txt file that ships with Windows 2000 Professional. Setup Manager is a graphical interface, and painlessly prompts you for answers to questions such as product ID number, type of installation, where installation files are located, and whether the computer will join a workgroup or domain. Make sure that you know how to obtain Setup Manager. Extract the files in the Deploy.cab file located on the Windows 2000 CD-ROM in the Support\Tools folder.

QUESTIONS

2.02: Using the Scripted Method

7. **Current Situation:** Jennifer's corporation has 250 computers running Windows 98, 150 running Windows NT 4.0 workstation, 175 brand-new computers with no operating system installed, and 15 servers running Windows NT 4.0 Server. The company is migrating to Windows 2000 products. Jennifer would like to use the tools available with Windows 2000 to automate the deployment. The 175 brand-new computers have identical hardware.

   Required Result: Automate the installation of all of the 175 brand-new computers.

Optional Desired Results:

1. Automate the upgrades of the Windows 98 and NT workstation computers.

2. Install with no user interaction.

Proposed Solution: Using the Setup Manager Wizard utility, create three different answer files. Choose unattended installation in Setup Manager, and check Fully Automated when prompted for user interaction level. Create one answer file for the Windows 98 machines, one for the workstations, and one for the 175 new machines. Use the switch /u when installing.

A. The proposed solution produces the required results and both of the optional results.

B. The proposed solution produces the required results and only one of the optional results.

C. The proposed solution produces the required results and none of the optional results.

D. The proposed solution does not produce the required result.

8. Mark is an administrator for a large Internet start-up company, and is setting up an unattended installation of Windows 2000 Professional using a script file. He typed in the following command to begin the application: Winnt32 /b/s: d: i386. Mark received an error message concerning the location of the answer file. What does Mark need to type to make the installation work properly?

A. Winnt /b /s:d:\i386 /u:d:\i386\unattend.txt

B. Winnt32 /b /s:d:\i386 /u:d:\i386\unattend.txt

C. Winnt32 /b /s:c:\i386

D. Winnt32 /b /s:d:\i386 /u

9. A client computer has been booted with a remote boot disk. Once the RIS server is contacted, in what order do the initialization activities occur?

A. TFTP, DHCP, and BINL

B. TFTP, BINL, and DHCP

C. BINL, DHCP, and TFTP

D. DHCP, BINL, and TFTP

10. Ron is planning a scripted installation of Windows 2000 Professional across his network. He is going to use the Setup Manager to help him create his answer file. Which of the following are parameters that he can include in his planning?

    A. Screen savers and desktop settings

    B. Location of home folders

    C. Installation path and product ID

    D. Time zone and language preference

    E. Both C and D

11. Jim is planning an unattended installation of Windows 2000 Professional for 45 new computers in his firm. None of the computers have operating systems on them, and their hardware and software requirements are similar to other computers on his network. He has used answer files before, and has experience installing Windows 2000 over a network. What is the best way for Jim to create an answer file for his newest unattended installation?

    A. Create from scratch.

    B. Modify an answer file he has used before.

    C. Modify the unattend.txt file that comes with Windows 2000.

    D. Use the Microsoft Management Console snap-in for creating answer files.

    E. Create the answer file using the Setup Manager.

12. When deploying an unattended installation, there are five choices for the level of user interaction. In an environment where security is a major concern, which of the five options below offer the two best choices for an unattended installation?

    A. Provide Defaults or Hide Pages

    B. Read Only or GUI-attended

    C. Provide Defaults or Read Only

    D. Fully Automated or Read Only

    E. Fully Automated or Hide Pages

Performing an Unattended Installation of Windows 2000 Professional

The previous section was an introduction to unattended installation of Windows 2000 Professional using the scripted method. The Setup Manager Wizard can be used to help perform a fully automated installation. Unattended installations use an answer file to provide automated answers to questions asked of users during setup. Answer files can be created using Setup Manager, by editing the generic unnatend.txt file that ships with Windows 2000, or they can be created from scratch. Summaries of important points follow.

■ The unattended installation of Windows 2000 Professional is done using the Winnt or Winnt32 command with the /u switch and specifying the location of the installation files and the answer file.

■ The user wishing to do an unattended setup may modify the default answer file using Notepad, or create a custom answer file using the Setup Manager Wizard.

■ The unattended installation method can be used either for a clean install or to upgrade a previously installed operating system.

■ If a Fully Automated installation mode is selected in the answer file, the user is not prompted for an administrator password.

exam
ⓦatch

Always read the Proposed Solution/Required Result questions carefully, but when addressing unattended installations over a network, make sure that the proposed solution includes creating a network share. A network share is a centralized shared folder on the network usually located on a file server where the installation files are stored. This folder also holds the necessary service packs or upgrades for the applications. The Winnt32 setup command permits use of up to eight source file locations when you use the /s switch.

QUESTIONS

2.03: Performing an Unattended Installation of Windows 2000 Professional

13. Jackie has created some setup scripts using the Setup Manager and has selected the Fully Automated installation option. She wants the users to choose their own display properties and regional settings. When the users started installation using the script, they did not see these options displayed to them. What is the problem?

   A. Windows 2000 does not allow user to specify display properties during installation.

   B. Windows 2000 Professional automatically configures regional settings.

   C. With the Fully Automated installation option, the users are not prompted to type in any information.

   D. None of the above.

14. Linda has created the perfect answer file for her company's unattended installation of Windows 2000 Professional, but has now decided she will need to change the Time Zone. What is the easiest way for Linda to change this? Should she choose an option from the Setup Manager shown here, or pick one of the other choices below?

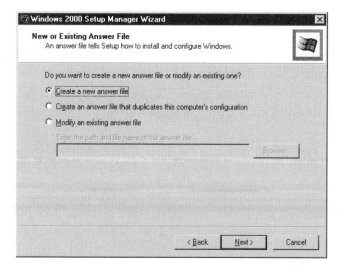

   A. Start over with the Setup Manager Wizard and create a new answer file.

   B. Open the Setup Manager Wizard and choose Modify an Existing Answer File.

   C. Open the answer file in notepad and change the line for Time Zone.

   D. Use the generic unattend.txt file that came with Windows 2000 Professional; it has the correct Time Zone settings that Linda wants.

   E. Use Setup Manager to create a new answer file that duplicates the computer she is working on.

15. Constance is using remote installation to install Windows 2000 Professional on computers in her company. She has clients whose network interface card is not equipped with a PXE boot ROM. These clients cannot be installed remotely without using the utility rbfg.exe. What exactly is rbfg.exe used for?

   A. To correct BootP error messages when installing over a network

   B. To ensure that the DHCP server is authorized in Active Directory

   C. To ensure that the router between the client and the RIS server is allowing requests to go through

   D. To create remote installation boot floppy disks to enable remote installation

16. Bob is trying to decide on an appropriate way to use disk duplication for his deployment of Windows 2000 Professional throughout his organization. He has decided to use Sysprep for some of the installations, and RIPrep for the others. Which of the following statements are true regarding Sysprep and RIPrep?

   A. Sysprep is only for upgrades, while RIPrep is for upgrades as well as clean installations.

   B. Sysprep does not support remote installations, and RIPrep only supports remote installations.

   C. There are no differences.

   D. The Remote Installation Preparation Wizard removes anything unique to the client, while Sysprep does not.

17. Merritt knows that there are many resources that must be available and working in order for RIS to be used for the installation of Windows 2000 to client computers. He cannot get RIS to work properly, but has the following services up and running perfectly: A DNS server, a DHCP server with the scope configured and activated, a server with RIS installed on the network, and client computers which have PXE boot ROM. What is missing?

   A. Merritt needs to run rbfg.exe before beginning installation procedures.

   B. Merritt needs to install the Windows 2000 Resource Kit.

   C. A Windows 2000 domain with Active Directory installed.

   D. None of the above; RIS should work properly with the aforementioned services. Check network connections and protocols.

LAB QUESTION

Objectives 2.01–2.03

You own your own company and run the network yourself. You have six Windows 2000 servers, one in each of six departments. Each department has 25 computers that all run Windows NT workstation, except for one department. You recently upgraded the domain controllers to Windows 2000 Server, and it went very well, and now would like to upgrade the client machines also. Each of the six departments has similar hardware and software configurations, except for the warehouse. They still run Windows 95 and use an old software program that you think will not run on Windows 2000. You have wanted to upgrade the software and retrain your employees in that area for a while anyway. You want to do all of the upgrading yourself to save money and ensure that the upgrades are done perfectly. You have decided to use the Remote Installation method to do the installations in the company.

The following are some steps that could help you perform a successful RIS-based deployment of Windows 2000 Professional. Try to find missing or incorrect steps or flaws in the planning.

1. Install Remote Installation Service on one of the servers using Control Panel | Add Remove Programs | Add Remove Windows Components. Run RISetup.exe from the command prompt. Configure RIS.

2. Ensure that you have a DNS server running on the network.

3. Create a DHCP scope on the DHCP server and activate it.

4. Install Windows 2000 Professional on a computer using RIS.

5. Install all business and custom applications on this computer and test it.

6. Run RIPrep on the test computer to make an image of the system and copy it to the RIS server.

7. Make Remote Boot Disks for the clients using rbfg.exe utility.

8. Boot the client computers using the Remote Boot Disk to run the client Installation Wizard.

9. When given a choice, select the image appropriate to the department.

QUICK ANSWER KEY

Objective 2.01

1. C
2. A
3. B
4. D
5. C
6. E

Objective 2.02

7. A
8. B
9. D
10. E
11. B
12. D

Objective 2.03

13. C
14. B and C
15. D
16. D
17. C

IN-DEPTH ANSWERS

2.01: Understanding Disk Duplication Methods

1. ☑   **C** is the correct answer. The proposed solution will be met by using the Sysprep utility to create an image for the 175 brand-new machines. The hardware is the same, a third-party image distribution program is available, and a volume licensing agreement is in hand.

    ☒   **A** and **B** are incorrect because none of the optional results are met. The first optional result is not met because disk duplication is only used for clean installations, not upgrades. The second optional result is not met because the switch /quiet would have to be added to Sysprep. **D** is incorrect because the required result is produced.

2. ☑   **A** is the correct answer. To run Sysprep on a computer, one must hold Administrator status.

    ☒   Because one must hold Administrator status, **B**, **C**, and **D** are incorrect.

3. ☑   **B** is correct because each of those must be available in order to use RIS.

    ☒   **A** is not completely correct because it does not address the issue of supported network adapters or PXE-based Boot ROM. **C** lists the sequence of protocol activities. **D** does not include necessities like AD, DNS, or DHCP.

4. ☑   **D** is the correct answer because both A and B are correct.

    ☒   Makeboot.exe creates the boot disks needed to perform a new installation of Windows 2000 Professional when there is no operating system on the computer already, and rbfg.exe is used to make boot disks for clients who do not meet Net PC specifications. **C** is incorrect because you do not have to be at the client computer to make the disks required.

5. ☑   **C** is the correct syntax to run Sysprep without generating a security identifier for the computer.

☒ **A** is not a valid command and is incorrect. /quiet is a command to run in quiet mode, so **B** is incorrect also. **D** is incorrect because sysprep32.exe is an invalid command.

6. ☑ **E** is the correct answer. **A** and **B** are both correct ways to run Sysprep.

☒ **C** is not a valid option. You must be in the correct folder to which the files were extracted from the CD-ROM.

2.02: Using the Scripted Method

7. ☑ **A** is the correct answer. The Setup Manager Wizard utility allows automated installations on computers with varying configurations. Setup Manager also allows upgrades, as well as clean installations. By choosing unattended installation and fully automated user interaction level in the Setup Manager dialog boxes, you can achieve the second optional result. The switch /u allows unattended installations.

☒ **B** and **C** are incorrect because both of the optional results are produced. **D** is incorrect because the required result is produced.

8. ☑ **B** is the correct answer. The switch /b causes no boot disks to be made, /s specifies the source path for the installation files, and the /u switch tells that it is an unattended install, and specifies the location of the answer file as d:\i386\unattend.txt.

☒ **A**, **C** and **D** are all missing parameters.

9. ☑ **D** is the correct answer: DHCP, BINL, and TFTP. When a computer is started using a remote boot disk, it first tries to contact the DHCP server for an IP address. Once achieved, the computer contacts the RIS server for the boot file. This is accomplished with BINL. TFTP then transfers the necessary boot files from the RIS server to the client computer.

☒ **A**, **B**, and **C** are not in the correct sequence.

10. ☑ **E** is the correct answer. Installation paths, upgrade options, target computer names, product IDs, the role of the computer, whether it will join a workgroup or domain, time zone, and network configuration information are all options that can be set using the Setup Manager.

☒ Screensavers, desktop settings, and location of home folders are not set using the Setup Manager, therefore **A** and **B** are incorrect.

11. ☑ **B** is the correct answer. Because Mark has used answer files before, and because the new computers have similar hardware requirements and software needs, the best way to create an answer file is to modify one previously used.

    ☒ **A**, **C**, and **E** are also ways to create answer files, but are not the best solution for this situation. **D** is not a way to create an answer file.

12. ☑ **D** is the correct answer. The two best choices for a network installation of Windows 2000 in unattended mode in a secure environment are Fully Automated and Read Only.

    ☒ **A**, **B**, **C**, and **E**. Provide Defaults allows changes to be input by the client, Fully Automated allows no interaction, Hide Pages allows interaction on pages where the administrator did not provide default information, Read Only allows interaction but no changes, and GUI-Attended requires manual input from the client. To address the security issues, one of the two most restrictive should be chosen.

2.03: Performing an Unattended Installation of Windows 2000 Professional

13. ☑ **C** is correct. When the Fully Automated installation option is chosen, users are not given prompts to change settings or properties.

    ☒ **A** and **B** are incorrect because display properties and regional settings can be configured during setup.

14. ☑ **B** or **C** would work, but to avoid any chance of creating more problems by having a syntax error using notepad, **B** is the best choice.

    ☒ **A** would take too long since an answer file is already written that is almost perfect, and **D** is not true since the CD Linda has does not know what time zone she is in, or her current configuration of computers. **E** is not the correct answer since this particular computer may not match the configuration she wants.

15. ☑ **D** is the correct answer. rbfg.exe is used to create remote installation boot disks.

☒   **A**, **B**, and **C** have nothing to do with rbfg. The other answers deal with protocols and issues related to troubleshooting and sending information across a network.

16.   ☑   **D** is correct. RIPrep allows computers that have multiple hardware configurations to use the same image for installation. Sysprep prepares a source computer for imaging.

☒   **A** is incorrect because Sysprep cannot be used for upgrades, only clean installs. **B** is incorrect because Sysprep is used to aid in remote installations. **C** is incorrect because of the difference stated in **D**.

17.   ☑   **C** is correct. In order for RIS to work properly there has to be a server on the network running Active Directory directory services.

☒   **A** is incorrect because the clients have PXE boot ROM and do not need client boot disks. **B** is incorrect because this is unnecessary software. **D** is incorrect because Active Directory is needed.

LAB ANSWER

Objectives 2.01–2.03

Most of the important steps are listed. The following important steps are missing:

1. After installing and configuring RIS, you must authorize the RIS server in the Active Directory. This has to be done from Start | Programs | Administrative Tools | DHCP.

2. Run the rbfg.exe utility and click on the Adapter List tab to view a list of supported adapters. Make sure that the client computers network adapters are supported.

3. Step 6 does not address the fact that there are six different departments. Although five of them are similar in nature, to assume that they could all use the same image is improper thinking. It would be wise to create six images. At the very least, two need to be made. One image should be made for the NT Workstations, and one for the warehouse department.

4. The Warehouse Department has special needs that should be addressed because they are running Windows 95, and need new application programs and training. Consideration should be given to training and installation of the new software before proceeding.

This procedure assumes that you have domain administrator rights and are the only one performing the remote installations. If you have some other persons who will help you in carrying out the deployment, you will need to give them rights so they can create computer accounts in the domain.

3

Implementing and Conducting Administration of Resources

M onitoring, managing, and troubleshooting access to different types of files and folders is a crucial part of administering a network, as well as a major part of Microsoft's exam 70-210. In order to successfully master either, learning the rules associated with file and folder permissions is crucial. You must be able to distinguish between the rules for local and network files and folders, permissions associated with shares and NTFS, moving and copying files and folders, compression and encryption, effective permissions if users are members of multiple groups, and possible conflicts when assigning permissions to shares, local machines, NTFS, and FAT drives.

NTFS permissions provide local and network security for your hard drives. To implement file and folder permissions that will be applied locally, you *must* be using NTFS for the file system on the partition. There is no such thing as local security for FAT file systems. A user's effective permissions are decided by the accumulation of permissions to a particular resource. Folders, files, and printers are examples of resources.

Monitoring, Managing, and Troubleshooting Access to Files and Folders

Monitoring, managing, and troubleshooting files and folders are everyday tasks for a network administrator, and may be heavily tested on the exam. Two specific management tools are compression and encryption. Compression allows file size to be reduced on an NTFS drive, and encryption is a process that makes information unreadable to protect it from unauthorized viewing or use. NTFS permissions control access to shared resources on a network, and can be set for items such as files, folders, and printers.

- The only form of compression you may use with Windows 2000 Professional is NTFS compression. Other compression schemes are not supported.

- Compression and encryption are mutually exclusive. A compressed file cannot be encrypted, and an encrypted file cannot be compressed. A file that is compressed may have an encryption attribute set, but it will lose its compression attribute.

- To modify compression from a command prompt, use Compact.exe. Compact.exe may be used in scripts or batch files to automate compression routines.

- NTFS permissions are the only form of local security for your hard drives. Unlike share permissions, they always apply, whether a user is logged on locally or over a network.

- NTFS file permissions include Full Control, Modify, Read & Execute, Read, and Write.

- Each of these NTFS permissions consists of a logical group of special permissions. These special permissions may be modified.

- File and Folder permissions are the same, except that folders contain one new permission, List Folder Contents.

- A user's effective permission to a file/folder is the accumulation of all the permissions he or she has been allowed, either as a member of a security group or individually. As with share permissions, a user's permission is the accumulation of the permissions he or she has through his or her individual account or group's permissions.

- There is an exception to this rule: Deny. Deny will always prevail except in one specific circumstance. If you create a share on an NTFS volume, make the share permission Deny and the NTFS permission Full Control, then when the user tries to access the share over the network, Deny applies. But if the user logs on locally, the permission is Full Control. Shares do not come into effect when a user is logged on locally.

exam

Ⓦatch

The topic of calculating effective permissions will probably be heavily tested on exam 70-210. The questions will most likely be scenario-based, or of the Proposed Solution/Required Result format, and will require careful study. Make sure you know that a user's effective permission to a file or folder is the accumulation of all of the permissions he or she has been allowed on NTFS drives. If both shares and NTFS permissions are assigned, it is the most restrictive permission of the final accumulation of the two that applies. Watch out for long, drawn-out questions that include a user who has been given the share permission Deny and the NTFS permission Full Control. Although it is tempting to memorize "Deny always means deny," this is not always the case. If the question adds that the user is logged on locally to the machine, remember that the permission will now become Full Control because shares do not come into effect when a user is logged on locally.

QUESTIONS

3.01: Monitoring, Managing, and Troubleshooting Access to Files and Folders

1. You plan to compress files and folders on your computer to free up space on your hard drive. It is possible to compress any volume under Windows 2000 Professional, even partitions. However, some files may not be compressed. Which of the following files and/or partitions are you unable to compress?

    A. Pagefile.sys

    B. Any encrypted files

    C. Administrator files

    D. System and boot partitions

2. You are planning to compress some of the files on your Windows 2000 Professional system and you are using NTFS as your file system. You do not have any encrypted files. What are some of the ways you can perform compression on the files on your computer?

    A. Run compact.exe /c from the command line.

    B. Run compact.exe /u from the command line.

    C. Right-click the appropriate file, choose Properties from the pop-up menu, choose the Custom tab, and then check the Compress contents to save disk space.

    D. Right-click the appropriate file, choose security, and then choose Compression.

3. Jessica is a member of two groups, Managers and Power Users. The Power Users group has the NTFS permission Full Control of a folder named "Client List." Managers have the NTFS permission Read & Execute, only. Jessica has been demoted from Manager to Sales Personnel, and is given the NTFS

permission Deny in the Managers group for the folder "Client List." She is not removed from either group. What are Jessica's effective permissions for the folder "Client List"?

A. Because Jessica is still a member of the Power Users group, she still has Full Control of the file.

B. Because Jessica is still a member of both groups, the least restrictive permission is assigned and she still has Full Control of the file.

C. Because Jessica is still a member of both groups, the most restrictive permission is assigned, and she has Read & Execute permission to the file.

D. Because Jessica has the Deny permission assigned from the Managers group, she is unable to access the file.

Questions 4–6   This scenario should be used to answer questions 4, 5, and 6.

Karen and John work for a large Internet company and each use a computer running Windows 2000 Professional. Their computers only have 2GB of hard drive space, and they are concerned about running out of room for saving their files. They have both decided to compress some files they do not use very much. However, after choosing a file to compress and right-clicking it, they are both unable to do this. They see the options shown below.

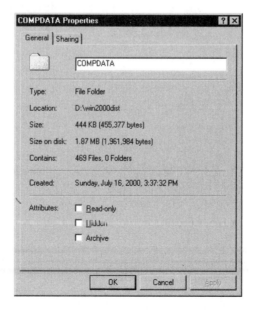

4. Why can't Karen access an option to compress the file, and what can she do about it?

   A. Karen does not have the compression utility installed on her computer. She needs to insert the Windows 2000 CD and choose Add Components.

   B. Karen cannot compress this file. If she chooses another file, compression will work.

   C. Karen's computer is using the FAT file system, and she needs to convert it to NTFS.

   D. Karen needs to run compact.exe from the command line.

5. John works for the same Internet company as Karen. He also has a 2GB partition, but is already running the NTFS file system. John works in the securities division and must encrypt all of his important files and folders as a safety measure. John would like to compress some of his larger files but is also unable to find a way to do this. Compact.exe does not work, nor does right-clicking the appropriate file. Since John is already running NTFS, what could be the problem?

   A. Encryption and compression are mutually exclusive; you cannot use both at the same time.

   B. John is trying to compress a file that is too large for the compression utility.

   C. John needs to run compact.exe from the command line.

   D. None of the above is true; John should reinstall Windows 2000.

6. John still wants to compress his files but is unable to remove encryption from his system due to security restrictions in his department. Which of the following is not a viable alternative to solving John's problem of a lack of disk space? (Choose all that apply.)

   A. Delete temporary Internet files and cache.

   B. Add more hard drive space using a removable drive or bigger hard disk.

   C. Remove photos and pictures and place on CDs or other similar media.

   D. Add more RAM.

7. Joe is assigning permissions for a folder on an NTFS drive that is accessed by the Accounting Department. He wants to give the members of the Accounting Department the ability to change certain permissions of the file or folder, such as Full Control, Read, and Write. What permission should Joe give each individual or group to change the permissions on a specific file or folder?

    A. Change

    B. Synchronize

    C. Read & Execute

    D. Full Control

    E. None of the above; the members of the Accounting Department will need to be placed in the Administrators group to be able to change permissions for a file or folder.

8. The Advertising Department's files have been moved from an NTFS volume to a FAT32 volume on the same computer. The accounting share permission has been reconfigured to point to the FAT32 volume and is set as Full Control. The Advertising Department's files were set to Change before the move. What are the effective permissions for users of the Advertising Department when they try to access the accounting share?

    A. Change

    B. Read

    C. Read & Execute

    D. Full Control

9. Sara is a member of the Finance Department. She has the NTFS permissions Read & Execute for a file on the company's main server. Sara is also a member of the Finance group, which has the NTFS permissions Write and Modify. What are Sara's effective permissions?

    A. Read

    B. Execute

    C. Write

    D. Modify

    E. All of the above

Managing and Troubleshooting Access to Shared Folders

A network consists of users, resources, software, and hardware. Users need resources and the ability to access them. On smaller networks or on resources that have ten users or less, you can use Windows 2000 Professional to address your needs and allow access using share permissions. There are only three permissions associated with a share on this type of system: Read, Change, and Full Control. A user's effective permission to a share is the same as in an NTFS volume; it is the least restrictive and accumulative. Make sure that you know the difference between the two, and are familiar with the bulleted points listed below.

- Folders, files, and printers are a few of the resources that may be shared with other users across your network. Resources on any file system may be shared, but all shared special actions are not available unless the share resides on an NTFS partition.

- The maximum number of users that may connect to a share on a Windows 2000 Professional computer is ten. This number may be lowered but never increased. If you want to limit the share to less than ten simultaneous users, you can do so. If you want more than ten simultaneous users, you need to upgrade to one of the Windows 2000 Server operating systems.

- There are only three permissions associated with shares: Full Control, Change, and Read.

- A user's effective permission to a share is the least restrictive permission he or she has been allowed. The exception to this rule is Deny. If a user, or a group a user belongs to, has the Deny permission, it overrides all other permissions.

- Share permissions have no local effect unless the person who is logged in at the local machine is accessing the resource through the share. Shares only apply to users attaching to your PC over the network.

- When both share and NTFS permissions are present, the user gets the *most* restrictive permission of the final accumulation of each of the two.

The big "gotcha" in this section is determining effective permissions when you have both share and NTFS assigned. Remember that when you only have share permissions to compare, you take the least restrictive, and the same is true for NTFS. But if you have a share permission and an NTFS permission to compare, it is the most restrictive of the two. Even more complicated than that is when you have multiple NTFS permissions and multiple share permissions. In that case you must first take the least restrictive of each category, and then the most restrictive of the result.

QUESTIONS

3.02: Managing and Troubleshooting Access to Shared Folders

10. Jennifer wants to create shares on the computers in her network at home. She has three computers and wants each to have access to all resources on the network. She is running Windows 2000 Professional, and is using the FAT file system. What steps must Jennifer follow to create these shares?

    A. Before Jennifer can create a share on this computer, she needs to upgrade to NTFS.

    B. Jennifer cannot create a share on a computer with the FAT file system; it must be upgraded to FAT32.

    C. Right-click the folder to be shared, select Properties, then Sharing. Choose Share This Folder, then set permissions.

    D. Right-click the folder, choose Sharing from the menu choices, and then name the share. Set permissions and concurrent connections.

11. Kay is a member of two groups: Payroll and Accounting. Both groups have share and NTFS permissions for a file called Salary.xls. The Payroll Department has share permission Full Control and NTFS permission Read. The Accounting

Department has share permission Read and NTFS permission Change. What are Kay's effective permissions to the file?

A. Full Control

B. Read

C. Change

D. Deny

Questions 12–16 This scenario should be used to answer questions 12, 13, 14, 15, and 16.

Current Situation: The company you work for has four departments: Publishing, Editing, Payroll, and Sales. Each department has approximately 25 members and each form a group in a Windows 2000 Professional domain called The Company. Some of the resources in The Company have shares assigned to them, and others have NTFS permissions. Some of the employees are members of more than one group, and the Network Administrator has been receiving complaints that these users are unable to access files, folders, and other resources with the correct permissions. Here are a few examples of the problems they are having:

12. Bob is a member of both the Publishing and Editing groups. He wants to use an expensive color laser printer in the Publishing Department, but is denied access. He has the NTFS permission Full Control in the Publishing group and cannot understand why he is unable to access the printer. What could be a reason for this?

    A. The printer is not working properly and needs to be restarted.

    B. The printer is not connected properly to the network.

    C. Members of the Editing group have the permission Deny for that particular printer.

    D. All of the above are possibilities.

13. Suzan is a member of both the Sales group and the Payroll group. The Sales group has a share permission to the client address book of Change, while the Payroll group has a share permission to Full Control. Suzan also has an NTFS

permission in the Payroll group, Read. Why is Suzan unable to modify the contents of this folder?

A. Suzan can modify the contents because she has Full Control permissions. This must be user error.

B. Suzan cannot modify the contents because she has only Read permissions.

C. Suzan has Change permissions but no permission to Modify.

D. Suzan has no access to the folder.

14. Billy wants access to the client address book folder. He is a member of the Sales group but has been denied access because he has been caught using the names and addresses in the address book for his personal use. You come to work on Monday and discover he has been tampering with the folder. How did he get access?

A. Billy had not been removed from the Payroll group, which has the share permission Full Control.

B. Billy is a member of the Payroll group, which has the NTFS permission to Read.

C. Billy accessed the folder from the computer on which it is stored.

D. Billy is a member of the Publishing group and has a share permission Change.

15. Jerry has both share and NTFS permissions to a particular folder. Jerry isn't sure how effective permissions are decided when both types of shares are involved, and is not able to access some of his files properly. You need to reassign some of the permissions assigned to Jerry to eliminate this problem. Which of the following describe this process correctly?

A. When both types of permissions are present, the user gets the *least* restrictive permission of the accumulation of each type. That is, if a user has the share permission Read, and the NTFS permission Full Control, that user is given the least restrictive permission; in this case, the user has Full Control.

B. When both types of permissions are present, the user gets the *most* restrictive permission of the accumulation of each type. That is, if a user has the share permission Read, and the NTFS permission Full Control, that user is limited by the most restrictive permission; in this case, the user has Read Only.

C. When both types of permissions are present, the user gets both. That is, if a user has the share permission Read, and the NTFS permission Full Control, that user has both Read and Full Control.

D. When both share and NTFS permissions are present, the NTFS permission is always chosen because it represents a higher security level over shares.

16. You want to give access to your files and folders and use NTFS permissions like Read, Read & Execute, Full Control, List Folder Contents, Modify, and Write so you can limit the access that users have to your files. However, after right-clicking a folder and choosing the Properties tab, the Read & Execute, Last Folder Contents, Modify, and Write permissions are not available. The only available permissions are Read, Change, and Full Control, as shown in the following illustration. Why are the other permissions unavailable?

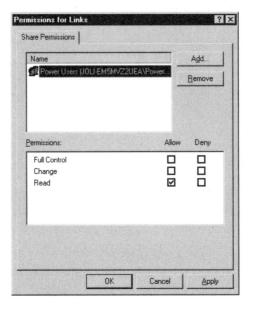

A. These special permissions can only be set when the file is open. Open the file, choose Tools | Online Collaboration, and set them there.

B. You do not have ownership of this file. Log on as Administrator, take ownership, and then right-click again. The permissions will be available at that time.

    C. After right-clicking the file, select Security instead of Properties. This is where you set permissions.

    D. The drive is formatted as FAT and needs to be formatted as NTFS. Use the convert utility to upgrade the drive.

17. Your boss wants to assign some special permissions to files and folders on his NTFS drive. He will apply these special permissions to one object only, and for one person only. Which of the following special permissions exist?

    A. Traverse Folder / Execute File

    B. Create Folders / Append Data

    C. Delete Subfolders and Files

    D. Grant Ownership

18. Sharon is a member of three groups that all have NTFS permissions assigned to them for a file called Money.xls. The first group has Read, the second has Modify, and the third has Write. In addition to this, Sharon has the share permission Full Control to this file. What is Sharon's effective permission regarding access to this file and its contents?

    A. Sharon can take ownership of this file because she has the Full Control share permission.

    B. Sharon can delete this file, but cannot launch binary executables.

    C. Sharon cannot copy this file to another location.

    D. Sharon can Read, Write, Execute, Modify, and Delete the file.

19. Jennifer wants to create a share for a file on her computer at home. She is running Windows 2000 Professional, and is using the FAT file system. What are the steps involved in creating a share for a file on a FAT volume?

    A. Jennifer cannot create a share for a file on this computer; she needs to upgrade to FAT32.

    B. Right-click the file to be shared, select Properties, then Sharing. Choose Share This File, then set permissions.

    C. Right-click the folder, choose Sharing from the menu choices, and then name the share. Set permissions and concurrent connections.

    D. None of the above are correct.

LAB QUESTION

Objectives 3.01–3.02

You are a Network Administrator for a large corporation and need to assign share and NTFS permissions for some groups and departments on your floor so that the following requirements are met:

1. Shared data should be available to network users both online and offline.

2. The offline data should improve the performance of your network.

3. A large numbers of users should be able to access the data.

4. The data should be protected from any access by the Internet group.

5. The Research and Development group requires complete access to the data.

You create a share, Downloads, on your Windows 2000 Professional computer. You accept the default share permissions. You give the Research and Development group Full Control of the share Downloads. You configure Automatic Caching of Documents for the share.

You configure NTFS permissions for the folder, giving Research and Development Full Control, and you specifically deny access to the Internet group.

Does this fulfill all of the requirements above? Please consider all that you have learned in this chapter while thinking about this question. You will see scenario-based requirement questions on some of your certification exams.

QUICK ANSWER KEY

Objective 3.01	
1.	A and B
2.	A
3.	D
4.	C
5.	A
6.	A, B, and C
7.	D
8.	D
9.	E

Objective 3.02	
10.	C and D
11.	C
12.	C
13.	B
14.	C
15.	B
16.	D
17.	A, B, and C
18.	D
19.	D

IN-DEPTH ANSWERS

3.01: Monitoring, Managing, and Troubleshooting Access to Files and Folders

1. ☑ **A** and **B** are the correct answers. Pagefile.sys is the swap file, and encryption and compression are mutually exclusive; they cannot be used simultaneously.

   ☒ **C** is incorrect because administrator files can be compressed. **D** is incorrect because both system and boot partitions can be compressed.

2. ☑ **A** is correct because the switch /c will compress the file. There are two ways to compress a file: either right-click the file, choose Properties from the pop-up menu, choose the General tab, Advanced Button, and check the Compress contents to save disk space; or run compact.exe from the command line.

   ☒ **B** is incorrect because the switch /u decompresses the file. **C** and **D** are incorrect because they do not have the correct tabs listed for enabling compression.

3. ☑ **D** is correct. Because Jessica has the Deny permission assigned from the Managers group, she is unable to access the file.

   ☒ **A**, **B**, and **C** are incorrect for this same reason.

4. ☑ **C** is correct. If an Advanced Attributes tab is not visible, you are not working on an NTFS volume. To compress data, it must reside on an NTFS partition.

   A is incorrect because the ability to compress files is installed automatically with Windows 2000. **B** is incorrect because this file can be shared. **D** is incorrect because the ability to compress files would be shown in this box under the Advanced tab if compression were available.

5. ☑ **A** is the correct answer. Encryption and compression cannot be used at the same time.

    ☒ **B** is incorrect because there is no file size limit for compression. **C** is incorrect because John has tried this already. **D** is incorrect because reinstalling will not solve the problem.

6. ☑ **A**, **B**, and **C** are all good ways to reduce the amount of data on a hard drive.

    ☒ **D** is not a good solution. RAM is memory, not permanent disk space, and will not solve the problem of a full disk drive.

7. ☑ **D** is the correct answer. The NTFS permission Full Control can be given to a group or individual to allow them to change the permissions of a folder or file.

    ☒ **A** is incorrect because Change is a share permission, not an NTFS permission. **B** is incorrect because it is not a valid permission. **C** is incorrect because Read & Execute do not allow a user to change permissions to a resource. **E** is incorrect because you do not have to be a member of the Administrators group to change permissions on a file or folder.

8. ☑ **D** is the correct answer. The fact that the Advertising Department's files were set as Change before the move does not mean that they will remain as Change after the move. Remember, when data moves from an NTFS partition to a FAT partition, all NTFS permissions are lost because FAT32 does not support File and Directory permissions.

9. ☑ **E** is the correct answer. Sara's effective permissions are a combination of all of the permissions listed above since all are NTFS.

    ☒ **A**, **B**, **C**, and **D** are incorrect because the effective permissions in this case are the accumulation of all the permissions assigned.

3.02: Managing and Troubleshooting Access to Shared Folders

10. ☑ **C** and **D** are both correct answers. To enable a share, choose the properties tab after right-clicking the folder. Then, select Share This Folder from the choices.

    ☒ **A** is incorrect because shares are specifically used on FAT volumes, not NTFS. **B** is incorrect because shares can be employed on both FAT and FAT32 volumes.

11. ☑ **C** is the correct answer. When calculating effective permissions when both share and NTFS are involved, first determine the least effective permission for each group, then the most restrictive of what is remaining. For Payroll, compare Full and Read, and take the least restrictive, Full. For Accounting, compare Read and Change, and take the least restrictive, Change. Now compare Full and Change and take the most restrictive, Change.

    ☒ **A**, **B**, and **C** are incorrect for this same reason.

12. ☑ **C** is the correct answer. Because Bob is a member of both the Publishing and Editing groups, and since the Editing group has no access to the resource, Bob will be unable to access it.

    ☒ **A** and **B** are incorrect because Bob is being denied access. If the printers were offline or not working properly, he would have received a different error message.

13. ☑ **B** is the correct answer. When comparing the share permissions, Change and Read, we take the least restrictive of Change for her effective share. However, when we compare that with her NTFS permissions, we take the *most* restrictive. When comparing Change and Read, Suzan's effective permission to the folder is Read.

    ☒ **A**, **C**, and **D** are all incorrect for these same reasons.

14. ☑ **C** is the correct answer. Share permissions only apply when the resource is accessed over the network. If Billy can access the folder from the computer on which it is stored, his share permissions do not apply.

    ☒ **A**, **B**, and **D** are incorrect because the permission Deny would override any other permissions assigned.

15. ☑ **B** is the correct answer. When both types of permissions are present, the user gets the *most* restrictive permission of the accumulation of each type.

    ☒ **A** is incorrect because it suggests the *least* restrictive, **C** is incorrect because it also represents the *least* restrictive, and **D** is incorrect because NTFS is not always chosen as the effective permission.

16. ☑ **D** is the correct answer. In order to set NTFS permissions, the drive must be formatted as NTFS. Once it is, right-click the file or folder to share, choose Properties, then Permissions.

    ☒ **A** is incorrect because this is not a way to access permissions. **B** is incorrect because you will still need an NTFS partition. **C** is not a way to set permissions.

17. ☑ **A**, **B**, and **C** are all valid special (advanced) permissions.

    ☒ **D** is incorrect. Ownership is always taken, but never granted. There is no member of any network who can assign ownership of an object to a certain user or group.

18. ☑ **D** is the correct answer. The accumulation of the NTFS permissions is Modify, and the share is Full Control. The more restrictive of these two is Modify. Modify is a combination of Read & Execute, Write, and Modify. The Modify permission allows Sharon to delete the file.

    ☒ **A** is incorrect because to take ownership of a file, she would need Full Control. **B** is incorrect because the ability to launch executables is allowed by the Read & Execute permission. **C** is incorrect because she is allowed to copy the file due to the Read permission.

19. ☑ **D** is the correct answer because shares on FAT drives are only available for folders and drives, not files. Be very careful when you read the questions!

    ☒ **A**, **B**, and **C** are incorrect for this same reason.

LAB ANSWER

Objectives 3.01–3.02

The plan outlined in the Lab Question fulfills many, but not all of the requirements.

1. Because the data is shared and configured for automatic caching for documents, it will be available online and offline.

2. Because the documents will be cached locally, network performance will improve.

3. This requirement is not met because you are using Windows 2000 Professional to allow access to the share. A maximum of ten users can access a share on Professional. To allow large numbers of users, you would need to upgrade to Windows 2000 Server.

4. The data is protected from access by the Internet group, although not in the best way possible. The default share permission of Everyone Full Control was left on the share, which could have caused problems, but the folder was locked down against the Internet group with NTFS permissions.

5. The Research and Development group has Full Control to the share, and Full Control for the NTFS permissions. They will have complete access to the data.

MICROSOFT CERTIFIED SYSTEMS ENGINEER

4

Implementing Printing and File Systems

I n this chapter, we'll cover two basic topics in Windows 2000 Professional management: printers and file systems. As a Network Administrator, managing, installing, and troubleshooting logical printers and print devices will be one of your main job functions. Printing in a Windows 2000 environment can involve local and network-interface printers, issues with drivers, and the management of print servers. Windows 2000 offers a new Internet printing feature, integration of printers within the Active Directory, and easy installation of all types of printers and print servers.

File systems require configuring and managing also. There are important differences between the types of file systems available, and it is imperative to know when you should use NTFS and when you should use FAT. File systems determine how data is written physically to the hard disk. Using NTFS allows you to use Professional's disk tools such as intelligent disk writing, disk logging features, and compression and encryption.

TEST YOURSELF OBJECTIVE 4.01

Connecting to Local and Network Print Devices

Printers can be accessed locally or from a network. Before making any decision regarding the type of printing to employ, you must consider not only the users' and company's printing requirements, but also where they will be located, and if print servers will be needed. Make sure you know how to install a printer, connect to a network printer, that printer drivers can be downloaded automatically to certain clients, and how to set up a printer pool. A feature new to Windows 2000 is Internet printing. By entering the URL of a print device, a user can print to that printer even if it is half way across the world. In order to use Internet printing features, Windows 2000 Professional must be running Personal Web Server. Be familiar with the following points:

- Applications send documents to be printed as a set of calls to the GDI API; they are interpreted by a driver into a form comprehensible to the particular printer.

- Because drivers are translators, every pairing of a particular operating system and a particular model of printer demands its own distinct driver.

■ Print jobs are held in a queue in the *print spooler*, where they are accessible and managed.

■ Printers, whether local or networked, must be *defined* locally before local applications can print to them.

■ Windows 2000 allows Internet printers to be defined locally.

■ Windows 2000 allows networked printers to be located through their Active Directory entries. This lets users search for printers by workgroup, name, and features, such as color printing or automatic stapling.

■ When system A defines system B's printer as a network printer, system A will download printer drivers from system B. This means that if you're making your printer a network printer, you have to load all the drivers for every system that might define your printer.

exam
ⓦatch

You might get tripped up on the exam if you are not completely familiar with the terms printer, logical printer, print processor, print router, print server, print spool, and print device. Remember that a printer and print device refer to physical equipment: a printer. But when you use the Add Printer Wizard you are actually creating a logical printer. Logical printers are software interfaces that allow the user to access printers from their computer. Print routers and print servers differ because the print router determines if the print job is local or not, and the server is the device used to manage the network printing setup. Make sure you are familiar with all of the terms above before attempting the exam.

QUESTIONS

4.01: Connecting to Local and Network Print Devices

1. Your company has 400 employees and seven departments. These departments are scattered across a large campus in five different buildings. Beverly emails you and says that the printer in her building is not working properly. Other

users are also complaining that their jobs are not printing. After walking to her building on the other side of the campus and examining the printer, you can't find a problem. Given this information, what is the most likely problem since so many of the users are complaining of an inability to print to the printer, and what is an appropriate solution?

A. The printer is working fine; the printer drivers on the users' machines need to be reinstalled.

B. There is nothing wrong with the printer, but there are many print jobs in the queue. The users need to be patient.

C. The printer was offline, out of paper, or out of ink, and someone fixed the problem before you arrived.

D. The spooler service has stalled. You should stop and restart the spooler service.

2. To add a new local printer at your computer, you have chosen to use the Add Printer Wizard. While using the wizard, Windows 2000 Professional did not automatically detect your printer and the following screen appeared. What are your options at this stage? (Pick the two best answers.)

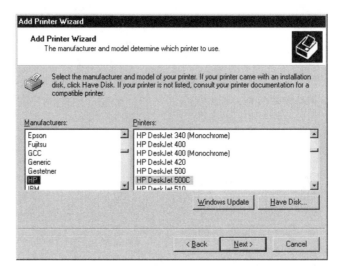

A. Install the printer driver that Windows 2000 has suggested in the dialog box above.

B. Click Have Disk and insert the disk that came with the printer.

    C. Insert the Microsoft 2000 Professional CD-ROM to see if the driver is available there.

    D. Click Windows Update and let the wizard find the appropriate driver from Microsoft's Internet Driver Database.

3.   Marilyn uses Excel 2000 exclusively in her job. She is frustrated because it seems almost every time she needs to print a workbook, she has to go through the printer's Advanced Properties box and change the settings. She always uses landscape, prints back to front, and only in black and white. She prints on legal size paper, not the usual $8^1/2 \times 11$. She approaches you with this concern, and adds that she does not always have to go through this, but it seems like she has to change the settings at least once a day. How can you help Marilyn?

    A. This is a software problem because she occasionally maintains the settings, but usually not. You choose to reinstall her Office applications.

    B. She does not have permission to change her print settings. Make her a member of the Power Users or Print group, and give her special permissions for this printer.

    C. There is no way to change these setting permanently. Tell Marilyn she'll just have to deal with this inconvenience.

    D. Have Marilyn make the changes by setting the properties from the printer icon instead of inside the Excel program.

4.   **Current Situation:** You are a member of a small network that consists of 21 computers. Four of these computers are Windows 95, four are Windows 98, ten are Windows 2000 Professional, and two are Windows 2000 Servers. One is a Windows 3.1 machine. You have configured one of the domain controllers to act as a print server for the network, installed a printer, shared it, and configured permissions appropriately.

Required Result: When all of the computers on the network make the first connection to the printer on the print server, the client computers must automatically download the printer driver from the print server, with the exception of the Windows 3.1 computer.

Optional Desired Results:

1.   Thereafter, all client computers should check for updated printer drivers each time they print, except for the Windows 3.1 computer.

2.   Allow the Windows 3.1 computer to print to the printer.

Proposed Solution: Make sure the drivers are available on the print server for all of the client computers. Manually install the printer driver on the Windows 3.1 computer.

A. The proposed solution produces the required results and both of the optional results.

B. The proposed solution produces the required results and only one of the optional results.

C. The proposed solution produces the required results and none of the optional results.

D. The proposed solution does not produce the required result.

5. Michael is trying to locate where the printer drivers are stored on the Windows 2000 print server mentioned in the previous question. He knows the folder has to be shared because his computer checks for updates to the drivers when he prints. He is unable to find the folder that contains these drivers. Where are they, and why is Michael unable to find the folder?

A. They are system files and only the Windows 2000 operating system has access to them.

B. They are in a hidden folder call Print$ in [*%system_root%*]\System32\ Spool\Drivers.

C. They are located in the D:\Documents and Settings\Administrator\ PrintHood folder.

D. They are in the D:\WINNT\system32\drivers folder.

6. Pat is trying to set permissions for the two printers in his small office. There are three people who continue to print to the expensive laser printer in the president's office, even though they have been asked not to, and he'd like to make sure that they are unable to do that in the future. The company had a network solutions provider set up their office and Web site, and install all the applications. Even though he has right-clicked the printers' icons, and chosen the Properties tab, he is unable to set any permissions for the printers. Pat has set permissions for folders before. What is wrong?

A. Pat is not a member of the Print Operators group.

B. The drive is formatted as FAT or FAT32, and must be formatted as NTFS to allow printer permissions.

   C.   Pat is trying to set permissions on a Windows 2000 Professional machine; printer permissions can only be changed from a Windows 2000 Server.

   D.   All of the above.

   E.   Only A and B.

7.   Your boss is complaining that unnecessary documents are being printed and wants to be able to interact with the printer's print queue. You assign him the permission Manage Printers, and tell him that he is now able to stop, start, resume, and delete documents from the queue. This morning you get an email from your boss saying that he is still unable to do this. Why can't your boss access the print queue?

   A.   The permissions are set appropriately; you need to explain to your boss how to work with the Printer Properties dialog box.

   B.   The employees have permissions that allow them to control their own print documents, and have set their printer properties to disallow deleting or editing their print jobs.

   C.   The correct permission is Manage Documents; you gave the permission to Manage Printers.

   D.   Your boss is not a member of the Print Operators group.

8.   Your employees are complaining that their documents have to wait on the print server an inordinate amount of time before they are printed. You realize that this is not only frustrating for them, but because of the high volume of printing, it is also wearing out your printers. You decide to purchase more printers and set up a printer pool. What are the requirements for a printer pool?

   A.   All print devices must be identical, or at the very least, use the same printer driver.

   B.   Users will need to receive instruction on how to choose available printers from the printer pool.

   C.   Make sure to place the printers in different physical locations so users will not all be waiting in the same area for their print jobs to complete.

   D.   All print devices must be network-interface devices.

Questions 9–11 This scenario should be used to answer questions 9, 10, and 11.

As a Network Administrator for a large company with 2,000 employees, part of your job is to install, configure, and troubleshoot the printers on the network. You have 15 printers, some of which are local, some network, some expensive laser printers, and many less expensive ink-jet printers. After 15 years with the company you are leaving to accept another position and are training a new Print Operator who will take over this part of your job. Ask your replacement to look at these common troubleshooting scenarios, and choose the best solution for each.

9. The CEO has to wait too long for his jobs to print to the laser printer on his floor. You have given him the highest priority for the printer pool, and his documents should print before anyone else's, but they do not. What should you do?

   A. Make him a member of the Print Operators group.

   B. Give him the permission to Manage Documents.

   C. Give him permission to Manage Printers.

   D. Adjust the printing priorities for the printer on his floor.

10. Windows 98 users complain that when a new printer driver is released, their co-workers who have Windows 2000 machines get the new driver, but they do not. What's going on?

   A. Windows 2000 operating systems will automatically look for a new driver to download each time they print; Windows 95 and 98 machines will not.

   B. Windows 2000 Professional is Plug and Play, and knows when a new driver is released. It obtains the driver from its driver database.

   C. Each time a new driver is released, the printer will need to be reinstalled at the Windows 98 machines. Because the printers will work fine with the old drivers, the Administrator has decided not to add them.

   D. As long as the print jobs do not generate any error messages, Windows 98 will not look for any new drivers. Once an error is generated, the operating system will locate and download the new drivers for the printer.

11. After connecting and installing a new local printer, loading the drivers that came from the manufacturer, and turning the printer on, when prompted during setup to print a test page, nothing happens. Which of the following answers could be the problem? (Choose all that apply.)

A. You need to obtain updated drivers from the manufacturer.

B. You have a bad cable from the computer to the printer.

C. The test page was redirected to a printer pool located on another floor.

D. The printer is configured to use an incorrect port.

TEST YOURSELF OBJECTIVE 4.02

Configuring and Managing File Systems

File systems are a very important part of the planning and installation of Windows 2000 Professional. You can choose from FAT, FAT32, and NTFS. The file system you choose will act as the interface between the operating system and hard disk. The FAT file system has many inefficiencies and a lack of scalability. NTFS has many positive attributes including high maximum partition size, disk logging features, compression and encryption features, and permission setting, which are the bread and butter of Windows 2000 security. Microsoft suggests you only use FAT or FAT32 when there is a need for a dual-boot system or a hard disk smaller than 2GB; otherwise, you should always choose NTFS. Know all of the following information thoroughly.

- A file system is a way of writing files to a hard drive. A file system knows where a file is located *physically* on the disk.

- FAT is the universal file system; many operating systems can natively read a FAT drive.

- NTFS is the NT operating system; only Windows NT and 2000 natively know how to read NTFS.

- FAT's maximum partition size is 4GB; NTFS' is 16 *Exabytes*—17 billion times larger.

- Microsoft recommends FAT for creating partitions 2GB and smaller.

- NTFS writes to disk intelligently, reducing drive head travel time.

■ NTFS contains disk-logging features, which makes disk recovery radically better.

■ NTFS allows compression and encryption of files and folders, although not at the same time.

■ NTFS allows file attributes such as permissions. Applications can create custom attributes.

■ All partitioning, formatting, and the like, formerly done from Disk Administrator, in Windows 2000 is done from the Disk Management pane of the Computer Management MMC, accessible from Programs | Administrative Tools.

e x a m
ⓦa t c h

Watch out for questions on the exam that address partitioning and formatting drives that are either unformatted, already contain data, unallocated, or are already defined as FAT or NTFS. Remember, you can only partition unallocated space. If a space is already partitioned, you'll need to delete that partition and create a new one. This, of course, will destroy any data on the partition. Also, if a question asks where to make these changes to the hard disk, make sure to pick Disk Management, and not Disk Administrator as it was previously called in Windows NT.

QUESTIONS

4.02: Configuring and Managing File Systems

12. You are trying to decide on a file system for your new computer. Your hard drive is 2GB, and you are not very concerned with security. You only have three workstations on your network and do not need to assign permissions to files and folders. You do, however, need to assign permissions to your printer. Which file system(s) can you choose?

   A. FAT

   B. FAT32

   C. NTFS

   D. CDFS

13. Notice below that Disk 0 is a basic disk. From the Computer Management window you can upgrade to a dynamic disk by right-clicking the disk in question. What are the reasons for upgrading your basic disk to a dynamic disk? (This computer is running Windows 2000 Professional.)

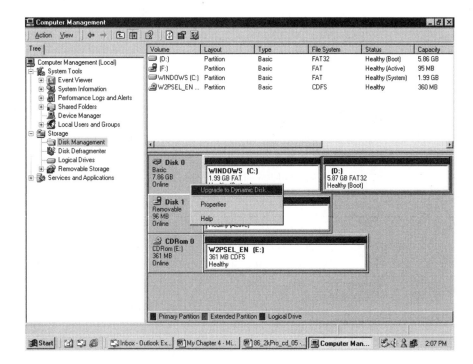

A. To create a single partition that will include the entire disk.

B. To create simple, spanned, and striped volumes.

C. You resize your partitions often, and do not want to have to reboot each time.

D. All of the above.

14. You have computers that have large volumes of 10GB or more each. You do not need security or permissions for printers, or need to use compression or encryption. What are the reasons why you would still choose NTFS over FAT in this scenario? (Choose all that apply.)

A. NTFS is more efficient than FAT because FAT's Master File Table (MFT) is smaller than NTFS' MFT.

B. NTFS is more efficient than FAT because FAT's clusters grow in direct proportion to the volume, making small files use up large amounts of disk space.

C. NTFS is more efficient than FAT when using large volumes because NTFS writes to disk intelligently, reducing file fragmentation.

D. NTFS is more efficient than FAT because NTFS writes to disk intelligently, placing small files near the Master File Table.

15. Your boss has a computer in his office that he configured and installed himself. He is able to access the network, print, and save files to the domain controller. He has some files he'd like to share with others in his immediate vicinity. He asks you for help because when he right-clicks the file that he wants to share and chooses Properties, he doesn't see anywhere to assign permissions to that file. How will you fix this problem?

A. He doesn't have the permission to assign permissions. Assign him the correct permissions from the server, and then have him reboot, take ownership of the file, and try again.

B. His computer is using the FAT file system. Convert it to NTFS before continuing.

C. His active directory is not set up properly.

D. He is using dynamic disks and needs to revert back to basic disk configuration.

16. You wish to format your partition as NTFS so that you can take advantage of Windows 2000's advanced features. Which of the following accurately describes the difference between disk logging and intelligent disk-writing?

A. Intelligent disk-writing is used to reduce drive-head transit times; while disk logging is used to store changes to file system integrity, like name changes, folder and directory movements, etc.

B. Intelligent disk-writing is used to store changes to file system integrity, like name changes, folder and directory movements, etc.; while disk logging is used to reduce drive-head transit times.

C. Intelligent disk-writing keeps track of a file's attributes, while disk logging is a built-in feature used to back up all active files in case of data loss.

D. None of the above describes the difference.

17. **Current Situation:** A new computer was purchased by the Networking Department in a large government office. Most of the computers at this location have been upgraded to Windows 2000 Professional and Server, although there are a few computers that still run Windows 98. Your job is to help with the planning process and the installation of the new computer.

    Required Results:

    1. The new computer must have disk logging, intelligent disk-writing, and allow permissions to be set for resources, files, and folders.

    2. The new computer must be able to dual-boot between Windows 98 and Windows 2000, so this department can test changes and applications for the older Windows 98 machines in the office.

    Optional Desired Results:

    1. Because this is a government facility and security is tight, you must be able to encrypt the data.

    2. Because the hard drive will contain photos and large graphics files, the data must also be compressed.

    Proposed Solution: Partition the hard drive space into different logical drives and make one NTFS and another FAT32, with the system files on the NTFS drive.

    What results does the proposed solution produce?

    A. The proposed solution produces the required results and both of the optional results.

    B. The proposed solution produces the required results and only one of the optional results.

    C. The proposed solution produces the required results and none of the optional results.

    D. The proposed solution does not produce the required result.

    Questions 18–20   This scenario should be used to answer questions 18, 19, and 20.

    Roger runs a large network with multiple departments and over 1,000 employees. He is running Windows NT 4.0 on the servers and Windows 2000 Professional on the majority of the workstations. He plans to upgrade the servers in the near future. He has configured the network so that the users save the greater part of their data on the servers to make backing it up more reliable and efficient. He also relies on NTFS permissions to allow access to printers and other resources. Roger is having a few minor problems maintaining order within his network.

18. Roger has sent out many memos concerning the available disk space on the servers, and has asked his users to delete unnecessary files and data. However, he has been unable to force the users to do this. What can Roger do?

   A. Use the per-disk, per-user disk quota available on all server versions of Windows to limit the amount of space made available to the user.

   B. Set up a RAID5 disk configuration to limit the amount of space the user has available.

   C. Upgrade the servers to Windows 2000, and use the per-disk, per-user disk quota to limit the amount of space available to the users.

   D. Set limits on the Windows 2000 Professional computers using the per-disk, per-user quota to limit how much data they can save to the server.

19. Roger doesn't have time to oversee every aspect of his users' daily work ethics and habits, but would like to let his users know when and how to defragment their drives. He has stated that they should defragment their drives at least once a month, when disk read and write is below average, or after a large amount of data has been deleted. How will he explain the process of defragmenting?

   A. Choose Start | Run and type in **MMC**. In the Microsoft Management Console select Action | Defrag. Select OK to begin defragmentation of the selected drive.

   B. Right-click My Computer and select Manage. Double-click Disk Defragmenter. Right-click the drive to be defragmented and select Analyze. If, after looking at the graphic, the drive seems fragmented, choose to defragment.

   C. Click Start | Programs | Administrative Tools | Performance. Double-click Disk Defragmenter. Right-click the drive to be defragmented and select Analyze. If, after looking at the graphic, the drive seems fragmented, choose to defragment.

D. Click Start | Programs | Administrative Tools | Services. Double-click Disk Defragmenter. Right-click the drive to be defragmented and select Analyze. If, after looking at the graphic, the drive seems fragmented, choose to defragment. Below is an example of a healthy drive.

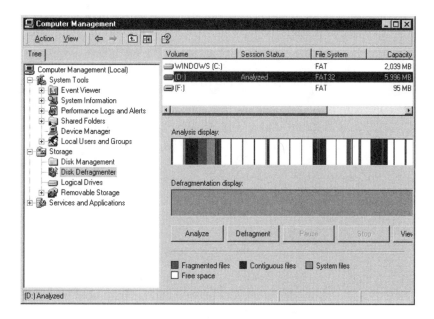

20. Roger would like his employees to save more data on their own hard drives and employ some sort of fault tolerance on their Windows 2000 Professional workstations to relieve him of some of his duties. What kinds of fault-tolerant schemes are available to his users?

   A. RAID5 (Disk striping with parity).

   B. Disk arrays.

   C. Mirrored disks.

   D. Fault-tolerant volumes.

   E. There are no fault-tolerant schemes supported in Windows 2000 Professional.

LAB QUESTION

Objectives 4.01–4.02

Current Situation: You manage, troubleshoot, and assign permissions for the local and network printers in a large government facility. You use the NTFS file system on your domain controllers and print servers. You have shared your printer and assigned permissions for employees in your building. Now, you need to write a document for your boss that explains exactly how the print process works, and the steps involved in moving a document from an application like Word 2000 to the actual physical printout on paper. Put the steps in order below by placing a 1 in the box for the first step, 2 for the second step, and so forth. Check your answers in the Lab Answer section later in the chapter.

- [ ] The application sends the document as a series of calls to an Application Program Interface (API) called the graphical device interface (GDI).

- [ ] The *print router* examines the print job, determines whether the print job is bound for a local or network printer, and then sends the print job to either a local spooler or the network spooler.

- [ ] The *print monitor* actually sends the data to the *printer*, and there the data is transformed into ink on paper.

- [ ] The driver takes the print job and translates it from GDI calls into model-specific instructions.

- [ ] The driver then sends the translated print job to the *print processor*.

- [ ] Word sends the document as a *print job* to the appropriate *print driver*.

- [ ] The *print processor* arranges the translated print job into routable form and sends the arranged, translated print job to the *print router*.

- [ ] The spooler holds the print jobs in a stack (typically first-in, first-out) and, as the printer becomes available, feeds each print job to the *print monitor*.

A QUICK ANSWER KEY

Objective 4.01

1. D
2. B and C
3. D
4. B
5. B
6. E
7. C
8. A
9. D
10. A
11. A, B, and D

Objective 4.02

12. C
13. D
14. B, C, and D
15. B
16. A
17. B
18. C
19. B
20. E

IN-DEPTH ANSWERS

4.01: Connecting to Local and Network Print Devices

1. ☑ **D** is the correct answer. The spooler service is a concern here because many users are complaining of an inability to print.

   ☒ **A** is incorrect because reinstalling all of the users' printer drivers is unnecessary. **B** is incorrect because patience will not help if the spooler service is stalled or hung up. **C** is incorrect only because **D** is a better answer, and the more likely explanation.

2. ☑ **B** and **C** are the best answers here. If the manufacturer's disk is available, it will most likely contain the drivers you need for the printer. The drivers may also be available on the CD-ROM.

   ☒ **D** is incorrect because the Windows Update is used to update system files and drivers already installed, and an Internet connection may not be available. **A** is incorrect because this may or may not be the appropriate printer on your system.

3. ☑ **D** is the correct answer. When you alter printing options from within an application, your changes apply only to that particular session. This means that if you close your application and reopen the same document, the Printing Preferences will reset to their default settings. The only way to apply universal, permanent changes is through the Printing Preferences window as accessed through the Printers window.

   ☒ **A** and **C** are incorrect for this reason. **B** is incorrect since you do not need to be a Power User or a member of the Print group to modify your print properties. Marilyn may not, however, have the ability to change these settings due to a lack of permissions.

4. ☑ **B** is the correct answer. Because the print server has a copy of the driver, the client computers will be able to automatically download the driver when a printer is added to their workstations, meeting the required result. By manually

installing the Windows 3.1 computer with the driver, the second optional result is met. The first optional result is not met since Windows 95 and 98 will not be able to download the updated printer drivers each time they print. Only Windows 2000 and NT computers will be able to do this.

5. ☑ **B** is the correct answer. The drivers are in a hidden shared folder called Print$ in the system root directory under System32, Spool, Drivers.

   ☒ **A**, **C**, and **D** are not the correct location of the drivers.

6. ☑ **E** is the correct answer. To modify permissions for printers, you must be a member of the Print Operators group, and the drive must be formatted as NTFS.

   ☒ **C** is incorrect because printer permissions can be assigned from Professional. **D** is incorrect because **C** is an invalid answer.

7. ☑ **C** is the correct answer. The Manage Documents allows groups to interact with the printer's print queue.

   ☒ Manage Printers allows groups access to the Printer Preferences for this printer, so **A** is incorrect. **B** is not an available permission or attribute for a print job. Finally, **D** is incorrect because an appropriate permission can be assigned without a specific membership to the Print Operators group.

8. ☑ **A** is the correct answer since the print devices must use the same driver.

   ☒ **B** is incorrect because the available printer choices will be transparent to the user. **C** is incorrect because it would be best to place all of the printers in the same physical location so users know where their documents should be picked up. **D** is incorrect because a printer pool can consist of local and network printers.

9. ☑ **D** is the correct answer because the CEO only wants to print to the printer by his office. Set the priorities only for that printer.

   ☒ **A**, **B**, and **C** are incorrect because the permissions do not affect the priority of a print job.

10. ☑ **A** is the correct answer. Windows 2000 operating systems will automatically look for a new driver to download each time they print; Windows 95 and 98 machines will not.

    ☒ **B** and **D** are incorrect because Windows 98 machines will never download updated drivers from the network, and do not have a database of possible upgrades to drivers. **C** is incorrect because a printer would not have to be reinstalled just because a new driver is released.

11. ☑ **A**, **B**, and **D** are correct. **D** is mostly likely, the selected port is incorrect. **A** and **B** could be also be correct answers, although the fact that the printer and drivers are new suggests this may not be the problem.

☒ **C** is incorrect because you are setting up a local printer, and there is no mention of a network.

4.02: Configuring and Managing File Systems

12. ☑ **C** is the only correct answer. Although it may seem that FAT or FAT32 could be correct because of the hard disk size, lack of need for security or permissions, and the fact that you only have three computers on your network, NTFS is required to assign permissions to printers.

☒ **A** and **B** are incorrect for this reason, and **D** stands for Compact Disk File System and is not applicable here.

13. ☑ **D** is correct. Dynamic disks allow for all of the above, including fault tolerance. However, fault tolerance is available only on Windows 2000 Server products, not on Windows 2000 Professional. Make sure if you receive a question concerning fault-tolerant schemes on the exam that you are aware of this!

14. ☑ **B**, **C**, and **D** are all good reasons for choosing NTFS over FAT in this case.

☒ **A** is incorrect because FAT does not have an MFT.

15. ☑ **B** is correct. You must be using NTFS to set permissions for files.

☒ **A** is incorrect because this situation would show the permission box, but it would be grayed out. **C** is incorrect since Active Directory is used on the domain controller. **D** is incorrect because basic or dynamic disks do not play a role in this question. Note: Reverting from dynamic disk to basic disk results in data loss.

16. ☑ **A** correctly describes the difference between disk logging and intelligent disk-writing.

☒ **B** is backward, and **C** is simply not accurate.

17. ☑ **B** is the correct answer. By partitioning the hard drive space into different logical drives and making one NTFS and the other FAT32, you use the full

range of security features for files that need it, while at the same time you have a space to put files for full heterogeneous interoperability. Remember, though, if you have a dual-boot system between an NTFS-enabled system like Windows 2000 Professional and an NTFS-illiterate system like Windows 98, when you boot up in Windows 98, you won't be able to read any of the files on the NTFS drive. However, this is not a required or optional result. Only one of the optional results is met. Depending on how you look at it, you can either compress or encrypt, but not both.

18. ☑ **C** is the correct answer. Per-disk and per-user quotas are solutions for limiting the amount of space a user can take up on a server, but this was not available natively before Windows 2000, and cannot be applied unless the servers are upgraded.

☒ **A** is incorrect for this reason, **B** is incorrect since RAID is a fault-tolerant scheme used for data recovery, and **D** is incorrect because this would have to be configured on the server.

19. ☑ **B** is the correct answer. The Disk Defragmenter tool is located under Computer Management.

☒ **A**, **C**, and **D** all offer the wrong paths to Disk Defragmenter.

20. ☑ **E** is the correct answer.

☒ Although **A**, **B**, **C**, and **D** are all valid fault tolerance alternatives, none are supported in Windows 2000 Professional.

LAB ANSWER

Objectives 4.01–4.02

1. Word sends the document as a *print job* to the appropriate *print driver*.

2. The application sends the document as a series of calls to an API called the graphical device interface (GDI).

3. The driver takes the print job and translates it from GDI calls into model-specific instructions.

4. The driver then sends the translated print job to the *print processor*.

5. The *print processor* arranges the translated print job into routable form and sends the arranged, translated print job to the *print router*.

6. The *print router* examines the print job, determines whether the print job is bound for a local or network printer, and then sends the print job to either a local spooler or the network spooler.

7. The spooler holds the print jobs in a stack (typically first-in, first-out) and, as the printer becomes available, feeds each print job to the *print monitor*.

8. The *print monitor* actually sends the data to the *printer*, and there the data is transformed into ink on paper.

MICROSOFT CERTIFIED SYSTEMS ENGINEER

5

Implementing, Managing, and Troubleshooting Disks and Displays

TEST YOURSELF OBJECTIVES

I n the last chapter, we addressed managing and configuring file systems. This chapter expands on these concepts and will cover implementing, managing, and troubleshooting file systems and their disk devices. Windows 2000 Professional has many tools to assist in disk management, including the Disk Manager snap-in, a disk defragmenting application, and Plug-and-Play capabilities. These tools are new in Windows 2000, and allow for more efficient computer management. Windows 2000 also supports basic and dynamic disks; multiple disks; and simple, spanned, and striped volumes. Managing and troubleshooting hard disks is a large part of a Network Administrator's job, and may be heavily tested on the exam. Be sure to know where and how to implement these tools, and when to use them.

Also covered in this chapter is the management of display devices. Implementing and troubleshooting these devices includes installing drivers, configuring settings, and installing multiple monitors. VGA mode is available from the advanced boot options menu if a basic video driver is needed.

TEST YOURSELF OBJECTIVE 5.01

Implementing, Managing, and Troubleshooting Disk Devices

Disk management includes much more than simply defragmenting the drives once a month, or installing new disks occasionally. Disk management and troubleshooting disk devices are excellent ways to maximize your computer's disk space through the use of dynamic disks and volumes; striped, spanned, or simple volumes; and removable disk devices. Although there are no available fault-tolerant schemes in Windows 2000 Professional, there are many ways to optimize performance. Disk Manager is a snap-in of the Computer Management console and allows changes to disks such as those listed below:

■ The Disk Manager snap-in of the Computer Management console replaces the Disk Administrator that was a part of Administrative Tools in Windows NT 4.0. It is now possible to perform online disk management.

■ Disk Management provides tools for creating, configuring, and managing disks and volumes. It also has a disk defragmentation utility.

■ Windows 2000 supports basic and dynamic disks, and basic and dynamic volumes. Dynamic volumes can exist on dynamic disks only.

■ A basic disk can be upgraded to a dynamic disk without restarting the computer, if it does not contain any system or boot files. The basic disk must have a 512KB sector size.

■ In case the computer has only a single disk, it can have either basic disk or a dynamic disk configuration. To have multiple configurations, there must be multiple disks in the computer.

■ Windows 2000 Professional supports simple, spanned, and striped volumes only. Fault-tolerant mirrored volumes or striped volumes with parity are not supported.

■ Dynamic volumes are not supported on removable storage media such as tape devices. These are also not supported on portable computers.

■ In order to manage disks on remote computers in a Windows 2000 workgroup environment, the user must have an identical account name and password on all computers where they want to run Disk Management.

exam
🐾 a t c h

Be fully aware that Windows 2000 Professional does not support any type of disk fault tolerance. Striped volumes only improve the read-write performance of a system; simple volumes contain disk space for a single disk, and spanned volumes include disk space from multiple disks (up to 32). Fault tolerance is the ability of a computer to respond to loss of data. Fault-tolerant systems such as disk mirroring (RAID1) and disk striping with parity (RAID5) are supported in the Windows 2000 Server operating system.

QUESTIONS

5.01: Implementing, Managing, and Troubleshooting Disk Devices

1. Bob is using Disk Management to add disks to his Windows 2000 Professional computer and manage his striped, spanned, and simple volumes on various workstations in his office. He also uses this tool to view and configure his file systems. What else can Bob do with the Disk Management utility?

   A. Set up fault tolerance.

   B. Defragment the disks.

     C. Remotely manage disk devices.

     D. B and C only.

2. You are using Device Manager to check the hardware on your system and make sure that everything is functioning properly. The following graphic illustrates what you see relating to your system. Even though everything seems to be working properly, you notice the yellow question mark shown below. What could this mean, and how can you repair it?

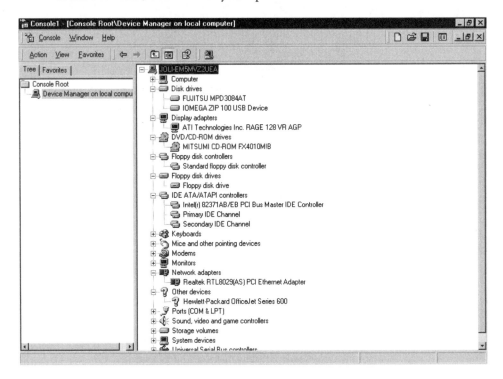

     A. The printer is not working properly due to a bad IEEE 1284 cable. Replace the cable.

     B. An incorrect driver has been installed, or the correct driver is unavailable. Replace the driver with one that is acceptable.

     C. The printer is out of ink, toner, paper, or is jammed. Repair the problem at the printer and the question mark will disappear.

     D. The printer is not online. Bring the printer online and the question mark will disappear.

3. Jennifer has just purchased a new computer for her office. She wants to have dynamic volumes with multiple partitions on her hard drive, and has installed Windows 2000 Professional. She is trying to use the disk management feature to upgrade it from a basic disk to a dynamic disk. However, she is unable to perform the upgrade. Why is this?

   A. The sector size of the disks is 512KB and needs to be at least 1024KB.

   B. The boot or system partition is not a part of a mirrored set.

   C. Jennifer has purchased a laptop computer.

   D. Jennifer's hard drive is not supported by the HCL.

   Questions 4–6   This scenario should be used to answer questions 4, 5, and 6.

   Most of the users on your network use Windows 2000 Professional and connect to a Windows 2000 Server located in another building. Many of the users have multiple drives on their computers, and each has special needs and requests concerning the configuration of their disks. How would you choose to configure the disks of the following three employees?

4. Joe has four small disks of 2GB each that he needs to fill with data. He is not concerned with speed, only with filling the first disk completely before saving to the second, third and so on. How will you configure the volumes on his dynamic disks?

   A. Simple

   B. Spanned

   C. Striped

   D. None of the above

5. Jimmy has 14 disks of 2GB each. He is concerned with read and write performance optimization of these disks. How will you configure the volumes on his dynamic disks?

   A. Simple

   B. Spanned

   C. Striped

   D. None of the above

6. Lucy has only one 10GB hard drive on her computer running Windows 98. She has a physical disk with three primary partitions and one extended partition. She is also concerned with the speed of her hard drive and disk optimization. How will you configure her disk?

   A. Simple

   B. Striped

   C. Spanned

   D. None of the above

7. Tim is using the Volume Properties sheet to manage the volumes on his drives. He hasn't backed up his data lately and has noticed that disk performance is also suffering. Under which tab of the Volume Properties sheet will he find these utilities?

   A. General.

   B. Tools.

   C. Hardware.

   D. Security.

   E. None of the above; the only place to defragment volumes or drives is in the Computer Management or MMC Console window under the Storage or Disk Defragmenter snap-in.

8. Disk quotas for various volumes can be set on a per-user basis in Windows 2000, and you need to enable this service. You share your computer with three other people who are saving too much data on the hard drive and you want to limit how much data they can save. You believe your computer meets all of the requirements for using Disk Quotas, because you have an NTFS volume, and use Windows 2000 Professional. When you try to enable disk quotas, however, the tab is not there. Why not?

   A. You are not looking at the Volume Properties sheet.

   B. You have not installed the Disk Quota snap-in.

   C. You are not logged on as an Administrator.

   D. You have a problem with the operating system and need to reinstall.

9. You think your computer has picked up a virus from a floppy disk one of your co-workers gave you. You received the error message "Missing operating system." Other users who have accessed this floppy are receiving the same message. You want to run the antivirus software that comes with Windows 2000 Professional to see if that will fix the problem. In what directory will you find this program if E:\ is the location of your CD-ROM?

   A. E:\AntiVirus\AVBoot

   B. E:\Valueadd\3rdparty\Ca-antiv

   C. E:\Valueadd\AVBoot

   D. E:\AVBoot\AntiVirus\MBR

TEST YOURSELF OBJECTIVE 5.02

Implementing, Managing, and Troubleshooting Display Devices

One of the lighter aspects of network administration is the management of display properties including adding, removing, and configuring display adapters; loading display drivers; and configuring multiple displays. Many of these properties can be configured without ever rebooting the system. Also, any user who has the right to load and unload device drivers can configure them. A new feature, which was not available in earlier versions of Windows NT, is multiple-display support. Listed below are some of the more important points to be familiar with in this section.

▓ Display devices are managed from the Settings tab of the Display Properties sheet. It is possible to change a number of display settings without restarting the computer.

▓ Plug-and-Play video adapters are automatically detected, and Windows 2000 installs suitable drivers.

▓ The Advanced tab of the Settings Properties sheet is used for advanced display configurations, such as updating display drivers and troubleshooting.

■ The user who wishes to change the display configurations must have sufficient privileges to load and unload device drivers.

■ Windows 2000 can be configured to have multiple monitors, and up to ten monitors are supported. The secondary display devices must not use any VGA resources.

■ In order to find out which of the installed display devices is primary and which is secondary, check to see which one is displayed in the BIOS information at startup.

■ When there is a problem with the display driver and the screen goes blank, VGA mode can be enabled from the Advanced Boot Options menu to load the basic video driver.

exam
ⓦatch

Be sure to know the steps involved in adding and configuring multiple displays (monitors). This will most likely make up one or two test questions because it is new to Windows 2000. Be able to distinguish between primary and secondary display devices and the requirements for each. The main requirement for the primary device is that it must be detected by the computer BIOS during system startup. Requirements for secondary devices include: ten as the maximum number of monitors allowed, the secondary monitor must have a Windows 2000–compatible driver, the monitors in the multiple-display configuration must use the PCI or AGP device, and the PCI or AGP device must not use any VGA resources because these are to be used by the onboard VGA device.

QUESTIONS

5.02: Implementing, Managing, and Troubleshooting Display Devices

10. Annette is a new employee and has just received access to the computer on her desk and to the network. She only works with word processing applications, and you have configured her computer and permissions for just this task. She spent all morning setting her screensaver, font sizes, and wallpaper, and after

changing some of the advanced options, her display is unviewable. What is the best way to deal with this problem?

A. Restart the computer in VGA mode, and change the offending setting.

B. Restart the computer. It will detect a problem and revert to a working setting.

C. Turn off the computer, remove the monitor, and replace it with another. Let Windows detect the new Plug-and-Play monitor.

D. Open the computer, and remove and reseat the video adapter. Close and restart the computer.

11. Jane is having problems with hardware acceleration after configuring some advanced properties of the display settings. How can Jane access the Troubleshooting tool for resolving the hardware acceleration problems in a display adapter?

A. By choosing Help from the Start menu

B. From the Advanced tab of Display Properties Settings screen

C. From the Effects tab of Display Properties

D. From Device Manager | Display Adapters

12. Lisa has caused her computer to boot to a blank black screen after configuring some of the display properties. She presses F8 after restarting her computer. What exactly is happening when she starts her computer using the Advanced Boot Options and selecting Enable VGA Mode?

A. The faulty display driver is automatically uninstalled.

B. The computer uses the Last Known Good Configuration for the display.

C. The display properties revert back to default settings and the computer boots normally.

D. The basic VGA display driver is loaded.

13. **Current situation:** You own an architecture firm and want to set up multiple monitors so your clients can have a large area to see their virtual plans and blueprints. You plan to install four monitors.

Required Result: Install the multiple monitors successfully, using all four to display the image that would have been shown on only one screen previously.

Optional Desired Results:

1. Make the screen resolution 1280 × 1084 pixels.

2. Enable scalability; later you want to change from 4 monitors to 16.

Proposed Solution: Purchase three additional PCI adapters and three more monitors. Install the adapters and their drivers, and connect the monitors. Notice during setup which adapter is primary and which is secondary. Configure the display settings to extend display to multiple monitors. Accept the default setting for display properties after multiple monitors have been configured.

What results does the proposed solution produce?

A. The proposed solution produces the required results and both of the optional results.

B. The proposed solution produces the required results and only one of the optional results.

C. The proposed solution produces the required results and none of the optional results.

D. The proposed solution does not produce the required result.

Questions 14–15   This scenario should be used to answer questions 14 and 15.

You own a publishing company and need to set up your desktop with predefined settings that include colors, screen area, font size, and effects that have been recommended by your Printing Department. Because certain colors and schemes do not print well, and uniformity is important, this task must be performed precisely. How will you make the following changes?

14. The screen area needs to be 800 × 600 pixels. After right-clicking the desktop, what comes next?

A. Choose Properties | Settings.

B. Choose Properties | Appearance.

    C. Choose Properties | Effects.

    D. Choose Properties | Settings | Advanced.

15. The Printing Department wants everyone to use a scheme with extra large icons, fonts, and menu bars so they show up well when screen shots are printed, and also to accommodate a few people with poor eyesight. However, they want to maintain the Windows Standard scheme for their computers. How can they do this?

    A. Right-click the desktop, choose Properties | Advanced options. Change the Display Font Size to Large. Under the Appearance tab, choose Windows Standard.

    B. Open Control Panel, double-click the Display icon, Settings tab | Advanced options. Change the Display Font Size to Large. Under the Appearance tab, choose Windows Standard.

    C. Right-click the desktop, choose Properties | Appearance. Under Scheme select Windows Standard (Extra Large).

    D. Open Control Panel, double-click the Display icon | Settings tab | Advanced options. Change the Display Font Size to Large. Under the Appearance tab, choose Windows Standard. Finally, check Large Icons under the Effects tab.

16. Management has decided that all employees need to use a screensaver and that it must be password protected. The setting should be applied so that after 15 minutes of inactivity, this security feature will be enabled. How do you accomplish this?

    A. There is no such feature in Windows 2000 Professional.

    B. The users will need to have special permissions assigned to them to accomplish this at their computers.

    C. Open Display from the Control Panel, choose Screen Saver, change the setting to 15 minutes, then choose Settings to assign a password.

    D. Both B and C are correct.

17. You've noticed that network traffic is higher than usual, and have traced this phenomenon back to the week you hired your new junior financial manager. After examining his computer, you notice he is using the following resources in his Display Properties Web settings. What conclusions can you draw from this?

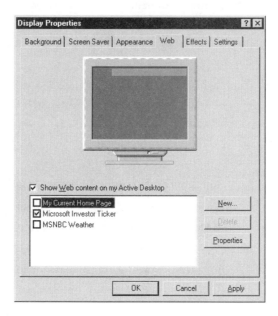

A. Your new financial manager is trading stocks over the Internet when he should be working. This explains the large amount of network traffic.

B. Your new financial manager is receiving a constant flow of information because he is using Active Desktop to view an investment ticker while at work. This explains the increased network traffic.

C. Active Desktop does not create or allow increased network traffic; there are built-in filters to manage this. Check the Device Manager for a faulty network adapter card.

D. There is no reason shown here to explain the higher network traffic. Use Performance Monitor and the event logs at your computer to determine where the traffic is coming from.

18. You've purchased and installed a new PCI display adapter and restarted the computer. Although the supplier told you that the adapter is Plug and Play, Windows 2000 did not detect it. How can you install the driver for this display adapter that is provided by the supplier?

    A. You cannot install the adapter because Windows 2000 accepts only Plug-and-Play adapters.

    B. From the Display Properties window under Settings.

    C. From the Control Panel, using Add/Remove Hardware.

    D. From the Device Manager, using Add the New Adapter utility.

19. You purchased an extra display adapter and monitor, and are installing these to enable multiple monitor configurations. After confirming which of these is primary and which is secondary in the computer's BIOS, you begin to install the drivers and commence configuration procedures. The installation of the new adapter fails. What are the possible reasons for this failure? (Choose all that apply.)

    A. The new adapter you purchased does not have a Windows 2000–compatible driver.

    B. The monitor is not on the HCL.

    C. You have not enabled multiple monitors in the Control Panel | Sounds and Multimedia.

    D. A and B.

LAB QUESTION

Objectives 5.01–5.02

You need to add a new hard disk to your computer and configure it, and then install multiple monitors on this same computer. Listed below are some of the steps required to do both of these installations. Review the steps carefully and note any unnecessary steps, steps that are left out, and/or incorrect steps. Perform the following steps to add another hard disk and then multiple monitors:

For the disk:

1. Shut down the computer and connect the hard drive to a free connector of the primary IDE cable. It will act as a slave drive, so you must set the master/slave configuration jumper to the slave position.

2. Start the computer. Log on to the system as an Administrator.

3. The disk will not be automatically detected. Choose Add/Remove Hardware.

4. Right-click the My Computer icon on the desktop, and select Properties. This opens the Computer Management console.

5. Computer Management will now detect this new disk and configure it appropriately.

For multiple monitors:

1. Confirm that the primary display adapter is using the available VGA resources.

2. Install the additional video adapter in a free PCI slot of the computer motherboard. When you restart the computer Windows 2000 will detect the adapter automatically.

3. You will be prompted to restart your computer. The video adapter is detected by the operating system, and the Add/Remove Hardware Wizard appears.

4. You are prompted to confirm that a correct adapter has been detected. The wizard asks you to select a driver for the adapter. Click Search. Click Next.

5. When prompted, insert the Windows 2000 Professional CD in the CD-ROM drive. Click OK.

6. The driver files are installed. Click Finish twice to complete the driver installation.

7. The additional adapters will be detected automatically. Wait until this procedure finishes before continuing.

8. Right-click the desktop. Select Properties from the drop-down menu.

9. From the Display Properties window, click the Settings tab. You will notice that more than one adapter is listed.

10. Select Detect and Configure Adapters from the Settings tab. This will only be available when installing multiple monitors.

11. Click the check box for Extend My Windows Desktop to This Monitor.

12. Choose any color scheme and resolution you wish for this secondary monitor.

13. Repeat steps 4 through 6 for each of the additional monitor.

QUICK ANSWER KEY

Objective 5.01		Objective 5.02	
1.	C	10.	A
2.	B	11.	B
3.	C	12.	D
4.	B	13.	C
5.	C	14.	A
6.	D	15.	C
7.	B	16.	C
8.	A and C	17.	B
9.	B	18.	C
		19.	D

A IN-DEPTH ANSWERS

5.01: Implementing, Managing, and Troubleshooting Disk Devices

1. ☑ **C** is the correct answer. Be careful with the wording of this type of question. The question asks what can Bob do with the Disk Management utility. The only other task he can perform with this utility is remote management of disks.

   ☒ **A** is incorrect because there is no fault tolerance included with Windows 2000 Professional. **B** is incorrect, because the Disk Defragmenter is included in the Storage snap-in, or as a stand-alone Disk Defragmenter snap-in, and is not in the Disk Management snap-in.

2. ☑ **B** is the best answer. Note that the question states, "everything seems to be working properly."

   ☒ Therefore, **A**, **B**, and **D** are incorrect. There is no mention of anything being physically wrong with the printer or the system. However, a yellow question mark indicates some sort of problem, and it is most likely a device driver issue.

3. ☑ **C** is the correct answer. Dynamic storage is not supported on portable computers or removable media devices.

   ☒ **A** is incorrect because a requirement for dynamic disks is that they be no larger that 512KB. **B** is incorrect, also. If the boot or system partition is a part of a mirrored set, this partition cannot be upgraded to a dynamic disk. **D** is incorrect because she already installed Windows 2000 Professional and the disk must have been supported.

4. ☑ **B** is correct. A spanned volume contains space from more than one hard drive. You may have from two to 32 drives on a spanned volume. The operating system writes the data on the disks in a sequential manner until the last of the hard drives is full.

   ☒ For this reason, **A** and **C** are incorrect.

5. ☑ **C** is the correct answer. A striped volume contains space from multiple disks (two-32) and makes it a single logical drive. The data on the participating drives is written simultaneously, thus enhancing the read-write performance of the system.

   ☒ **A** and **B** are incorrect for this same reason.

6. ☑ **D** is the correct answer. Because her physical disk is divided into three primary partitions and one extended, it is configured now as a basic disk. Dynamic disks are not supported under Windows 98, and offer another reason to choose **D** as the correct answer.

   ☒ **A**, **B**, and **C**, are all incorrect because Lucy is using Windows 98 and not Windows 2000.

7. ☑ **B** is the correct answer. The Tools tab under the Volume Properties sheet offers these utilities.

   ☒ **A** is incorrect since this tab lists label, type, file system used, and free space on the volume. **C** is incorrect because this dialog box is used to check properties of the hard drive and provides troubleshooting tools. **D** is incorrect because you would use this tab to set NTFS permissions for the volume.

8. ☑ **A** and **C** are correct. The Quota tab is located in the Volume Properties sheet, and in order for it to be accessed, you must be logged on as an Administrator.

   ☒ Disk Quota is not a snap-in, making **B** incorrect, and **D** will not solve the problem of the inability to see the Quota tab.

9. ☑ **B** is the correct location of the antivirus software that comes with Windows 2000 Professional on the CD-ROM.

   ☒ **A**, **C**, and **D** are all bogus directories.

5.02: Implementing, Managing, and Troubleshooting Display Devices

10. ☑ **A** is the best answer. Windows 2000 Professional offers this option for just this dilemma.

   ☒ **B** is incorrect because restarting the computer will result in the same problem, which will not be solved automatically by the operating system.

C and D are drastic measures and unnecessary in this case. If the monitor or display had malfunctioned without any user intervention, these might have been good solutions.

11. ☑ **B** is the correct answer. The Advanced tab of the Display Properties Setting screen offers tools to troubleshoot hardware acceleration problems.

 ☒ The Help tool will tell you how to resolve the problem, but it is not where you gain access, making **A** incorrect. **C** is incorrect because the Effects tab does not offer troubleshooting tools of this type. **D** is incorrect because the Device Manager is used to solve problems involving drivers and inoperable devices.

12. ☑ **D** is correct. The basic VGA driver is loaded so the computer can be booted, at which time the settings problems can be resolved.

 ☒ **A**, **B**, and **C** are all incorrect for the reason provided in the explanation of answer **D**.

13. ☑ **C** is the correct answer. By following all of the steps written in the proposed solution, you can successfully install multiple monitors. However, the optional results are not met. To change the settings from the default to 1280 × 1084 pixels, you'll have to set it manually, and Windows 2000 Professional only allows multiple monitors up to ten.

 ☒ **A** and **B** are incorrect as neither of the optional results are met. **D** is incorrect as the required result is met.

14. ☑ **A** is the correct place for changing the screen area size.

 ☒ Appearance is the tab for setting schemes and colors, making **B** incorrect. Effects are for setting visual effects and changing icons, making **C** incorrect. The Advanced tab of the Settings tab allows you to change font size and compatibility.

15. ☑ **C** is correct. If the Printing Department wants to use a scheme with extra large icons, fonts, and menu bars, only **C** can be correct.

 ☒ **A** and **B** only change the font sizes, and **D** changes the font and icon sizes but not the appearance of the menu bars. This makes these three answers incorrect.

16. ☑ **C** is the correct answer. This describes the correct way to set a screensaver password on a user's computer.

 ☒ **A** is incorrect because this feature is available. **B** is incorrect because a user will not need special permissions to do this.

17. ☑ **B** is the correct answer. The Web tab in the Display Properties window allows for Active Desktop, which enables users to have information sent directly to their desktops from the Internet.

☒ **A** is incorrect because the traffic generated in this instance would not cause noticeable changes in network traffic. **C** is incorrect because there are no built-in filters to manage how the information is received. **D** is incorrect because Active Desktop will cause increased traffic.

18. ☑ **C** is the correct answer. Any new device that is not detected automatically by the Windows 2000 operating system can be added using the Add/Remove Hardware applet, as long as Windows 2000 supports it.

☒ **A** is not true; devices do not have to be Plug and Play for Windows 2000 to accept them. **B** is incorrect because you cannot add an adapter using the Display Properties window. **D** is incorrect because there is no such utility.

19. ☑ **D** is correct. Both **A** and **B** can cause a new monitor or adapter to function incorrectly or not at all. The driver must be suited for Windows 2000, and the monitor should be on the HCL.

☒ **C** is incorrect because configuration of multiple monitors is not done under the Sounds and Multimedia icon of Control Panel.

LAB ANSWER

Objectives 5.01–5.02

For the disk:

1. Shut down the computer and connect the hard drive to a free connector on either the Primary or Secondary IDE cable. If it is a secondary device on the cable, it will act as a slave drive. You must then set the master/slave configuration jumper to the slave position.

2. Start the computer. Log on to the system as an administrator.

3. The disk will be automatically detected if it is a Plug-and-Play device, and Windows 2000 will configure a suitable driver for it.

4. Right-click the My Computer icon on the desktop, and select Manage. This opens the Computer Management console.

5. Select Disk Management to view your hard disk configurations.

6. Now, from the Action menu, select Rescan Disks. A new disk will be added to the right-side pane of the console. Configure your disk using the Action menu. You may not need to restart your computer.

For multiple monitors:

1. Confirm that the primary display adapter is *not* using any VGA resources.

2. You must shut down the computer before installing the additional video adapter in a free PCI slot of the computer motherboard. When you restart the computer Windows 2000 will detect the adapter automatically.

3. You will be prompted to restart your computer. The video adapter is detected by the operating system, and the Add/Remove Hardware Wizard appears.

4. You are prompted to confirm that a correct adapter has been detected. The wizard asks you to select a driver for the adapter. Click Search. Click Next.

5. When prompted, insert the Windows 2000 Professional CD in the CD-ROM drive. Click OK. You can also select Have Disk.

6. The driver files are installed. Click Finish twice to complete the driver installation.

7. You should repeat steps 2 through 6 for each additional device you wish to add.

8. Right-click the desktop. Select Properties from the drop-down menu.

9. From the Display Properties window, click the Settings tab. You will notice that more than one adapter is listed.

10. Click the monitor number for the primary display device. Select the adapter for this monitor. Choose any color scheme and resolution you wish. Select the monitor number for the secondary display device. Select the adapter for this monitor.

11. Click the check box for Extend My Windows Desktop to This Monitor.

12. Choose any color scheme and resolution you wish for this secondary monitor.

13. Repeat steps 4 through 6 for each of the additional monitors.

MICROSOFT CERTIFIED SYSTEMS ENGINEER

6

Managing and Troubleshooting Hardware Devices

TEST YOURSELF OBJECTIVES

I n this section we will cover hardware issues that concern mobile computer users, input/output devices, drivers, multiple processing units, and the installation and configuration of network adapters. Managing and configuring hardware is an important part of an administrator's duties.

Windows 2000 offers more accessibility than ever before for mobile computer users. This includes hardware improvements like new power management schemes and card services. Card services allow the laptop user to access the same levels of technology that are currently available to desktop users. With the advent of caching offline files, users can also download files from a network server and use that data even when they are not connected to the network. A synchronization manager is available to manage offline files once they are utilized.

Other hardware issues involve input/output devices and network adapter cards. Both are managed through Device Manager and include all hardware that connects to a system. Mice, keyboards, monitors, scanners, and printers all have to be configured using proper drivers and must be on Windows HCL to function properly. Network cards allow users to connect to other computers, and upgrades made to Windows 2000 make many of the configuration changes available without a reboot. Windows 2000 Professional also supports multiple processors and can have up to two processors on a single machine.

TEST YOURSELF OBJECTIVE 6.01

Implementing, Managing, and Troubleshooting Mobile Computer Hardware

With the advent of computer and network technology, the need for mobile computing arose. This need was first recognized for only a few mobile users and technicians. However, as users and employers became more dependent on their computers, it became apparent that users could work from anywhere, as long as they could access the network. Windows 2000 addresses these mobile users' needs with improved mobile hardware support, power management features, and card services.

- Windows 2000 offers improved hardware support over Windows NT, incorporating all of the hardware improvements supported in Windows 95 and Windows 98.

- The power management schemes supported by Windows 2000 are Advanced Power Management (APM) and Advanced Configuration and Power Interface (ACPI).

- Power Management must be enabled and supported by both the computer's BIOS and the OS in use.

- Card Services allow laptop users to take advantage of the same technology available to desktop computer users by incorporating these features into PCMCIA devices.

exam
ⓦatch

Know the difference between the two available power management options: APM and ACPI. APM is a legacy power management scheme that is supported by older BIOSes. The main goal of APM was to allow the hardware to be shut down or disabled after a period of inactivity, and re-enabled when needed by the user. This scheme had its faults, however, and shut down when there was inactivity on the keyboard or mouse. If a program was running in the background, sometimes data loss resulted. ACPI is a newer specification to not only cleanly power down components when not needed, but also to power the components back up in the event of network or modem activity, or even scheduled tasks.

QUESTIONS

6.01: Implementing, Managing, and Troubleshooting Mobile Computer Hardware

Questions 1–3   This scenario should be used to answer questions 1, 2, and 3.

Current Situation: Tabitha has an older laptop that she uses for business trips. Her company has recently upgraded all of their computers to Windows 2000

Professional, and even Tabitha's laptop has received the upgrade. Below is a screen shot of her Power Management window.

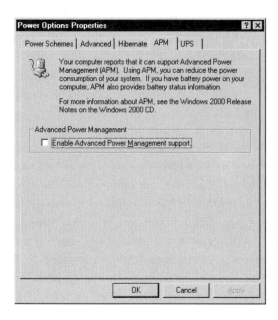

1. Tabitha is fed up with the current power management scheme she uses, APM, and wants to switch to ACPI. Can she do this?

   A. Yes. However, APM/ACPI support is determined by Windows 2000 Setup. Since the network administrator chose APM for the power management scheme when installing, the only way to switch to ACPI is to reinstall.

   B. No. The computer's BIOS supports only one of the schemes, and it is displayed in the CMOS setup.

   C. Yes. The user makes the choice between APM and ACPI. If her computer's BIOS supports one of the schemes, it will be displayed in the CMOS setup.

   D. Yes. Press F8 when Windows 2000 boots and choose Advanced Boot Options. Choose from the power management schemes available.

2. Tabitha's computer has APM enabled, and this is causing problems when she tries to resume working after her computer has gone into standby mode. Sometimes nothing happens and she has to reboot the computer from the reset button. What is the most efficient way to solve this problem?

   A. Replace the BIOS with a newer version.

   B. Boot into Safe mode and delete the following file: %systemroot%\system32\drivers\ntapm.sys

   C. Find the APM information in the registry at HKLM/Hardware, and change the setting from 1 to 0.

   D. Replace the PCMCIA bus with a newer model.

3. Tabitha understands that ACPI is an enhanced version of APM and both provide the same functions. Since she has APM already, she wants to know when and how she can upgrade to ACPI. She knows that ACPI is a newer technology, and expands the capabilities of APM. Which of the following is correct?

   A. An upgrade will be available with the first Windows 2000 Service Pack.

   B. Have the network administrator change the file %systemroot%\system32\drivers\ntapm.sys to %systemroot%\system32\drivers\w2kacpi.sys and install an appropriate BIOS.

   C. Obtain an upgrade disk from the manufacturer of the BIOS in her laptop, and upgrade it. Then, reinstall Windows 2000.

   D. There is currently no way to upgrade to ACPI from APM.

4. Your brand-new computer keeps turning itself off when you go to lunch or take a coffee break. You don't mind if your monitor shuts down, but you don't want the hard drives to power off. Where do you configure Advanced Power Management on a Windows 2000 Professional computer?

   A. Power Options applet in Control Panel

   B. Hardware profiles

   C. Device Manager

   D. Power Manager

TEST YOURSELF OBJECTIVE 6.02

Managing and Troubleshooting the Use and Synchronization of Offline Files

The Offline Files and Synchronization feature in Windows 2000 Professional allows users to keep local copies of files that are stored on a central file server, and have them available at all times. Individual files, folders, mapped network drives, or even Web pages can all be made available, even when the user is not connected to the network, and changes made to the offline item can be synchronized manually or automatically. This can be extremely useful for mobile laptop users who are not always connected to the network, but need to have access to network resources.

■ Offline Files allows a user to locally cache frequently used files, folders, and Web pages that are normally stored on remote servers, and access those files even when the computer is not connected to the network.

■ Changes made to the locally cached copy of the files are synchronized when the computer connects to the network again.

■ The Synchronization Manager is used to manage offline folders once they have been set up.

exam
ⓦatch

Make sure you know the steps for configuring and using offline files and folders. The new tests may include more hands-on questions and you may be asked to perform the task of configuring folders for offline use. Remember that a share must be created on the network server first, but this test will see if you know how to configure offline settings for Windows 2000 Professional. From a "Professional" point of view remember these things: under Folder options, Enable Offline Files must be checked, and you'll use the Advanced option to specify which files and folders will be available. The Offline Wizard will help in the configuration of the rest of the process.

QUESTIONS

6.02: Managing and Troubleshooting the Use and Synchronization of Offline Files

5. Joseph has just begun using Offline Files and Folders on his laptop computer. He was reprimanded yesterday because no changes had been made to his part of the project when his boss checked the server files. Joseph knows that he did the work. What happened?

    A. Joseph did not check the radio button Synchronize All Offline Files Before Logging Off and no changes were made on the server.

    B. Joseph had not checked the radio button Enable Reminders that would have reminded him to synchronize his files before logging off.

    C. Joseph did not check the box Enable Offline Files.

    D. Joseph did not synchronize with the server before logging off, and has lost all of his data.

6. **Current Situation:** You are setting up the use of offline folders on your network so the group Travel will be able to access these files while they are away. You have already created an NTFS share and assigned permissions on the network server, which is running Windows 2000 Server. All of the clients use Windows 2000 Professional.

    Required Result: Increase the performance of the Offline Folders features when accessed from a Windows 2000 Professional computer using the caching features of Windows 2000. Set up and configure the Professional machines to use Offline Files and Folders.

Optional Desired Results:

1. The Professional machines should synchronize all offline files before logging off.

2. The Professional machines should place a shortcut to the offline folders on the desktop.

Proposed Solution: In the Caching Settings dialog box, enable caching, and accept the default option in the Caching drop-down box. On the Professional computers, map a drive to the shared folder. Select Tools | Folder Options | Offline Files, and check Enable Offline Files, as well as all of the other options available.

What result does the proposed solution produce?

A. The proposed solution produces the required results and all of the optional results.

B. The proposed solution produces the required results and only one of the optional results.

C. The proposed solution produces the required results and none of the optional results.

D. The proposed solution does not produce the required result.

TEST YOURSELF OBJECTIVE 6.03

Implementing, Managing, and Troubleshooting Input and Output (I/O) Devices

Input and output devices, hardware, and peripherals are connected to the computer via serial, parallel, USB, PS/2, SCSI cards, and through a network. These devices allow interaction between the user and the computer itself. Managing and troubleshooting these devices requires selecting the correct driver software and confirming that the device is on the HCL; and driver signing verifies that Microsoft has fully tested the driver. Device Manager is the central location to troubleshoot and configure hardware and I/O devices.

■ The information needed to configure and troubleshoot hardware and I/O devices is contained in the Device Manager.

■ All hardware requires driver software to enable it to work with the operating system. Hardware intended for use on a Windows 2000 computers must be on the Microsoft Hardware Compatibility List (HCL) and have a Windows 2000– specific driver.

■ Updated drivers can be provided by the hardware manufacturer or found on the Windows Update Web site.

exam

ⓦatch

If you have multiple devices configured on your system that conflict with each other or are using conflicting hardware settings, errors will be displayed in Device Manager with a yellow exclamation point icon superimposed on the device icon. This usually signifies an error or conflict involving the memory range or I/O ports. You may also see an error here for a device that is using an incorrect driver. Each hardware device installed on the computer is shown in Device Manager and has a Properties sheet associated with it. This sheet contains information about the device including device type, manufacturer, location of the device, problems and conflicts, a place to uninstall or update the driver, version of the files, and resources used.

QUESTIONS

6.03: Implementing, Managing, and Troubleshooting Input and Output (I/O) Devices

7. You purchased a scanner on a whim because it was on sale. When you got it home, you began the installation without reading the accompanying material. Now, every time you try to use this USB device, the computer hangs up and

stops responding. What might have caused this problem, and how can it be corrected? (Choose all that apply.)

A. The driver you are using is for Windows 98 and not 2000. Check the manufacturer's Web site for drivers that will allow you to install to your Windows 2000 computer.

B. The scanner is not on Microsoft's HCL. Call Microsoft Support Services and ask them to help you configure the device.

C. You have an incorrect version of the driver. Check Microsoft's Web site to see if they have any new drivers for this scanner available.

D. You are using a motherboard that has the VIA chip set. Update with the newer chip set version.

8. Tom was looking at the Device Manager to find out who the manufacturer was for his network adapter card, and he noticed a yellow question mark on the printer icon. After right-clicking the printer in question, he pulled up the following Properties sheet. His printer has been working fine. What does this mean?

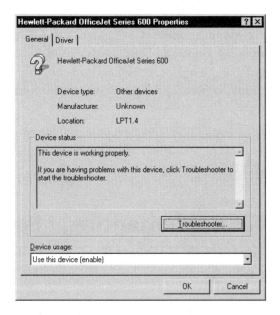

A. No driver has been installed because a driver is not needed for this device.

B. The driver needs to be updated or is the incorrect driver.

C. You need to click the Troubleshooter button and reinstall or update the driver.

D. This device has been disabled.

9. **Current Situation:** Tina's computer is set up with a video card, sound card, modem, keyboard, and mouse. She also had a printer and scanner installed in a piggyback fashion from the single parallel port on the back of her computer. She is using Windows 2000 Professional on a computer that is three years old.

Required Result: Install a PCI network adapter card and driver that is on the HCL, but not detected as Plug and Play.

Optional Desired Results:

1. After installation you notice in Device Manager that the NIC was installed using IRQ5. This is the same IRQ that is being used by the sound card. Resolve the I/O or IRQ conflicts.

2. Verify that the NIC works properly.

Proposed Solution: Turn off the computer and insert the new NIC in an open PCI slot in the computer. Restart the computer, insert the manufacturer's driver disk, and install the driver accepting the default settings. Restart the computer again if necessary, open up Device Manager, and right-click the new NIC. On the Resources tab, click Change Settings to modify the memory range and I/O ports to ones that are not being used.

What result does the proposed solution produce?

A. The proposed solution produces the required results and all of the optional results.

B. The proposed solution produces the required results and only one of the optional results.

C. The proposed solution produces the required results and none of the optional results.

D. The proposed solution does not produce the required result.

Updating Drivers

Updating drivers is sometimes necessary to resolve bugs with the driver, or to allow for features that have been added. Device Manager presents a convenient way to perform these upgrades, and offers the Upgrade Device Driver Wizard. This wizard asks you to choose between searching for an updated driver and selecting a driver from a list of drivers that Windows 2000 already knows about. The wizard will also warn you if the driver is not digitally signed by Microsoft, and will give you the option of canceling installation of the updated driver.

- Drivers need to be updated periodically to improve performance and fix bugs.
- Driver updates are performed on hardware that is already installed.
- Driver updates are performed from Device Manager.

e x a m

Ⓦatch

When using the Upgrade Device Driver Wizard and specifying the path to the driver files window, be aware that even though you may only type in something like A:\drivers\Windows2000, the wizard will still look in its own operating system for appropriate drivers. In addition to the locations you've specified, it will also search %systemroot%\inf, which contains previously loaded drivers and drivers that are included on the Windows 2000 CD. It may offer you more than one choice of drivers, and will inform you of any digital signatures.

QUESTIONS

6.04: Updating Drivers

10. Brian is a member of the Programming Department and knows that there are driver files located on the Windows 2000 Professional CD his company just

purchased. He wants to browse these files to see all of the drivers available. What is the name and location of these driver files? (E:/ is the CD-ROM.)

A. E:/VALUEADD/DRIVER.CAB

B. E:/SUPPORT/DRIVER.CAB

C. E:/I386/DRIVER.INF

D. E:/I386/DRIVER.CAB

11. **Current Situation:** You have a computer that has Windows 2000 Professional and numerous games installed on it. You want to upgrade the driver for the video card because the upgraded driver promises to offer better resolution, respond faster, and have more onboard features.

Required Result: Upgrade the driver through the Device Manager.

Optional Desired Results:

1. The driver should be digitally signed.

2. Verify there are no I/O or IRQ conflicts.

Proposed Solution: Open Device Manager and right-click the video card. Open the Properties sheet. Click on the Driver tab and choose Update Driver. Insert the floppy disk that was sent by the manufacturer in the A drive, and check the floppy drive box in the Locate Driver Files window. If the Digital Signature window appears, choose Yes and continue. Select Finish to close the wizard. Verify that the device is working properly in Device Manager.

What result does the proposed solution produce?

A. The proposed solution produces the required results and all of the optional results.

B. The proposed solution produces the required results and only one of the optional results.

C. The proposed solution produces the required results and none of the optional results.

D. The proposed solution does not produce the required result.

12. Elizabeth is installing an updated driver for her NIC, and was told the new driver is in the shared files on the network server. She thinks the file is called

Upgrades or Updates but she isn't sure. When the Upgrade Device Driver Wizard asks for the location of the files to copy, what should Elizabeth do?

A. Pause installation of the new driver until she can ask someone the exact location of these files.

B. Stop installation of the new driver until she can ask someone the exact location of these files.

C. Browse the network server for the possible folders, have the wizard search all of the specified search locations, and report on drivers that are found.

D. Elizabeth should look for an updated driver on her Windows 2000 Professional CD-ROM.

TEST YOURSELF OBJECTIVE 6.05

Monitoring and Configuring Multiple Central Processing Units

Windows 2000 products offer support for multiple Central Processing Units (CPUs). For an operating system to be able to use multiple processors, it must be able to divide its workload into controllable slices, and have power over when and how these slices will be sent to the processor. An operating system that can do this is said to be a *multitasking* operating system. A scheme called Pre-emptive Multitasking is used in Windows 2000, and involves the use of a portion of the operating system called the *kernel*. The kernel is responsible for scheduling applications for the processor in such a way that applications can share these slices of time while reducing the possibility of having to reboot the system if a program hangs or crashes. The kernel is able to remove the offending program from memory, and the rest of the system is unaffected.

■ Windows 2000 Professional supports up to two Intel CPUs on a single machine. These two processors work together under the direction of the Windows 2000 kernel to efficiently schedule and run several applications at once.

■ While the Windows 2000 kernel will load balance between the processors, individual applications can be given preference to run on one processor, and the rest of the system will share the remaining processor.

e x a m

ⓦ a t c h

To use multiple processors you must install drivers to convert your computer from its previous configuration of a single processor to a multiple-processor configuration. Make sure you know the steps involved that are listed here. In Device Manager, double-click Computer. Right-click the description of your computer and choose Properties. Choose the Driver tab, click Update, and follow the guidelines of the Upgrade Device Driver Wizard. Here's a gotcha: Watch out if the question has you do this, but does not mention anywhere that you have multiple processors. You must have multiple processors installed to upgrade to the driver successfully!

QUESTIONS

6.05: Monitoring and Configuring Multiple Central Processing Units

13. Sam wants to install Windows 2000 Professional on his computer that has two MIPS processors installed. His boss says the installation of the operating system and configuration of these multiple processors will fail. Sam doesn't think so. Who is right?

   A. Windows 2000 supports multiple processors of all types including MIPS. Sam is right.

   B. Windows 2000 only supports multiple processors that are Intel-based or Digital Alpha. Sam's boss is right.

   C. MIPS is an Intel-based processor, and they are both correct.

   D. At the release of Windows 2000, only Intel-based and Digital Alpha CPUs were supported. Now there is an updated driver that allows MIPS processors to work. They are both correct.

14. Gary has a multiple-processor computer that is running Windows 2000 on an NTFS volume. He wants to make sure he is using both CPUs efficiently, and

wants to check the CPU usage and CPU history graphs. What will he have to do to look at these graphs?

A.   Open Task Manager and click the Applications tab.

B.   Open Task Manager and click the Processes tab.

C.   Open Task Manager and click the Performance tab.

D.   Double-click the System icon in Control Panel, Advanced tab, and Performance Options.

15.   Shelby is a member of the group Junior Programmers and was working on a project concerning device driver signing with his co-worker Shelly. Shelby and Shelly both have NTFS Full Control permissions to all of the files and folders in the Junior Programmers group. While taking a break from their work, Shelby decided to click Update Driver in the window shown below. His computer only has a single processor. He has access to the driver files needed to perform this upgrade. What happened after he completed this procedure?

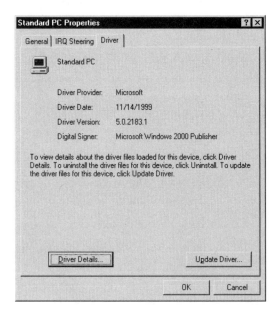

A.   The computer crashed. If a single processor machine is upgraded to one for multiple processing, the computer will no longer function.

B.   Nothing happened. Since there was only one processor, the upgrade was unsuccessful.

C. The upgrade worked great. The computer CPU use was optimized after the new driver was installed.

D. It depends on the configuration of the system board. There is not enough information to know what happened.

TEST YOURSELF OBJECTIVE 6.06

Installing, Configuring, and Troubleshooting Network Adapters

Network adapters allow users to connect their local machines to a network. Previously, adding network cards was a tedious and time-consuming process, but with the addition of Plug and Play in Windows 2000, the task just got easier. With many NICs, drivers are already included on the Windows 2000 CD. This means that most drivers can be automatically installed and configured. Unlike Windows NT, you can now change domains, register your computer with a new WINS or DNS server, even change protocol bindings, and the changes will take effect immediately. No more rebooting for these tasks!

- Network adapters (also known as network interface cards, or NICs) are used to connect a computer to a network. NIC drivers are configured through Device Manager.

- Windows 2000 supports Plug-and-Play network adapters, and will configure them automatically.

- Configuration changes made to network adapters no longer require a reboot to take effect.

exam
ⓦatch   *Don't be fooled by questions that give you the names of icons, applets, and applications that were used in Windows NT 4.0 when asked how to configure, install, update, or manage network cards. Remember, in NT4 you could add and remove NIC drivers, change domain membership, configure protocols, and change protocol binding orders, all from a single Control Panel applet. In Windows 2000 these items have been moved around a bit. NIC and driver configurations are now performed from the Device Manager. Domain association is managed from the Network Identification tab in the System applet in Control Panel, and protocols and bindings are configured on a per-connection basis from Network and Dial-up Connections in Control Panel.*

QUESTIONS

6.06: Installing, Configuring, and Troubleshooting Network Adapters

16. Sally needs to make some changes to her network settings, but is unable to reboot her computer at this time. Which of the following can't Sally do without having to reboot her computer?

   A. Sign on to a new WINS server.

   B. Change her computer's IP address.

   C. Move from a workgroup into a domain.

   D. Uninstall a PCI bus network card.

17. You want to uninstall this network adapter and install a combination card. You are changing offices and your new office has different requirements. Look at the following illustration. How do you access this window?

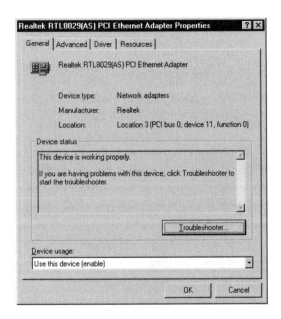

A. From Control Panel | Network and Dial-up Connections; right-click local area connection | Properties | Configure.

B. From Control Panel | System | Hardware tab | Device Manager | Network Adapters, select the adapter, right-click, and choose Properties.

C. Right-click My Computer | Properties | Hardware | Device Manager | Network Adapters; select the adapter, right-click, and choose Properties.

D. All of the above.

E. Only B and C.

18. Your boss gives you a new computer that has two NICs installed. Because you only make one connection, you assign both of them the same TCP/IP address. What will happen?

A. This will optimize performance because the first NIC to log on will maintain the connection, but if the connection is dropped, the other NIC will take over.

B. It won't make any difference. One NIC will be used to log on and the other will not be used.

C. You can never use the same TCP/IP address twice, not even on the same computer.

D. One will be the primary NIC and the other the Secondary. Configure the settings in the protocol bindings in the Network and Dial-up Connections panel.

LAB QUESTION

Objectives 6.01–6.06

This chapter covered many aspects of hardware support, implementation, management, and configuration. In order to fully integrate all of the available options in Windows 2000 Professional, including allowing power management features to be available, the use of smart cards, incorporating offline files, addressing compatibility issues, network interface card requirements, and requirements for multiple processors, you need to make sure you have the proper hardware to begin with.

Current Situation: Suppose you are starting a company from scratch. You have the money necessary to buy the very best equipment. You want to incorporate as much of Windows 2000 Professional's offerings as you can. Here is a list of things you'd like to incorporate into your new company. In the blank space beneath each item, write down the necessary hardware requirements for each.

1. ACPI Power Management.

2. Card Services for your laptops.

3. Laptop users should be able to access the network by phone or Ethernet.

4. Ability to use and store large offline files on users' computers.

5. Hardware must be easy to install.

6. Updated drivers must be easy to find.

7. Machines must be upgradeable to multiple-processor configurations.

8. Network adapter cards must be easy to configure.

9. Security must be a high priority.

10. Operating system crashes must be avoided as much as possible.

QUICK ANSWER KEY

Objective 6.01
1. B
2. B
3. D
4. A

Objective 6.02
5. A
6. D

Objective 6.03
7. A, C, and D
8. B
9. B

Objective 6.04
10. D
11. B
12. C

Objective 6.05
13. B
14. C
15. A

Objective 6.06
16. D
17. D
18. C

IN-DEPTH ANSWERS

6.01: Implementing, Managing, and Troubleshooting Mobile Computer Hardware

1. ☑ **B.** The user does not make the choice between APM and ACPI. APM is a legacy power management scheme that is supported by older BIOSes.

   ☒ In **A**, even though the first sentence is true, the network administrator does not have the option to choose the power management scheme. **C** and **D** are also incorrect because the scheme is determined by the BIOS and Windows 2000 Setup.

2. ☑ **B.** The %systemroot%\system32\drivers\ntapm.sys. can be deleted to solve any APM-related problems. These may include the system not shutting down properly, problems after resuming, and general system instability when entering a reduced power mode.

   ☒ **A** and **D** are hardware replacements and although they may solve the problem, they represent unnecessary expenditures of time and money. **C** is incorrect because it is never a good idea to change settings in the registry, and it is not an appropriate solution anyway.

3. ☑ **D.** There is no way to upgrade from APM to ACPI at this time.

   ☒ **A**, **B**, and **C** are incorrect. None of the other answers describe a way to upgrade.

4. ☑ **A.** The Power Options applet in Control Panel is used to configure power management functions on hardware that supports either the ACPI or APM specification.

   ☒ **B** is incorrect. Hardware profiles allows you to select at the boot which drivers and services will be loaded, and is not related to power management. **C** is incorrect because the Device Manager enables you to view the properties and configuration of all of your hardware. Power management is not performed in the Device Manager. **D** does not exist as an application.

6.02: Managing and Troubleshooting the Use and Synchronization of Offline Files

5. ☑ **A.** One of the settings on the Folder Options/Offline Files tab is to synchronize your work with the server before logging off. If this box is not checked, the user has to remember to do it manually.

   ☒ **B** is incorrect because this allows tool-tip balloons to appear in the taskbar to remind the user when the network has been disconnected or reconnected. **C** is incorrect because he obviously has enabled offline files and is using them already. **D** is incorrect because the data will still be on Joseph's laptop.

6. ☑ **D.** Although this was a good start, at no time did the proposed solution address specifying which files and folders were to be available offline. To do this you would need to right-click the drive letter in Explorer of the drive you mapped previously. From the context menu, select Make Available Offline. A wizard will appear to guide you through the steps.

   ☒ **A**, **B**, and **C** are incorrect as the proposed solution does not meet the required result.

6.03: Implementing, Managing, and Troubleshooting Input and Output (I/O) Devices

7. ☑ **A**, **C**, and **D** are correct. Checking these two Web sites offers the best way to locate a newly released driver for a product. **D** is a problem that is documented on Microsoft's TechNet Web site and can be resolved using the appropriate patches.

   ☒ **B** is incorrect. If you phone Microsoft and tell them you have a device that is not on the HCL, the first thing they'll do is tell you to get one that is, or call the manufacturer to locate a new driver.

8. ☑ **D.** The driver needs to be updated or is the incorrect driver even though the operating system believes it to be working properly.

   ☒ **A** is incorrect because all hardware devices of this type need a driver. **C** is incorrect. To reinstall or update the driver, choose the driver tab, and reinstall or update from there. **D** is incorrect because when a device is disabled it is not given a yellow question mark on its icon.

9. ☑ **B.** The proposed solution will correctly install the NIC and driver, and will solve the conflict with the sound card. However, at no point was the NIC checked to see if it was actually working properly and sending and receiving data, making the second optional result incorrect.

   ☒ **A** and **C** are incorrect because one of the optional results was met. **D** is incorrect because the required result was met.

6.04: Updating Drivers

10. ☑ **D.** All of the drivers available at the time of release are located in the folder driver.cab.

    ☒ **A**, **B**, and **C** are all incorrect choices because they do not exist.

11. ☑ **B.** The required result is met by following the steps in the proposed solution to use Device Manager. The second optional result is met by verifying that the device is working properly after installation. The first optional result is not met. If the Digital Signature window appears, it is only to tell you that there is NOT a digital signature, and to ask you if you want to proceed. By answering Yes, you are accepting the update anyway.

    ☒ **A** and **C** are incorrect because one of the optional results was met. **D** is incorrect because the required result was met.

12. ☑ **C.** During installation of an updated driver, Windows will search all of the specified search locations and report on drivers that are found.

    ☒ **A** and **B** are incorrect because she thinks she knows where the files are and what name they are under. She can probably find the files by browsing. **D** is incorrect because her company might have a newer driver than the one on her CD.

6.05: Monitoring and Configuring Multiple Central Processing Units

13. ☑ **B.** Since Windows 2000 supports only Intel-based or Digital Alpha Processors, beware of questions that refer to non-Intel processors such as PPCs or MIPS. Since these processors are not supported under Windows 2000, there is no upgrade path for them.

☒ **A** is incorrect because MIPS is not supported. **C** is incorrect because MIPS are not Intel-based. Finally, **D** is incorrect because this has not happened.

14. ☑ **C.** Open Task Manager and click the Performance tab. This is the correct place to see the CPU usage and history graphs.

☒ **A** and **B** are both valid tabs under Task Manager, but do not point to the correct place to see the required data. **D** is incorrect because this is the place you set application response time.

15. ☑ **A.** The computer crashed. The decision to upgrade a single processor to a multiple processor must include the availability of multiple CPUs in the computer.

☒ If a computer with only one processor is upgraded to multiple processors, it can no longer function. **B**, **C**, and **D** are all incorrect for this reason.

6.06: Installing, Configuring, and Troubleshooting Network Adapters

16. ☑ **D.** Many of the configuration changes in Windows 2000 networking do not require a reboot to take effect. However, the PCI bus does not support removal of its devices without rebooting like a USB device would, so in order to remove a PCI network card the system must be rebooted.

☒ **A**, **B**, and **C** can all be applied without rebooting.

17. ☑ **D.** All of the choices offer correct ways to arrive at the window shown.

18. ☑ **C.** In order for computers to be uniquely identified on the network, each NIC must be configured with a unique address. Network addresses are configured in the Network and Dial-up Connections applet in Control Panel.

☒ **A**, **B**, and **D** are incorrect for this reason.

LAB ANSWER

Objectives 6.01–6.06

1. **ACPI Power Management**   Computers should have newer BIOSes that support ACPI. Older BIOSes only support APM.

2. **Card Services for your laptops**   To make this work well, install a USB port in the laptops.

3. **Laptop users should be able to access the network by phone or Ethernet**   Install a combo network card in all of the laptops.

4. **Ability to use and store large offline files on users' computers**   Make sure that any computer that will be using offline files has plenty of storage room available.

5. **Hardware must be easy to install**   All hardware should be on the HCL.

6. **Updated drivers must be easy to find**   If the hardware installed is from a well-known manufacturer, is on the HCL, and is new, updated drivers should be available.

7. **Machines must be upgradeable to multiple-processor configurations**   Choose Intel-based CPUs and make sure that each computer has two.

8. **Network adapter cards must be easy to configure**   Make sure they are on the HCL and are Plug and Play. Check to see if Microsoft supports the card during installation.

9. **Security must be a high priority**   Install NTFS, and assign NTFS permissions.

10. **Operating system crashes must be avoided as much as possible**   Use the Pre-emptive Multitasking capabilities of Windows 2000 Professional.

MICROSOFT CERTIFIED SYSTEMS ENGINEER

7

Monitoring and Optimizing System Performance and Reliability

TEST YOURSELF OBJECTIVES

Monitoring and optimizing system performance and reliability is an important part of running a successful and efficient network. Windows 2000 Professional offers many tools to assist you in system performance issues. Driver Signing is available to inform you whether drivers have been tested by Microsoft and are safe to use. A Task Scheduler is offered to aid in performing routine tasks such as disk defragmenting, drive cleanup, or backing up data, and can be scheduled to run any program, at any time, and as often as needed.

Also included are tools to help an administrator locate and solve problems before they cause damage. Performance logs and alerts, hardware profiles, and data recovery are important applications tools. System Monitor can be used to measure most any aspect of your network. Disk cache usage, memory usage, physical and logical disk issues, processor usage, and overall system performance are just a few of the items to examine when monitoring system performance.

TEST YOURSELF OBJECTIVE 7.01

Managing and Troubleshooting Driver Signing

Windows 2000 products use drivers that have been digitally signed by Microsoft, and Device Manager is available to verify the signature of any driver on any system by choosing the Driver tab. This digital signature ensures the driver's stability and quality, and guarantees that it has been tested extensively. When installing new drivers, a warning box will appear if the driver you are installing is not digitally signed. A user can configure driver signing to ignore warnings, warn, or block the installation of unsigned drivers.

- Verification that drivers have been certified by Microsoft is accomplished using Driver Signing.

- The three settings for driver signing are Ignore, Warn, and Block.

- You can see which existing drivers are signed using the System File Checker.

- The log file for the System File Checker is called SIGVERIF.TXT.

exam
ⓦatch

There are two ways to track the digital signature of files in Windows 2000 Professional. One way is to use Device Manager, as stated previously. Another way to check the signature of files is to use SFC, a utility used at the command line. There are syntax requirements for using this utility, as well as optional parameters. Syntax and optional parameters are listed here. Make sure you are familiar with this option and its syntax in case it comes up on the exam. SFC [/scannow] [/scanonce] [/scanboot] [/cancel] [/quiet] [/enable] [/purgecache] [/cachesize=x] are the syntax and options.

QUESTIONS

7.01: Managing and Troubleshooting Driver Signing

1. Garth and Doug work at a secure government facility in New Mexico and are in charge of the security of data, integrity of programs, and backing up of users' data each day. Garth is a member of the Research group, and Doug is a member of the Administrators group. Doug has set the options as shown below. Garth has a program he wants to install but cannot because of the digital signature restrictions. What will he need to do to install his program?

A. Garth needs to uncheck the box that says Apply Setting as System Default, and then change the radio button to Warn.

    B. Doug will have to change the settings to allow installation of these files.

    C. The program cannot be installed. These settings were configured at installation by an administrator, and cannot be changed.

    D. Garth needs to uncheck the box that says Apply Setting as System Default, and then change the radio button to Ignore.

2. **Current Situation:** You have just taken over a small network in an attorney's office. You need to verify that existing files on your office computers are digitally signed using the File Signature Verification tool.

    Required Result: Use the File Signature Verification tool to check if the files on the system have been signed.

    Optional Desired Results:

    1. Create a log file from the results of the file verification.

    2. Uninstall any drivers that do not have a digital signature.

    Proposed Solution: From the Start menu, select Run. In the Run dialog box, enter **sigverif** and click the OK button. Under the Advanced Options | Logging tab, click the radio button to enable logging, and save results to an existing log file.

    What result does the proposed solution produce?

    A. The proposed solution produces the required results and both of the optional results.

    B. The proposed solution produces the required results and only one of the optional results.

    C. The proposed solution produces the required results and none of the optional results.

    D. The proposed solution does not produce the required result.

3. You are concerned about the amount of signed and unsigned drivers and files on your workstation. You want to use the System File Checker (SFC) utility to keep track of the digital signatures of the files. You'd also like to perform this

scan of files the next time you boot your computer, but not every time. What syntax is required to do this?

A. SFC [/scanboot]

B. SFC [/scanonce]

C. SFC [/quiet]

D. SFC [/scannext]

TEST YOURSELF OBJECTIVE 7.02

Configuring, Managing, and Troubleshooting the Task Scheduler

Task Scheduler is a tool included with all Windows 2000 products that will allow a user to schedule tasks that are done often. An administrator can use the Task Scheduler to schedule program backups to take place when there is little or no network traffic, schedule scripts to run in the morning, or run disk cleanup utilities as often as necessary. These tasks can be scheduled to run daily, weekly, when the computer boots, or even when a user logs on. Programs can also be set to run. You can even schedule your CD-ROM drive to play your favorite CD every day at lunchtime.

- You can use the Task Scheduler to schedule when programs or batch files run.
- You can schedule a task by date, time, or by interval.
- Tasks are stored as a file with the extension .JOB.
- You can set a username and password for the task.
- Tasks can be assigned permissions to specify who can manage them.
- You can manage tasks on remote computers.

exam
Watch

One interesting note: if a scheduled task runs for an account that is different from the user's account who is currently logged in, then the task will run invisibly to the logged-in user. This could be a potential trick question and answer. If the question asks you to troubleshoot why a task is not running, it may actually be that another user is logged on instead of the user the task was assigned for.

QUESTIONS

7.02: Configuring, Managing, and Troubleshooting the Task Scheduler

4. Tina teaches classes to students who have never used Windows 2000 Professional. Each day, a new group of students comes in. Tina has set up the following task to run on all of her computers in her classroom. What else could she set up using the Advanced Properties?

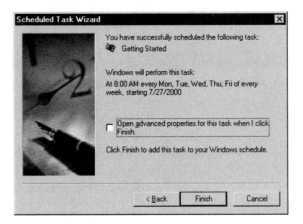

A. She can set multiple schedules.

B. She can change permissions for this task.

C. She can disable this task.

D. All of the above.

5. Jack is an administrator for a large company that is spread across a large campus. He has created Scheduled Tasks to run on users' computers for backup, scanning for viruses, and cleaning up users' mailboxes. He wants to

access the Scheduled Tasks on the other computers without actually walking over to them. Can he do this, and if so, how?

A.   No. If Jack wants to administer the Scheduled Tasks on another user's computer, he will need to log on locally to that computer.

B.   Yes. Jack can access these computers by browsing with My Network Places.

C.   Yes. Jack can access these computers using Network Neighborhood.

D.   No. Jack is not allowed access to others' Scheduled Tasks, even if he is an administrator.

TEST YOURSELF OBJECTIVE 7.03

Optimizing and Troubleshooting the Performance of the Windows 2000 Professional Desktop

Maintaining a successful network includes optimizing that network to run at peak performance levels as much as possible. Even in a healthy network, an administrator spends many hours observing how the network acts and responds to the demands placed upon it. Windows 2000 Professional offers many tools to evaluate network demands including the System Monitor, Performance Logs, and Administrator Alerts. The System Monitor can evaluate and access almost any aspect of a network including CPU usage, physical disks, processes, threads, paging files, and memory.

- The Microsoft Management Console (MMC) has a Performance snap-in that includes System Monitor and Performance Logs and Alerts.

- System Monitor can be used to collect data for memory usage, processor utilization, network activity, and more.

- A bottleneck is a component of the system as a whole that restricts the system from operating at its peak.

- The performance of your hard disk can be degraded due to fragmentation.

- The Disk Defragmenter can remove the fragmentation of your files.

- You can use the Task Manager to administer and configure processes.

In System Monitor, there are many objects and counters you can monitor and measure. Some of the questions on the exam will no doubt give you a scenario describing a usage problem, and ask you which aspect of your network you would monitor. For instance, if you think the processor in a computer is not handling the requests being sent to it, what should you monitor? Answer? The %ProcessorTime should not exceed 85 percent for a sustained period of time. If you think you are having memory shortage problems or excess paging, check the Available Bytes and Pages/sec counters. There are literally thousands of combinations of objects to monitor, and you should be familiar with the most common ones, and their maximum and minimum percentage and usage levels.

QUESTIONS

7.03: Optimizing and Troubleshooting the Performance of the Windows 2000 Professional Desktop

6. Anna thinks that she may need to add some more memory to her computer because she uses applications that require a tremendous amount of graphics files, and these files have been slower to respond to the application than normal. What counter should she measure from the list offered under the Memory Performance Object, and what levels should she watch for?

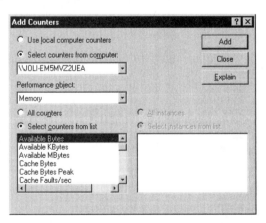

A. Watch the Available Bytes counter. If it goes under 4MB, she should add more memory.

B. Watch the Pages/sec counter. If it reaches 20, she should add more memory.

C. Watch the Pages/sec counter. If it reaches 20, she should add more hard disk space.

D. All of the above.

E. Only A and B.

7. Tiffany thinks that there is a bottleneck with a few of the hard disks on her network, and she needs to examine the performance of these disks using System Monitor. What will she need to do to enable this feature of monitoring the physical and logical disks?

A. Nothing. Simply choose the Physical Disk and Logical Disk objects in System Monitor, and choose the appropriate counters.

B. Run diskperf /y at the command line and restart the computer.

C. Diskperf is no longer available in Windows 2000. This is a command line utility from Windows NT.

D. Run diskperf /on to enable monitoring of disks.

Questions 8–10 This scenario should be used to answer questions 8, 9, and 10.

Current Situation: After adding 25 new employees and workstations to an existing network, the network begins slowing down. Users complain that it takes too long to access their files and applications on the three servers in the company. You have examined the network using System Monitor, but since the 25 workstations are new, there is no baseline of activity to compare it to. The following questions describe some of the measurements of objects in your network. Decide if a problem is occurring with these objects, and if so, choose an appropriate solution.

8. %CPU Interrupts/sec is at 98 percent.

A. Check for a bad driver.

B. Upgrade the CPU.

C. Add more memory.

D. This value is acceptable.

9. Memory, Pages/sec is at 12.

   A. Add more RAM.

   B. Add more hard disk storage.

   C. Place the paging file on another drive.

   D. This value is acceptable.

10. % Disk Time reaches 96 percent.

    A. Upgrade the hard disk to a higher speed disk.

    B. Create striped volume sets across different physical disks.

    C. See if the drives are fragmented and defragment the drives as needed.

    D. All of the above.

    E. This value is acceptable.

TEST YOURSELF OBJECTIVE 7.04

Using Performance Logs and Alerts

You can use Performance Logs and Alerts to collect, view, and receive information about local or remote computers on your network. You can monitor the same objects as those in System Monitor to receive alerts when defined thresholds are met. These are important tools to use when creating baselines and gathering statistical information about network performance. This information can be viewed from inside System Monitor, or in any spreadsheet software program of your choice, where data and information can be sorted and analyzed.

- The Performance Logs and Alerts allow you to collect data from local and remote computers to measure performance. This data can be logged and viewed in System Monitor, or it can be exported to Excel or to a database.

- The comment configuration option allows you to enter a description of the log file you are creating.

- Alerts allow some action to be performed when a performance counter reaches a particular threshold.

- Task Manager allows you to monitor applications, processes, and different performance statistics.

exam
ⓦatch

You can use the Performance Logs and Alerts MMC snap-in to configure your logging and alerts, and these logs can be configured in many different formats. Be sure to know the choices for the types of log files you can create and their extensions. The log file types are Binary and binary circular (.BLG), text-csv (.CSV), text –tsv (.TSV), and circular and sequential trace files (.ETL). Remember also that when setting the maximum size of a log file, be careful that it is not larger than the free space on the drive or larger than your disk quota. If the log runs out of disk space, an error will occur.

QUESTIONS

7.04: Using Performance Logs and Alerts

11. John wants to monitor all the processes, services, and drivers that are running on his computer. He'd also like to see the process name, process ID (PID), the percentage of CPU time being used, and the elapsed time using the CPU and memory usage. Where is the best place for John to view this information?

    A. System Monitor

    B. Task Manager

    C. Scheduled Tasks

    D. The latest System Monitor log file

12. **Current Situation:** You are devising a plan for using System Monitor to create and log statistics about the performance of your network. You plan to use these statistics for analyzing what happens to your network during peak usage times, as well as non-peak hours. You will create log files to import to other applications to be analyzed.

    Required Result: You must be able to view the log file using Excel.

    Optional Desired Results:

    1. Verify that the maximum size of your log file is not larger than the available disk space where the file will be stored.

    2. Enable alerts for CPU usage over 95 percent.

Proposed Solution: Use System Monitor to create logs for the required objects. Set the log type as Binary Circular. Accept the defaults for log file size. Create an alert to notify the administrator of the network when CPU usage is over 95 percent.

What result does the proposed solution produce?

A. The proposed solution produces the required results and both of the optional results.

B. The proposed solution produces the required results and only one of the optional results.

C. The proposed solution produces the required results and none of the optional results.

D. The proposed solution does not produce the required result.

TEST YOURSELF OBJECTIVE 7.05

Managing Hardware Profiles

Hardware profiles are available for clients who utilize laptop computers and other mobile computing devices, and have different hardware configurations determined by their location. A mobile computer user may need one configuration for a docked laptop, and another when that user is not at a docking station. Profile changes may include information concerning the type of keyboard or mouse the user has, how that computer will configure power management, and even how the computer will connect to a network.

- Hardware profiles allow you to have multiple hardware configurations.
- Hardware profiles are commonly used for portable computers with docking stations.
- You can create new hardware profiles by copying an existing one and then editing it.
- You cannot delete the hardware profile that you started Windows 2000 with.
- You can use the Device Manager to disable devices in hardware profiles.

exam

Watch

Usually with multiple profiles, the user is asked which profile he or she would like to start the system with, by being offered a menu of choices. A user can also configure the time the system will wait before defaulting to one of them. If presented with a question involving these choices, there is an exception to the rule. If you have a portable computer, you can have it automatically detect whether or not it is connected to a docking station. Windows 2000 can query the BIOS for a Dock ID to determine if it is docked or not. Then it will automatically start with the correct profile. Be aware that this is an option.

QUESTIONS

7.05: Managing Hardware Profiles

13. Jessica is using her computer at work, and decides to make a new hardware profile for herself. She sometimes switches offices and needs another profile to address the changes. She uses Control Panel to open the System icon, chooses the Hardware tab, and sees there is already a profile created and configured. Jessica knows she did not create this profile for herself. How did the profile get there?

    A. Her administrator configured it when she became a member of the domain.

    B. The profile is created by default when Windows 2000 is installed.

    C. Jessica's administrator created the profile when she became a member of the workgroup.

    D. A and C are both correct answers.

14. Jim's administrator has configured his laptop to have two profiles, one for its docked state, and one for undocked. The administrator has set the number of seconds to zero, so the computer will always boot to the default state of being docked because Jim is usually at the office. Jim leaves town on business and can not get his computer to come up in its second profile. Every time it boots, It

automatically chooses profile 1. What can Jim do to override the default during startup?

A. Select Control and press C during the system prompt.

B. Click the Windows icon on the keyboard during system prompt.

C. Press the SPACEBAR during the system prompt.

D. Press ESC during the system prompt.

15. **Current Situation:** You work for a large printing enterprise with many departments. Your assistant just received a laptop that he will use in-house and while away on business. When he is at the office he works mainly in your department, but also assists in two other departments. One of these departments has requirements that involve specialized devices and services. The other department requires that he have a certain color desktop, screensaver, and color scheme. While in all of these departments, his laptop will be docked.

Required Result: Set up the laptop to work with your department.

Optional Desired Results:

1. Set up the laptop to work in the department requiring specialized drivers and services.

2. Set up the laptop to work in the department requiring special color schemes, screensavers, and desktop.

3. Set up the laptop with a profile when he is away on business.

Proposed Solution: Install Windows 2000 on the assistant's laptop. After installation, configure his desktop with the colors and screensaver requirements of Department #2. Create one other profile called Special. Configure the profile Special to access the specialized devices and services of Department #1.

What result does the proposed solution produce?

A. The proposed solution produces the required results and both of the optional results.

B. The proposed solution produces the required results and only one of the optional results.

C. The proposed solution produces the required results and two of the optional results.

D. The proposed solution does not produce the required result.

TEST YOURSELF OBJECTIVE 7.06

Recovering Systems and User Data

Backing up data is crucial for a network to function efficiently. Administrators spend many hours making sure that a system can be restored in the event of catastrophic data loss. Windows 2000 offers many ways to prepare for and recover from such an event, and includes tools such as Backup and Recovery, Restore Wizards, Safe mode, the Recovery console, and Startup and Recovery options. Be familiar with the following information concerning Windows 2000 Backup, Recovery, and Restore utilities.

- You can use the Backup utility to back up files, folders, and the System State.

- If you back up an NTFS volume, then it should be restored to an NTFS volume.

- You can choose from the following types of backup: Normal, Incremental, Differential, Copy, and Daily.

- You can back up all files if you have Backup Operator or Administrator privileges.

- Safe mode can be used to isolate faulty drivers, services, and applications.

- You start Safe mode by pressing F8 at the Boot menu.

- The Recovery console can be used to repair Windows 2000 when your computer will not start.

- The Startup and Recovery dialog box allows you to choose which operating system is loaded by default, and how long to wait for the user to select an operating system to load.

exam **Watch**

There are five different types of backups that can be performed. Make sure you are completely comfortable with all types and know when and how to implement them before attempting this test. The ways to perform backups are listed here, with a short description of their characteristics. **Normal:** *This will back up all files that are selected and mark them as being backed up. This type is also commonly referred to as a Full backup.* **Incremental:** *This will back up all files that are selected that have changed since the last Normal or Incremental backup performed, and marks them as being backed up.* **Differential:** *This will back up all files that are selected that have changed since the last Normal or Incremental backup, but does not mark them as backed up.* **Copy:** *This will back up all selected files without marking them as backed up.* **Daily:** *This will back up all selected files that changed the day the backup was performed, without marking them as backed up.*

QUESTIONS

7.06: Recovering Systems and User Data

16. Dave employs many security measures to keep his network safe. He uses RAID5, NTFS, and has an ERD (emergency repair disk). He uses a UPS (uninterruptible power supply) at all times, and has extra copies of all of his applications like Office 2000, Windows 2000, and his drivers; and all have a digital signature from Microsoft. He uses ACPI (Advanced Configuration and Power Interface) as a power management tool, and all of his computers are brand new. Dave also has a firewall to keep out hackers, and virus-checking software. What else should Dave be doing to keep his network safe?

   A. Nothing. Dave has plenty of security measures in place already.

   B. Dave should install a Proxy Server.

   C. Dave should back up his data on tape or other media. RAID5 is not sufficient.

   D. Dave has gone over the top. He should remove some of these security features; they are causing performance degradation on his network.

17. **Current Situation:** You suspect that the main server for your network has a corrupt registry. Luckily, there is a backup copy of the System State on tape. You want to use the Recovery console to restore the registry, but it has not been installed.

   Required Result: Install Recovery console to the main server.

   Optional Desired Results:

   1. Copy files from the hard drive to magnetic tape in case Recovery console fails and the data is inaccessible.

   2. From the prompt, run the command FDISK to view system partitions and system information.

   Proposed Solution: Log on as an administrator. Start the computer from the Windows 2000 CD-ROM, and choose the Recovery Console option.

What result does the proposed solution produce?

A. The proposed solution produces the required results and both of the optional results.

B. The proposed solution produces the required results and only one of the optional results.

C. The proposed solution produces the required results and none of the optional results.

D. The proposed solution does not produce the required result.

LAB QUESTION

Objectives 7.01–7.06

Current Situation: Brett administers a large network of 400 users. He has recently upgraded all of the workstations to Windows 2000 Professional, and is concerned with the monitoring and optimization of the system performance and reliability of the network. He is utilizing many of the tools offered by Microsoft to make this monitoring more efficient. Listed below are some of the decisions he has made regarding this optimization. Which of the following choices are good decisions, and which decisions should be changed?

1. On Driver Signing, Brett has chosen Warn as a default setting for his users.

2. He has used System File Checker to determine which files have been signed and which have not on his systems.

3. He is using Task Scheduler to perform backup and disk cleanup jobs, and performs the backups during the workday so he can monitor their progress.

4. He uses Task Scheduler to manage tasks on remote computers.

5. He uses System Monitor to collect data about his network, and creates logs of the information.

6. He defragments his hard disks on the servers daily.

7. He defragments his workstations on Monday, Wednesday, and Friday.

8. He monitors hard disk usage on the servers daily, so he can notice any strains on the servers.

9. He has his computers set up to notify him if the %Processor Usage reaches 100 percent at any time.

10. He creates and maintains hardware profiles for his mobile computer users.

11. He backs up his data with a Full backup each day, so he can quickly and efficiently restore his network if there is a failure.

A QUICK ANSWER KEY

Objective 7.01

1. **B**
2. **B**
3. **B**

Objective 7.02

4. **D**
5. **B**

Objective 7.03

6. **E**
7. **B**
8. **A** and **B**
9. **D**
10. **D**

Objective 7.04

11. **B**
12. **D**

Objective 7.05

13. **B**
14. **C**
15. **C**

Objective 7.06

16. **C**
17. **C**

IN-DEPTH ANSWERS

7.01: Managing and Troubleshooting Driver Signing

1. ☑ **B.** Because Block is on, and the Apply Setting as System Default is checked, an administrator will have to log on to change the setting.

   ☒ **A** and **D** are incorrect because Garth is not logged on as an administrator. **C** is incorrect because the program could be installed if the settings were changed.

2. ☑ **B.** By using sigverif at the Run command, the application will be started, and by clicking the radio button to write a logging file, the first optional result is met. The second optional result is not met because there is no option to uninstall unsigned drivers while using this utility, and this action would probably bring down an existing system.

   ☒ **A** and **C** are incorrect because one of the optional results was met. **D** is incorrect because the required result was met.

3. ☑ **B.** The scanonce switch causes the SFC utility to scan at the next system restart.

   ☒ **A** is incorrect because it scans at each boot. **C** is incorrect because it replaces all incorrect system file versions without prompting the user. Finally, **D** is not a valid switch for the SFC utility.

7.02: Configuring, Managing, and Troubleshooting the Task Scheduler

4. ☑ **D.** All of the options listed can be set through advanced options.

5. ☑ **B.** Using My Network Places, an administrator can access Scheduled Tasks on any computer across the network.

   ☒ **A** and **D** are incorrect for this reason. **C** mentions Network Neighborhood, which is in Windows NT, not Windows 2000.

7.03: Optimizing and Troubleshooting the Performance of the Windows 2000 Professional Desktop

6. ☑ **E.** Only A and B state the correct counters and their appropriate limits. Available Bytes tells how much memory is available at any given time, and Pages/sec describes how often the paging file is used to swap information to and from the hard disk.

    ☒ **C** is incorrect because adding more hard disk space will not address the immediate issue of not having enough memory to run the applications.

7. ☑ **B.** Because monitoring hard disks will slow down the performance of the network, it must be enabled at the command line and then rebooted.

    ☒ **A** and **C** are incorrect for this reason. **D** is not the correct syntax; there is no /on switch for diskperf.

8. ☑ **A** and **B** are correct. Bad drivers can generate excessive interrupts, and upgrading the CPU will help if this is not the case.

    ☒ **C** will not affect CPU usage directly, and is incorrect. **D** is incorrect because the CPU Interrupts/sec is too high.

9. ☑ **D.** If the Pages/sec is under 20, this is not the source of the bottleneck.

    ☒ **A** and **B** are incorrect. Adding more RAM or more hard disk storage is not necessary. **C** is also incorrect because placing the paging file on another drive is not necessary.

10. ☑ **D.** This in an unacceptable value and needs attention. Upgrading the disks to a higher speed may solve the problem. Creating striped volumes across physical disks will increase read/write time. The disks may need defragmenting.

    ☒ **A**, **B**, and **C** are incorrect individually, because all of them are what need to be addressed. **E** is incorrect as this value isn't acceptable.

7.04: Using Performance Logs and Alerts

11. ☑ **B.** Task Manager can be used for different tasks, and allows you to monitor applications, processes, and different performance statistics. Task Manager has three tabs: Applications, Processes, and Performance. The information above can all be found under the Performance tab of Task Manager.

☒ **A** is incorrect because System Monitor is not the best choice here. All of the requirements can be accessed in one area of Task Manager. The Scheduled Tasks utility does not offer this information, making **C** incorrect. **D** is incorrect because the latest System Monitor log file does not contain all of this real-time information.

12. ☑ **D.** The creation of the log file is a good start; however, saving the log file in the format Binary Circular will not allow the administrator to view the file using Excel. This is a counter log file that stores the data in a binary format. Thus, the required result is not met. The first optional result is not met since the acceptance of default settings does not guarantee that there will be enough hard drive space for the file. The second optional result is met with the creation of the CPU usage alert.

☒ **A**, **B**, and **C** are incorrect because the proposed solution does not meet the required result.

7.05: Managing Hardware Profiles

13. ☑ **B.** A default profile is created when the installation of Windows 2000 takes place.

☒ **A** and **C** are incorrect because the administrator did not create this profile. If there had been two profiles listed, **A** and **C** might have been correct.

14. ☑ **C.** The easiest way to bypass the default settings when the timer is set to zero is to press the SPACEBAR during the system prompt.

☒ **A**, **B**, and **D** will not do anything to solve this problem.

15. ☑ **C.** By installing Windows 2000 on the laptop, a default profile is created. If you make this default profile with the color schemes necessary for Department #2, then this profile will work for both your department and that one. This takes care of the required result and the second optional result. By creating a second profile Special, you have addressed the first optional result. The third optional result is not met, since no profile has been created for the times that he will be away and his computer will not be docked.

☒ **A** and **B** are incorrect because the proposed solution meets none of the optional results. **D** is incorrect because the required result is met by the proposed solution.

7.06: Recovering Systems and User Data

16. ☑ **C.** There should always be backup copies of data available on tape, CD-ROM, or other media.

    ☒ **A** and **D** are incorrect because all of the items listed are necessary to keep a network from harm. **B** is incorrect because Dave already has a firewall in place.

17. ☑ **C.** It is possible to install and run the Recovery console when problems occur. It is not a requirement that it be installed prior, making the required result correct. However, neither one of the optional results are met because while in Recovery console a user cannot copy files off the hard drive to some other media for security reasons, and only commands that are supported by the Recovery console can be used at the prompt; FDISK is not one of them.

    ☒ **A** and **B** are incorrect because the proposed solution meets none of the optional results. **D** is incorrect because the required result is met by the proposed solution.

LAB ANSWER

Objectives 7.01–7.06

1. Warn is an appropriate choice if you trust your users to make appropriate choices regarding driver signing. The user still has the option of installing an unsigned driver. Block may be a more appropriate choice for such a large network.

2. Although it mentions that Brett is using System File Checker, there is no mention of what he has chosen to do about files that are not signed. Brett should have a plan in place to replace the unsigned files.

3. If Brett is performing these backups and disk cleanups during the day, this will have a negative impact on the network. These tasks should be performed when the network is not so busy.

4. Using Task Scheduler to manage tasks on remote computers is good!

5. If Brett uses System Monitor to collect data about his network, and creates logs of the information, he should also be examining that information on a daily basis to look for potential problems or bottlenecks.

6. Defragmenting his hard disks on the servers daily is not necessary. Once a week would suffice.

7. Defragmenting his workstations on Monday, Wednesday, and Friday is also too much defragmenting. Once every two weeks would suffice.

8. Monitoring hard disk usage on the servers daily WILL cause a strain on the servers. He should not be monitoring this all of the time.

9. If Brett is alerted every time the %Processor Usage reaches 100 percent, he may receive a lot of alerts. Some applications utilize 100 percent of the processor occasionally.

10. The fact that he creates and maintains hardware profiles for his mobile computer users is good.

11. Doing a Full backup every day, so he can quickly and efficiently restore his network if there is a failure, is not the best choice for backing up the data. He should intersperse Incremental, Differential, Copy, and Daily.

MICROSOFT CERTIFIED SYSTEMS ENGINEER

8

Configuring and Troubleshooting Users' Profiles and the Desktop Environment

TEST YOURSELF OBJECTIVES

8.01   Configuring and Managing User Profiles

8.02   Configuring and Troubleshooting Desktop Settings

8.03   Configuring and Troubleshooting Accessibility Services

This chapter covers the management of users' profiles, desktop settings, login scripts, policies, and accessibility services. In order to maintain an efficient network, or even a single shared computer, these areas of configuration make management easier to administer and more enjoyable for the user. For example, if two users share a computer, and one is excessively neat with his files and desktop, and the other is incredibly messy (scattering folders all over the desktop and wild screensavers), these two users may have a hard time working together and sharing the same computer. In a case like this, the management of this computer becomes an issue.

Another type of configuration and management problem may occur when there are local computer policies, users who roam, or scripts that may be required to run when users log on. Making a computer accessible to users with special needs may also be necessary. With Windows 2000, all of these issues can be addressed and configured, making the network run more efficiently, and keeping the users happy.

TEST YOURSELF OBJECTIVE 8.01

Configuring and Managing User Profiles

Configuring and managing user profiles allows users to have separate identities when they log on to a computer. Group membership and passwords determine what a user can and cannot accomplish while at the computer, and is the key to maintaining security in a network. Roaming profiles and home folders allow individualization of identities, permit users to take their settings with them when they sit at other computers, and give them a place of their own to store their documents.

- You must have Administrator status to manipulate Users and Passwords.

- Users and Passwords will let you add and remove users, change group membership, and manipulate the user profile and home folder.

- Group membership is the key to security; what a user can or cannot do depends almost entirely on what groups he is a member of.

- To create a roaming profile, set all accounts to a profile on a server.

- Roaming profiles have profile paths that point to server folders.

- You can create a login script for a user, which will run whenever the user logs on.

- Your home folder is where many applications will save to by default.

e x a m

ⓦa t c h

When multiple users are sharing a computer and each has a username and password, each user logs on and gets his or her settings on the desktop, and each user has access to the resources at the computer. When users create shortcuts on their desktops, only a .LNK file is created in their desktop folder; however a move will change the location of the file. For example, Jack moves the file Client List, instead of creating a shortcut for it. When Jim logs on later at the same computer, he will not be able to see the file in its normal position because Jack has moved it. Always teach users to create shortcuts on computers they share.

QUESTIONS

8.01: Configuring and Managing User Profiles

Questions 1–4   This scenario should be used to answer questions 1, 2, 3, and 4.

Current Situation: Jackie and Merritt share a computer at work. They both have a username and password, and a connection to the Internet. They have separate desktop settings, passwords, and home folders. Jackie mostly uses financial programs and data, while Merritt generally uses a CAD program for design work. They always log on to their own desktop, and do not know each other's passwords.

1. Jackie is changing departments and needs to change her Internet configuration, but Merritt does not need to change his. What will happen if Jackie changes her Internet connection?

    A. Because they share a computer, Merritt's connection will be changed also, and he'll have to reset all of his settings and his email address.

    B. Because they share a computer, Merritt's connection will be changed also, but he can retain his email and configuration settings.

    C. Because they share a computer, Merritt's Internet connection will change. If the computer had two modems or NICs, it would not.

    D. Nothing will be different when Merritt logs on.

2. Merritt has removed his Connect to the Internet icon from his desktop, all of his shortcuts, and the Recycle Bin icon. Jackie logs on and even though she can still access her shortcuts and her Internet connection, she no longer sees the Recycle Bin icon. Why can Jackie still access everything but the Recycle Bin?

   A. The shortcuts and Internet connection are stored in each user's Desktop folder as files, but the Recycle Bin is not. Therefore, a move or deletion of the Recycle Bin will affect the entire computer.

   B. The shortcuts and Internet connection are stored in each user's Documents and Settings folder, but the Recycle Bin is not. Therefore, a move or deletion affects the computer as a whole.

   C. Each user's shortcuts and Internet connections are stored in the user's Profile folder, but the Recycle Bin is not. A move or deletion of the Recycle Bin affects the computer as a whole.

   D. None of the above.

3. The administrator of the network suspects that Merritt has been doing more surfing on the Web than working. He wants to check Merritt's local user profile for proof of this. Where is the information about his local user profile stored, and where can the administrator find the information he is looking for?

   A. D: | Documents and Settings | MerrittB | Local Settings

   B. D: | Winnt | MerrittB | Local Settings | History

   C. D: | ProgramFiles | MerrittB | Local Settings | History

   D. D: | Documents and Settings | MerrittB | Local Settings | History

4. Since Jackie has been promoted, she needs to be added as a member of the Accounting group. You plan to achieve this using Local Users Manager. You have right-clicked Jackie's username and chosen Properties from the menu. Put the following steps in the order that they will be completed to add Jackie to the Accounting group.

   1. Choose the Accounting group from the queue of groups.

   2. Click on the Member tab.

   3. Choose Add from the window.

   A. 3, 2, then 1.

   B. 2, 3, then 1.

C. 1, 3, then 2.

D. It is listed in the correct order: 1, 2, and 3.

5. As a network administrator for a small company, you add users and profiles rarely. Recently, you added a user who logged on with the password you had given him. He did irreparable damage to your network and you got the blame. The new employee claimed he did not cause this damage, and you must have sabotaged the system using his account and password. What should you have done when setting the username and password properties to avoid this?

   A. Set the password option as Account Disabled.

   B. Set the password option as Account Locked Out.

   C. Set the password option as User Cannot Change Password.

   D. Set the password option as User Must Change Password at Next Logon.

6. The users on your network are only familiar with the applications they use daily. They input data, do data processing, and create documents. You want to make sure that the employees' software programs stay up-to-date, but do not want the users to have any hand in the installations. What group policy feature can you employ to achieve this?

   A. Administrators can manage software installation and upgrades using the Software Installation and Maintenance options.

   B. Administrators can manage the Synchronization Manager from User Data Management options in group policy.

   C. Administrators can manage remote installations using the Remote OS Installation features of group policy management.

   D. None of the above is available to manage upgrades to software installations.

7. You need to create a logon script for some of your users, so certain programs and applications will be run when they log on or when they log off. You have already set a path for this file in the Login Script box of the Properties Profile tab on your clients' computers. What options are available for you to write these scripts?

   A. VBScript

   B. DOS Batch files (.BAT and .CMD)

    C. JavaScript

    D. All of the above

    E. A and C only

8. Todd has been moved from the Programming Department to the Research and Development Division of his company. Todd needs to be removed from the Programming group. How is this achieved? (Select all that apply.)

    A. Highlight Users and Passwords, right-click the Groups tab, find the User, and click Remove.

    B. Right-click Users and Passwords, go to the Advanced Properties menu, open Local Users and Groups, open Programmers, double-click the user, click the Member Of tab, select the group, and click Remove.

    C. Open Users and Passwords, go to the Advanced Properties menu, under Advanced User Management click the Advanced button, open Users, double-click the user, click the Member Of tab, select the group, and click Remove.

    D. Right-click Users and Passwords, choose Open, go to the Advanced Properties menu, under Advanced User Management click the Advanced button, open Groups, choose Programmers, double-click it, find the user, select the user, and click Remove.

9. A user on your network has three accounts: an administrator account, a personal account, and a training account. When this user wants to make a configuration change to his desktop while logged on as administrator, the change does not take effect on his personal account or his training account. What can you do as an administrator to synchronize these accounts, so that changes to one account will affect all three?

    A. Copy the folders of the administrator account to the folders of the other two accounts.

    B. Combine the three accounts into one account using the Users and Passwords icon in Control Panel.

    C. Change the profile path in the training and personal accounts to the path in the administrator account.

    D. This is not yet possible in Windows 2000 Professional.

10. There are four members of the Planning and Zoning Department at the local city hall who are working on a project called Town Square. Each of the four members is working on a separate area of the planning which includes landscape, building codes, water and electric, and blueprints. These employees have all been told to save their work to a common folder on the city's main server, but most of the time these documents end up in the My Documents folders on their computers. This is making it impossible to back up the data regularly, and for the other members of the Planning and Zoning Department to access the files. What is the best way to solve this problem?

   A. Make them all use "thin clients" with no ability to store their files locally. Force all work to be done on the server.

   B. Give them all roaming profiles.

   C. Give each a local path to a shared home folder.

   D. Give each a local path to his own home folder.

TEST YOURSELF OBJECTIVE 8.02

Configuring and Troubleshooting Desktop Settings

Local computer policies are used to configure desktop settings for computers that may be used by more than one employee, or to restrict a user from making certain changes to the system or desktop. If a local computer policy is in effect for a computer, anyone that sits at that computer is affected. These restrictions give the administrator as little or as much control over a user's desktop as he or she deems necessary. If an administrator wants a password-protected screensaver on everyone's computer, it can be done. Local computer policy is not the highest level of security, but it can be effective at the local level.

- Local computer policy is a snap-in to Microsoft Management Console (MMC).
- Changes made inside local computer policy/user configuration are all local computer-wide; that is, they apply to all users who sit at that computer.

■ Changes made to policy are *meta-configurational*; that is, they don't simply change the desktop environment, but set the principles by which users can change their own environments.

■ Disabling icons and Start menu items through local computer policy only removes the icons; the users can still access these items through Windows Explorer or the command line.

■ Local computer policy is the weakest form of policy; it is overridden by policy set at any higher level, as in domain group policy at the server level.

exam
ⓦatch

As stated earlier, local computer policy is the weakest of all security options. You may set local computer policies for a workstation, only to have them not work at all when the user logs on to the network. The reason this happens is because there are other policies that will override the local computer policy, such as group policy at the server level. Policies are hierarchical, and server policies must either be in agreement, not set to anything in particular, or turned off, if local policies are to prevail.

QUESTIONS

8.02: Configuring and Troubleshooting Desktop Settings

11. Randy and Kim share duties as network administrators at a high-security factory that makes top-secret parts for fighter planes. Randy wants everyone to conform to the same desktop settings, and have restricted access to their desktop environments. Kim has suggested that Randy configure this local computer policy from the group policy snap-in for the MMC, but Randy knows another way to access it. In which two ways can Randy enable this service?

A. Run gpedit.msc from the Run menu.

B. Link to Group Policy editor from Active Directory.

C. From the icon for group policy in Control Panel.

D. Select Run from the Start menu, and type **mmc /a**. Use the Add/Remove button to add group policy.

12. Sammie sets the local computer policy to include restrictions in the Control Panel such as removing (hiding) the System icon and the Add/Remove Programs icon. The next day she notices that this same computer does not have the restrictions enabled. What happened?

A. The user changed the policy to disable in the Local Computer Policy properties box.

B. The user is logged in to a network, and the group policy at the Server level is overriding the local settings.

C. The administrator did not reboot the computer after making these changes.

D. The user logged on as someone else at the local computer.

13. Lori wants to use templates to assist in setting a local computer policy for a workstation that has three different users and logons. She wants to restrict access to as many objects as possible, leaving only the necessary applications, icons, and applets for these employees. Which of the following is available for configuration? (Choose all that apply.)

A. Remove Documents from the Start menu.

B. Disable adjusting desktop toolbars.

C. Hide all icons on the desktop.

D. Allow TCP/IP advanced configuration.

E. Don't run specified Windows applications.

14. Lately, you've noticed from your alert logs and statistics that there have been numerous logon attempts and failures at a specific computer on your network. You want to enable a local policy that addresses local account lockout and

lockout duration for this computer. Using the illustration below, choose the correct sequence of events for doing this.

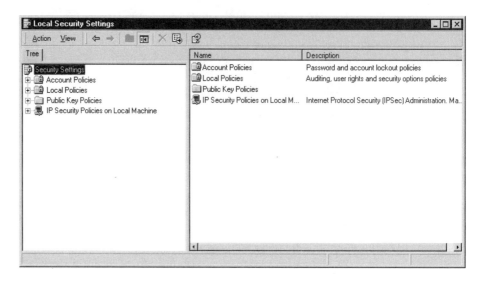

A. Account Policies | Account Lockout Duration. Configure the options in this Window.

B. Local Policies | Security Options. Scroll down to Lockout Options. Configure here.

C. Public Key Policies | Security Options | Lockout Options.

D. Account Policies | Security. Configure objects here.

15. You are setting up computers for a kiosk where users will log on as guests and have access to the Internet. You want all of the guests to log on and receive the same desktop appearance, as well as uniform policies disallowing downloading files, accessing certain sites, and access to Control Panel icons. However, you'd like to be able to log on with an existing roaming user profile when maintaining and managing these computers. How should you set this up?

A. Change the local security policy to meet the needs of the guests.

B. Place restrictions on the guest profile using security policies and group policies.

C. Change the local computer policy to address the needs of the guests.

D. On the guest account enable the following: Don't Save Settings on Exit, Disable Adjusting Toolbars, and Hide All Icons on Desktop.

16. Janice is using the local security policy snap-in to configure users' desktops. She thinks she has a good idea of what most of the policies do, but is not familiar with a few she'd like to set. She doesn't know if Hide All Icons on Desktop just hides the icons, removes the programs from the computer, or restricts the user from those applications. Where can Janice go to find out what this restriction really means?

A. Microsoft TechNet

B. Microsoft Help

C. Microsoft Windows Update

D. The Explain tab of the Policy dialog box

17. Bobby uses his computer to perform many different types of tasks, and utilizes almost all of the items on his menu bars every day. He is tired of the menus that only show what he's used recently, instead of all of the available tools. How can Bobby make sure that all of the options are always available on the menus?

A. Disable changes to Taskbar and Start Menu settings.

B. Enable Do Not Keep a History of Recently Opened Documents.

C. Disable Personalized Menus.

D. Disable Shortened Menus.

18. **Current Situation:** You are working for a small Internet start-up company and many users have to share computers. You want to set a group policy for each of the computers that are shared, and set it up in such a way that the computers are secure, conform to company standards, and revert to their original settings when users log off.

Required Result: No user shall run programs that are not on the acceptable use policy list mandated by the company.

Optional Desired Results:

1. Disable access of Control Panel from the Start menu.

2. Disable access of Control Panel from Windows Explorer.

Proposed Solution: Enable the policy restriction Do Not Run Specified Windows Applications, and make sure the policy list mandated by the company is covered there. Next, choose Disable Programs on the Settings menu and include Control Panel.

What result does the proposed solution produce?

A. The proposed solution produces the required results and both of the optional results.

B. The proposed solution produces the required results and only one of the optional results.

C. The proposed solution produces the required results and none of the optional results.

D. The proposed solution does not produce the required result.

TEST YOURSELF OBJECTIVE 8.03

Configuring and Troubleshooting Accessibility Services

Windows 2000 products offer many options to assist in the computing requirements of people that have accessibility needs. Most of these will look similar to those previously offered in Windows NT and 9x operating systems. Some of these options can be used to assist users without disabilities, like large icons, toolbars, and fonts, for those who sit a good distance from their monitors. Problems may occur when users try to set these options themselves, and users may be unable to change them back to their original settings. If you've ever changed the settings of Custom Font Size to 200 percent, you know what I mean!

- StickyKeys, FilterKeys, ToggleKeys, SerialKeys, MouseKeys, and On-Screen Keyboard can be very useful for mobility-impaired users, depending on the type of impairment.

- HighContrast, Magnifier, and Narrator are very useful for vision-impaired users.

- SoundSentry and ShowSounds are very useful for hearing-impaired users.

■ All accessibility settings are configurable either through the Accessibility Options pane from Control Panel, or from the Accessibility menu inside Start menu | Programs | Accessories.

exam

ⓦatch

There may be a question or two on the test that will address the differences between Sticky Keys, Toggle Keys, Filter Keys, and Serial Keys. These are simple concepts, which only require memorization on your part. Make sure you know the differences between them, and what they are used for. Also, know how to turn these features on and off, and their available sound options.

QUESTIONS

8.03: Configuring and Troubleshooting Accessibility Services

19. You've recently hired a hearing-impaired programmer to work in the Development Department of your company. You need to enable Accessibility Sound options on his computer. He is not interested in receiving a message on his desktop each time the computer makes a sound, only when he is using his caption-enabled programs. He wants these programs to enter Captioning mode when they start up. Which of the following should you enable?

A. SoundSentry

B. ShowSounds

C. ApplicationsSounds

D. SoundShow

20. For your visually impaired employees, you choose to use High Contrast options. These include White on Black and Black on White. However, for a few of these users this is not sufficient and they need other options. Which of the following could you also employ to assist these users? (Choose all that apply.)

A. The Narrator, which uses a speech synthesizer to read typed data

B. The Magnifier, which opens a window to typed data, similar to how a magnifying glass works

     C. The VoiceWriter, which allows the user to speak and have the words typed in the computer

     D. Enlarged Keyboard Support, which allows double-size keyboard drivers to be loaded for access to extra-large keyboards

21. You have an employee who recently had a stroke. He can use a mouse, but is unable to type with a keyboard. What can you do to enable this employee to type data without using the physical keyboard, and, if this is available, how will you enable it? (Choose all that apply.)

     A. There is no way to allow this employee to type data without a keyboard unless third-party accessories are used, such as high-tech eye-movement hardware and software.

     B. Microsoft Windows 2000 Professional includes a virtual keyboard that can be accessed with a mouse and can be enabled with Start menu | Programs | Accessories | Accessibility | On-Screen Keyboard.

     C. SerialKeys will let you use some alternative input device for keyboard input, and can be accessed under Control Panel | Keyboard Options.

     D. In Control Panel | Mouse | Advanced tab you can configure options for setting mouse movements to emulate keyboard strokes.

22. Mike doesn't have any disabilities, but still uses some of the accessibility options that are available in Windows 2000. One of his favorites is Toggle Keys. How did Mike enable Toggle Keys?

     A. He keeps hitting extra keys and his sentences tend to look like this: "rthis iss the qway to ggo."

     B. He uses alternate input devices for typing, such as voice recognition hardware.

     C. He has trouble holding down two keys at once because he types so fast.

     D. He presses the TAB key a lot when he doesn't mean to.

23. Sally and Theresa are setting up a kiosk at their local community college, and they have taken all of the necessary precautions to make sure that users who log on as guests cannot damage the system. They are currently trying to install a

touch-screen monitor that offers a menu of choices. They have set up the On-Screen Keyboard from the Control Panel, Accessibility Options icon, but the touch-screen monitor does not work. Why is this?

A. On-Screen Keyboard is for using eye-blinks to type data into a computer.

B. On-Screen Keyboard is for using a mouse to type on a graphical keyboard.

C. On-Screen Keyboard is for seeing a representation of your keyboard on the screen.

D. This touch-screen monitor is not on the HCL.

LAB QUESTION

Objectives 8.01–8.03

You are starting a small business that will create architectural plans for new homes in the area. You have the six employees who are listed below along with their respective positions. You need all of the desktops at your company to look alike, so when customers interact with your salespeople and architects, the plans and accompanying documents will all look the same. Also, these six people will access all of the computers in the network, depending on their needs and location. One of your employees is visually impaired. All of the working documents should reside in a single shared folder, and all workstation operating systems run Windows 2000 Professional.

Employees

Lisa, sales director

Ron, CEO and founder

Linda, lead architect

Bill, attorney (Bill is visually impaired.)

Mary Anne, graphic artist

Marilyn, junior architect

There are three main goals that need to be accomplished: the desktops need to look alike, there has to be a server that can hold a shared file where all of the users can store data, and Bill needs accessibility options configured.

Following is an example of how to configure each of these three items. After reading through this explanation, note anything that is excluded, or incorrectly described or configured.

Configuring Desktops to Be Alike

Create a mandatory user profile for each user except Bill, which contains the desktop environment, application settings, and network connection configurations. Create this mandatory roaming user profile and apply it to all of the employees except Bill. Here are the steps:

1. Create a generic user account that you can use as a template to create user profiles.

2. Log on as the administrator of the account, and configure the desktops appropriately.

3. Log off and reboot the computer.

4. Log on as administrator and locate the NTUSER.MAN file and change it to NTUSER.DAT.

5. Create a group that contains the five users, and call it Employees.

6. Move this file to the group that contains the members of the company, and apply the mandatory user profile.

Storing Users' Work in a Shared Folder on a Network Server

Follow these steps:

1. Create a server that uses FAT as its file system.

2. Create a folder on this server.

3. Remove the Everyone group and add the Employees group. Give them Read permissions.

4. For each user account, under Properties, and Profile tab, provide the path to this shared folder.

5. Click the Connect box, and specify a drive letter for this connection.

Configuring Bill's Accessibility Options

Follow these steps:

1. For Bill, create a separate profile that allows him to configure his desktop as needed.

2. Under Accessibility Options, choose Display and High Contrast.

3. Make Bill's profile mandatory.

4. Change Bill's profile path to the shared folder on the server.

5. Click the Connect box, and specify the drive letter for this connection.

QUICK ANSWER KEY

Objective 8.01

1. D
2. A
3. D
4. B
5. D
6. A
7. D
8. C and D
9. C
10. C

Objective 8.02

11. A and D
12. B
13. A, B, C, D, and E
14. A
15. B
16. D
17. C
18. D

Objective 8.03

19. B
20. A and B
21. B and C
22. D
23. B

IN-DEPTH ANSWERS

8.01: Configuring and Managing User Profiles

1. ☑ **D.** Each user can have separate settings and desktop configurations, and can even have separate Internet connections.

 ☒ **A** is incorrect because each user can have a separate profile on the machine, and both do not need to use the same Internet connection. **B** is incorrect because the connection will not be changed. If the connection were changed, however, he would need new email and configuration settings. **C** is incorrect because the connection does not have to change. The issue of having two modems or NICs does not affect the problem shown here.

2. ☑ **A.** Shortcuts and Connect to the Internet icons are stored in each user's Desktop folder as files, and are executed when a user logs on. However, the Recycle Bin is not in the Desktop folder, but is an entity that relates to the computer as a whole. If one of these users deletes the Recycle Bin from the desktop, it will affect all of the other users' desktops.

 ☒ **B** and **C** are incorrect because these settings are not stored in the Documents and Settings folder or Profile folder. **D** is incorrect since **A** is the correct answer.

3. ☑ **D.** The user profiles are stored under Documents and Settings where D:\ represents the system drive. The History folder contains information on Internet History.

 ☒ **A** is incorrect because the History folder is under the Local Settings folder and **D** gives more path depth than A does. **B** is incorrect because the folder Winnt is not where the user profiles are stored. **C** is incorrect because Program Files is not where the user profiles are stored.

4. ☑ **B.** 2, 3, and then 1 is the correct order of adding a member to a group using Local Users Manager. First the Member tab must be chosen, then Add

from the options given, and finally the appropriate group to which she should belong is chosen. Make sure that you can answer this type of question, in case a question on the exam asks you to *show* what you can do.

☒   **A**, **C**, and **D** list the incorrect order of these steps.

5. ☑   **D.** If this option had been set, then the new employee would have had to change the password before logging on to the computer, and the damage to the computer could not have been done by you since you would not have known the password.

☒   **A** is incorrect because the new employee could never have logged on. **B** is incorrect because lockouts occur when some security measure has been breached, like number of incorrect logon attempts. These are set in group policy. **C** would not have solved the problem; in fact, **C** could have been what caused the problem!

6. ☑   **A.** Software installations can be managed by group policy, thus eliminating the users' interaction from this process.

☒   **B** and **C** are not the correct areas to manage software upgrades. **D** is incorrect because **A** is the answer.

7. ☑   **D.** Logon scripts can be written in any Windows script host support language, and the options for these are all listed above.

☒   **E** is incorrect because **B** is also a correct answer.

8. ☑   **C** and **D** are correct. You can remove a user from a group from the Local Users and Groups console, either through the user's list of groups, or the group's list of users.

☒   **A** and **B** do not allow you to access the tabs and windows necessary for removing a user.

9. ☑   **C.** If a user has more that one account and wants configuration changes of the desktop to follow him across all of the accounts, the profile path will need to be changed.

☒   **A** is incorrect because copying the folders will not produce the result intended. **B** is incorrect because this cannot be configured from the Users and Passwords icon in Control Panel, and **D** is incorrect because A is the answer.

10. ☑   **C.** By creating a shared folder on the server, and giving these four employees a local path to this folder, almost everything they do can be saved here automatically.

☒   **A** is incorrect because it is such a drastic measure, and the problem can be solved in a much easier way. **B** would not solve the problem, and would, in fact, cause unnecessary traffic. **D** would give each of them a path to a home folder on the server, but it would not be shared. In order to allow each employee access to the others' work, a shared folder is needed on the server.

8.02: Configuring and Troubleshooting Desktop Settings

11.   ☑   **A** and **D** are correct ways to access and configure group policy and local computer policy.

☒   **B** is incorrect because the Active Directory that includes group policy editing is a feature only available in Server. **C** is incorrect because there is no icon in the Control Panel for group policy.

12.   ☑   **B.** This is a common problem. If local security settings are configured, and the computer is a member of a network, those settings will be overridden by any other policy that has more clout.

☒   **A** is incorrect because the user would have to have administrator status to make these changes. **C** is incorrect because the computer does not have to be rebooted. **D** is incorrect because this is a local computer policy that affects everyone who logs in at this computer.

13.   ☑   **A**, **B**, **C**, **D**, and **E** are correct. *All* of the answer choices can be configured under the templates menus in the group policy snap-in.

14.   ☑   **A.** The lockout duration and configuration is under Account Policies, not any of the others.

☒   **B**, **C**, and **D** are all incorrect because the lockout duration and configuration is not any of these choices.

15.   ☑   **B.** By restricting the guest account, you will restrict all users who log on as guests without making universal changes to the computer.

☒   **A** and **C** are incorrect because these will make local changes to the computer, and you only want changes to the guest account. **D** is incorrect because it will not accomplish all of the required security needs.

16. ☑ **D.** The Explain tab contains information on the policy and how it functions.

☒ Although you may be able to find the information from **A** or **B**, it is not the best way. **C** is a utility that uses the Internet to update Windows components or operating systems. (The Hide All Icons on Desktop option just removes the icons from the desktop and nothing else. Users can still use Explorer to find these items.)

17. ☑ **C.** Personalized menus are those menus that show what you usually use. Pressing the DOWN-ARROW key, or waiting a second or two can access the others.

☒ **A** and **B** will not solve Bobby's problem and are incorrect, and **D** is not a valid menu option.

18. ☑ **D.** If you want to prevent users from running specified programs, but do not also remove the ability for them to access the command prompt, you have not really secured the system. If your users know how to run a program from a command prompt, they can still enable any program they want. The first optional result is met since you have successfully removed the Control Panel from the Start menu; however, the second optional result is not met because this does not remove Control Panel access from Windows Explorer.

☒ **A**, **B**, and **C** are incorrect because the required result was not met.

8.03: Configuring and Troubleshooting Accessibility Services

19. ☑ **B.** When turned on, ShowSounds tells caption-enabled programs to enter Captioning mode. Speech and sounds will be captioned in whatever way the program is set up to caption.

☒ **A** is incorrect because SoundSentry substitutes visual displays for sounds. SoundSentry lets you pick from various substitutes, like pop-up windows and words flashed in the caption bar. **C** and **D** are not valid sound accessibility options and are incorrect.

20. ☑ **A** and **B** are correct. Narrator and Magnifier are the two options available, in addition to High Contrast, which a user can configure for support.

☒ **C** and **D** do not exist.

21. ☑ **B** and **C** are correct. Microsoft Windows 2000 Professional does offer a keyboard that shows on the monitor, and can be accessed with a mouse. **C** is also a way to use alternative input devices, and is found under Control Panel | Accessibility Options.

    ☒ **A** is incorrect because this option is available, although there are third-party hardware and software that may be helpful. **D** is incorrect because this is not an available option.

22. ☑ **D.** The toggle key is used to make a sound when this key is pressed.

    ☒ **A** represents FilterKeys, **B** is for SerialKeys, and **C** is for StickyKeys, making those three answers incorrect.

23. ☑ **B.** On-Screen Keyboard is used for people with disabilities who cannot use a keyboard, allowing them to use a mouse instead.

    ☒ **A** and **C** are incorrect explanations for the On-Screen Keyboard. **D** could possibly be an issue, but given the scenario, it is not the best answer.

LAB ANSWER

Objectives 8.01–8.03

The three main goals to be accomplished are as follows: desktops need to look alike, the users' work is stored in a shared folder on a network server, and Bill needs accessibility options configured.

Configuring Desktops to Be Alike

Notice the changes below in numbers 2, 3, 4, and 6.

1. Create a generic user account that you can use as a template to create user profiles.

2. Log on as this generic user, and configure the desktops appropriately. You should not log on as the administrator, but as the generic user you will use to create the profile.

3. Log off. (No need to reboot.)

4. Log on as administrator and locate the NTUSER.DAT file and change it to NTUSER.MAN. The previous choice was listed backward.

5. Create a group that contains the five users, and call it Employees.

6. Copy this file to the group that contains the members of the company, and apply the mandatory user profile.

Storing Users' Work in a Shared Folder on a Network Server

Notice the changes in 1, 2, and 3.

1. Create a server that uses NTFS as its file system. FAT does not offer much in the way of security. You should use NTFS whenever possible.

2. Create a folder and share it on this server. Remember to share the folder!

3. Remove the Everyone group and add the Employees group. Give them Full Control. If you only give the users Read permissions, they will have a pretty hard time doing any work. They need Full Control over their files.

4. For each user account, under Properties, and Profile tab, provide the path to this shared folder.

5. Click the Connect box, and specify a drive letter for this connection.

Configuring Bill's Accessibility Options

Notice the change in 3.

1. For Bill, create a separate profile that allows him to configure his desktop as needed.

2. Under Accessibility Options, choose Display, and High Contrast.

3. Do not make Bill's profile mandatory. It is probably better to leave Bill's profile so that it isn't a mandatory because he may need to make changes later.

4. Change Bill's profile path to the shared folder on the server.

5. Click the Connect box, and specify the drive letter for this connection.

MICROSOFT CERTIFIED SYSTEMS ENGINEER

9

Configuring Multilanguage Support and Using Windows Installer

TEST YOURSELF OBJECTIVES

9.01   Configuring Support for Multiple
        Languages or Multiple Locations

9.02   Installing Applications by Using
        Windows Installer Packages

M any decisions must be made when creating and running an efficient network including planning, deployment, security, hardware, and software issues. However, when a network needs support for multiple languages and locations, then additional configuration is necessary. If people in your business are spread out in different countries, then you will need to plan your Windows 2000 deployment to permit those people to correspond regardless of the language they speak. Windows 2000 Professional meets these needs with multilanguage support.

Also covered in this chapter is the matter of installing new software safely. Windows 2000 Professional offers Windows Installer Packages to guarantee that executable files, registry settings, and other components are installed in the correct locations and will function properly. This, of course, is a very important issue.

TEST YOURSELF OBJECTIVE 9.01

Configuring Support for Multiple Languages or Multiple Locations

When clients on a network need to communicate in different languages, or if Windows 2000 needs to be installed using a country's native language, then support for multiple languages is employed. Every country in the world has characters and number formats that are unique to them, and support for these plays a large part in the acceptance of Windows 2000 across the globe. Windows offers RTL and APIs that allow developers of software the ability to easily change the version of the applications to fit the local needs of the user. Without this, programmers would have to create separate programs for each language.

- Windows 2000 Professional can be installed using one of 24 possible localized versions. These localized versions display the User Interface and help files in the local language.

- ASCII and EBCDIC are character sets that allow English characters and letters to be displayed in files. Other character sets exist to support other languages.

- UNICODE is a single character set that supports characters from most of the world's languages. Applications and documents that use UNICODE do not need to switch between character sets to display information in multiple languages.

▨ RTL and other APIs exist to allow developers to create applications that can be displayed correctly in each localized version of Windows 2000. Without these features, a developer would need to create separate programs for each language.

▨ Locales are groups of preferences and settings relating to how a user's local language and customs change how information is formatted. There are three types of locales: User, Input, and System.

▨ User locales control how numbers, currency, dates, and times are displayed with regard to the language and country configured.

▨ Input locales are used to map an input method, such as a keyboard or speech-to-text software, to an installed language.

▨ System locales determine which character set and font files will be used.

Here is an excerpt from Microsoft's Web site concerning Multilanguage support: "When you use the Muisetup.exe tool to install multilanguage user interface files to support additional languages from the Windows 2000 Multilanguage-version CD-ROM, the %systemroot%\muisetup.log contains installation and uninstallation logging information. The log contents are in English, except for error codes returned from system calls, which will be logged in the language previously chosen by the user running the Muisetup.exe tool." Make sure that you know the names of these installation and log files, just in case a question appears on the exam.

QUESTIONS

9.01: Configuring Support for Multiple Languages or Multiple Locations

1. Jack is using an older PC that uses the character set EBCDIC for alphabet representation. He wants to write and send an email to a friend who lives in

France. Even though Jack speaks and writes French fluently, he is unable to write the letter. Why is this? (Pick the best answer.)

A. There are no characters to represent the needed accents in the EBCDIC set.

B. His operating system can only accept data written in English.

C. His keyboard does not have the necessary keys.

D. He'll have to change to ASCII to write the letter.

2. You support a network that has offices in Japan, Germany, France, and the United States. You run mostly Windows products and are responsible for selecting and implementing new software applications to be deployed worldwide. One of the programs you'd like to use does not have a Bi-directional Application Programming Interface, or RTL-API. What does this mean to you?

A. Nothing. This is not a necessary consideration when choosing software applications.

B. It will affect your users slightly, but is not a major concern since most of the users speak both their native languages and some English.

C. It should concern you as an administrator. This enables you to obtain multilanguage versions of the applications.

D. This only concerns programmers and administrators who need access to the VB code controls, to modify the program to suit their specific company's needs.

3. You have clients on your network from the United States and Israel. You are planning to deploy Windows 2000 across this network and need to take advantage of the multilanguage and locales support that is available. In what order would the deployment of these two take place?

A. Install support for different locales, and then install localized versions of the operating system.

B. Install localized versions of the operating system, and then install support for different locales.

C. Install localized versions of the operating system, and then install support for Bi-directional Application Programming Interface.

D. Install support for the Bi-directional Application Programming Interface, and then install localized versions of the operating system.

Questions 4–6   This scenario should be used to answer questions 4, 5, and 6.

Current Situation: Although the company you work for is based in the United States, you have many clients and business associates overseas. You are required to establish locale settings for some of the users in your office who communicate with these overseas clients. They must be able to communicate effectively using all types of applications including text-based, currency, and accessibility of the clients' local programs. Answer the following three questions that address this issue.

4. You have a Russian client who is trying to run a non-UNICODE application written for the Hebrew language version of Windows 95. Which type of locale settings would you change?

   A. Input locales.

   B. System locales.

   C. User locales.

   D. This is not an issue that can be addressed with locales.

5. You support a user who wants to use an Italian keyboard to type information in Italian, and use a microphone with speech-to-text software to insert German text into a manuscript. Which type of locale settings would you change?

   A. Input locales.

   B. System locales.

   C. User locales.

   D. This is not an issue that can be addressed with locales.

6. You have a user in your office who needs to conduct business with different countries. He wants his English clients to see currency formatted with the British Pound symbol (£), and American English users to see currency formatted with the dollar sign ($) symbol. Which type of locale settings would you change?

   A. User locales.

   B. System locales.

   C. Input locales.

   D. This is not an issue that can be addressed with locales.

7. Deb has a user in her office who wants to use speech-to-text and voice recognition software and hardware to input data into her computer, instead of using the keyboard. Deb doesn't want her client to have to be involved with the intricacies of the program, just to have the capability to use it. Which of the following choices offers assistance with this situation?

   A. Input Method Editor.

   B. Control Panel | Accessibility Options.

   C. Control Panel | System icon.

   D. *.NLS files are used for configuring the speech settings.

8. Your boss has asked you to configure and control network-wide settings that will determine which Language Groups are available and which System and User locales are to be used. What is the best way to accomplish this?

   A. Store the information about language options and locales in the registry for all users to access.

   B. Store the configurations under Control Panel | Regional Settings on the PDC.

   C. Create the settings as part of your group policy, and have them automatically applied when a person logs on Active Directory.

   D. Create the settings as part of the local computer policy for all of the computers in the network.

9. Jeremy is an administrator for a large, international firm. This firm has domains in three countries and is having trouble with computer names, account names, and passwords containing illegal characters. Each country has multilanguage support and multiple locales configured and running smoothly. How can the problem of these illegal characters be solved?

   A. Disable multilanguage support and multilocale support at all of the workstations, and only enable this support at the server levels. Configure network-wide policies for the servers.

   B. Enforce a policy whereby user and computer account names are all stored in one language, regardless of location.

C. Check the local software requirements in each country, and compile a list of characters that should not be used. Enforce local policies disallowing these characters.

D. Let DNS and DHCP servers create names for all of the accounts for computers and users. This will solve the problem of illegal characters, as well as any issues that arise from duplicate names on the network.

TEST YOURSELF OBJECTIVE 9.02

Installing Applications by Using Windows Installer Packages

As applications become increasingly complex, so do their installations. Applications and programs make changes to the registry, insert DLL files, contain registered components, and include executable files. Figuring out a way to install these programs successfully and reliably is an important part of an administrator's or programmer's job. Windows Installer is available in 2000 to assist with these concerns by preventing applications from overwriting system files, enabling a rollback to a state prior to installation if the install fails, offering a scripted unattended installation, and even repairing a corrupt installation.

- Most Windows applications consist of executable files, registry settings, and other components that must be installed in certain locations to function correctly.

- Software vendors might provide their own utilities to create these settings and install applications.

- Windows 2000 Installer technology is an updated way to handle software installations. All required files, settings, and installation logic are contained in a single file with an .MSI extension.

- Special applications will be required to help create MSI files. One such utility is included on the Windows 2000 CD.

- These applications create the MSI file by looking at a system before and after an application is installed, and looking at the net changes between the two configurations.

- The resulting MSI file can be installed locally by a user, or deployed automatically using Active Directory and group policy.

exam

Ⓦatch

An administrator can assign Windows Installer (.MSI) packages so that clients have very little interaction with the installation process. To do this, click Group Policy and choose Edit, decide if you want to edit the user or computer policy, and double-click Software Settings. Right-click Software Installation, then New, then Package. Next, browse to the .MSI file you want to deploy, open it, and choose Configure Package Properties, then OK. Under Deployment, click Assigned and then Basic. Note that the administrator may need to edit the .MSI file to adjust parts of the installation.

QUESTIONS

9.02: Installing Applications by Using Windows Installer Packages

10. Lisa has just purchased a new computer that has Windows 2000 already installed, and is reinstalling her favorite applications. Previously, Lisa was using Windows 95 to do business-related tasks like creating invoices, bookkeeping, and inventory. She has reinstalled an older program that she used for creating business forms, and has rebooted the computer. Now she keeps getting DLL errors. Which of the following is most likely happening?

A. The application is not supported by Windows 2000 and will not work properly.

B. The support DLL files that Microsoft provides as part of Windows have been changed or replaced.

C. The support DLL files that the developer has provided for the application have been changed or replaced by the operating system.

D. The DLL files have been moved to another location by the installation of the application.

11. Eddie has been having problems with his older operating system and keeps getting DLL errors. He has been unable to repair these, and has decided to upgrade his system to Windows 2000. What will the new Windows Installer technology do for Eddie, and how will this help him avoid these errors in the future? (Choose all that apply.)

    A. A software package created for Windows Installer can roll back a system to its original state, if the installation fails for whatever reason.

    B. It can prevent applications from overwriting common system files or files created by another application.

    C. It can attempt to repair a corrupted installation by keeping a log of what files were installed at the original install date, and replace those files if necessary.

    D. It can be scripted to allow the application to be installed automatically without a user's intervention.

    E. It can be configured to install only some components of an application to conserve disk space on the client, and those missing components can be automatically installed later, if the missing component is needed.

12. You are planning deployment of a network-wide proprietary graphics application, and you want to create an Installer Package to make sure your systems can recover if the installation is not successful. You have the Veritas Installer Lite software console installed and running. Put the following steps in order to achieve the creation of this Installer Package.

    A. Browse through the items listed and verify that each file, folder, and registry entry that you manually created is shown in the Editor window.

    B. Process the before and after snapshots.

    C. Right-click the MSI file and select Edit with WinINSTALL LE from the context menu that appears.

    D. Specify the name of the application.

    E. Choose a temporary location for the Discover application to store its files as it creates the package.

    F. Select Start | Programs | VERITAS Software | VERITAS Software Discover.

13. After the creation of the Installer Package in the previous question, you are ready to deploy the new graphics program throughout your network. You thought about using Active Directory setup, or making the MSI file available on the file server for manual installation, but have instead decided to use the option of deployment through group policies. Which of the following types of group policy would you choose if you wanted the software to be automatically installed?

    A. Published to users

    B. Assigned to users

    C. Assigned to computers

    D. Published to computers

14. The Programming Department has just finished creating a software program for use in your network. It is not a Windows 2000–certified product, and you are not sure you want to deploy the program for fear it may cause irreparable damage. What should you do?

    A. Deploying a custom or in-house application is one of the reasons to use a repackager.

    B. The application has probably been thoroughly tested and is okay to install.

    C. Install any Microsoft Service Pack prior to deployment of this new application.

    D. Use the Microsoft Deployment Wizard to install this application safely.

15. Jane wants to create an Installer Package using WinINSTALL, but the application currently has an SMS Installer Package with it. Can Jane use this SMS Installer Package with Windows Installer, and if so, how is this done?

    A. Jane can use the SMS Installer, but she needs to edit it using the registry editor.

    B. Jane cannot use the SMS Installer because SMS and WinINSTALL packages are not compatible.

    C. SMS and Windows Installer Packages are not compatible, but the SMS package can be converted using a utility found in SMS 2.0 SP2.

    D. SMS and Windows Installer Packages are interchangeable and require no editing or conversion.

16. After creating an Installer Package for an application for your network, you need to determine a way to deploy the Installer application among your users. It is a very small file and won't be too difficult for users to install themselves. Which of the following are appropriate ways to deploy this package? (Choose all that apply.)

    A. By email

    B. By Network Share

    C. Assign or publish through group policy

    D. Use Systems Management Server

17. You need to create an Installer Package for your local division that contains a proprietary CAD program that is very large. Because of this, you want to perform this Installer Package on the main server so you will have enough room to create the "before" and "after" shots. Since this is the company's main server, however, you are concerned about the number of reboots necessary for creation of the package. Which of the following is true?

    A. No reboots are necessary during this process.

    B. No reboots are necessary during this process except those required by the application's installation.

    C. The only reboot that is necessary is the one following the "before" shot.

    D. Two reboots are necessary, one following the "after" shot, and one upon completion of the package.

LAB QUESTION

Objectives 9.01–9.02

You are the lead network administrator for a large, international company. Your main focus and concerns are security, stability, and reliability of the network across great distances. Communication between users of the different countries is another major factor. The users must be able to communicate via email, shared documents, and the acceptance and usefulness of each other's data must be addressed. You have many American workers located in these overseas countries. Some of these users utilize specialized keyboards native to their countries only, and some use speech-to-text software.

You have been asked to plan and deploy the international and multilanguage features of Windows 2000, as well as to address issues regarding the security and reliability of the network. What are some of the things that you could use from this chapter to assist with these needs? Consider multilanguage needs, multiple locales, and Windows Installer features. List as many things as you can think of.

A QUICK ANSWER KEY

Objective 9.01

1. **A**
2. **C**
3. **B**
4. **B**
5. **A**
6. **A**
7. **A** and **B**
8. **C**
9. **B**

Objective 9.02

10. **B**
11. **A, B, C, D**, and **E**
12. **F, D, E, B, C**, and **A**
13. **B** and **C**
14. **A**
15. **C**
16. **A, B**, and **C**
17. **A**

IN-DEPTH ANSWERS

9.01: Configuring Support for Multiple Languages or Multiple Locations

1. ☑ **A.** The EBCDIC character set contains 256 letter, character, and number representations, but does not offer the required accents to properly formulate the spelling and pronunciation of French words.

    ☒ **B** is incorrect because the operating system doesn't know if you are writing a letter in English or French. **C** is incorrect because keyboards will usually contain the required keys. **D** is incorrect because ASCII only has 128 characters available, and would not solve the problem at hand.

2. ☑ **C** is correct in stating that it enables you to obtain multilanguage versions of the applications.

    ☒ **A** and **B** are incorrect because multilanguage versions of an application are necessary to have successful deployment in a worldwide situation. **D** is incorrect for this reason, also.

3. ☑ **B.** The first step is to install the operating system, and the version is determined by the country and language. The second step is to install support for a specific locale, which takes into account the user's language, culture, and environment.

    ☒ **A** does not describe the process in the correct order. **C** and **D** are incorrect because the Bi-directional Application Programming Interface provides a way for programmers to create dialog boxes in their programs that can automatically format themselves correctly, depending on the language.

4. ☑ **B.** System locales are system-wide settings used to determine which character set and font files will be used on the system. The default System locale is UNICODE-based. Changing the System locale to another language, or a non-UNICODE language, will allow certain localized applications that require a specific language to be present, to run.

    ☒ **A, C,** and **D.** These options do not allow changes to the System locale.

5. ☑ **A.** Input locales are per-user settings that match an input language with a method to input text.

☒ **B, C,** and **D.** These options do not allow changes to the Input locales.

6. ☑ **A.** User locales are per-user settings that control the formatting that will be applied to dates, times, numbers, and currency.

☒ **B, C,** and **D.** These options do not allow changes to this operation.

7. ☑ **A** and **B** are correct. The Input Method Editor is a software service installed in Windows 2000 Professional that provides common services for inputting text into an application from various sources; and Control Panel | Accessibility Options can be used to assist in configuration of hardware using Serial Key devices.

☒ **C** does not offer an area to configure this type of hardware and software, and **D** represents National Language Support files that do not have anything to do with the current situation.

8. ☑ **C.** An administrator can create language-related settings as part of an organization's group policy, apply those group policies to a user or organizational unit, and have them automatically applied when a person logs on Active Directory.

☒ **A** is incorrect. The settings that control which Language Groups are available, and which System and User locales are to be used, are stored in the Windows 2000 registry. From there, an administrator has the ability to control them using group policy. **B** is incorrect because this is not a workable solution. **D** is incorrect because it is not the most efficient way to create and configure these settings.

9. ☑ **B.** The solutions for this problem are to choose names for user and computer accounts that only contain letters and numbers; have passwords made of mixed-case letters, numbers, and symbols; ensure your naming convention is inline with the standards and requirements for other software components; and enforce a policy that user and computer account names are all stored in one language, regardless of location.

☒ **A** is incorrect since this would defeat the purpose of enabling multilanguage support for the users. **C** is incorrect because this may still cause universal naming problems. **D** is incorrect because DNS and DHCP do not create names for accounts and users.

9.02: Installing Applications by Using Windows Installer Packages

10. ☑ **B.** A problem arises if you install an older application on a system that replaces a DLL file. The replaced DLL file might cause other applications that depend on a later version of this file to function incorrectly.

    ☒ **A** is incorrect because it is assumed the program has been installed and there are DLL errors. **C** is incorrect because the application changes DLL files and not the operating system. **D** is incorrect because DLL files are not usually moved but changed or replaced.

11. ☑ **A, B, C, D** and **E** are correct. It is important to know that every choice is a characteristic of Windows Installer, as well as how to create an Installer Package.

12. ☑ **F, D, E, B, C,** and **A.** In order to create an Installer Package in Windows 2000, these steps must be performed in this order.

13. ☑ **B** and **C** are correct. Assignment refers to mandatory installation of software. Software assigned to a user will be installed under that user's profile, wherever that user logs on. Software assigned to a computer will be automatically installed on that computer, and is available to whoever signs on to that computer.

    ☒ Publication refers to the non-mandatory installation of the application, making **A** incorrect. **D** is not a valid option.

14. ☑ **A.** Repackaging is another term for creating an Installer Package.

    ☒ **B** is a bad idea because you are uneasy about the program. **C** is incorrect because Service Packs will not address issues with in-house programs. **D** is incorrect because there is no Microsoft Deployment Wizard.

15. ☑ **C.** SMS and Windows Installer Packages are not compatible, but the SMS package can be converted using a utility found in SMS 2.0 SP2.

    ☒ **A** is incorrect because the registry editor is not an appropriate place to create, edit, or convert Installer Packages. **B** is incorrect because conversion can take place. **D** is incorrect because a conversion is necessary, and the two are not interchangeable.

16. ☑ **A**, **B**, and **C** are correct. It is possible to send small Installer Packages across email platforms, by Network Share, or through group policy.

☒ However, **D** is incorrect because SMS and Windows Installer are not compatible.

17. ☑ **A.** The entire process can be completed without a reboot of the computer.

☒ **B**, **C**, and **D** are incorrect because no reboots are required.

LAB ANSWER

Objectives 9.01–9.02

Make sure that all of the users have operating systems that support UNICODE, like Windows 2000.

Require that all software installed offer multilanguage versions (by writing the application to make use of the RTL-API, UNICODE, and other topics from this chapter).

Enable multilanguage support on all of the workstations and servers, and install the necessary languages and locales.

Configure Input locales, when necessary, to be one of the installed Language Groups; and the input method configured, IME. This will allow a user to use a Greek keyboard to type information in Greek, and a microphone with speech-to-text software to insert Spanish text into a document.

Make sure that each computer that needs to communicate with another, or to share a document from another country, has the required currency, numbers, time, and dates configured for effective communication.

Plan a strategy for the names of computers and accounts that will work for all of the countries involved, thus eliminating issues arising from illegal characters.

Use Windows Installer Packages to ensure the security of the network after new software is installed.

Use group policy or Active Directory to install software, lessening user error problems:

- Hardware and software must support multiple languages and present the Windows User Interface to each user in the appropriate local language.

- The expansion manager should have the UI for all countries installed.

- Per-user and per-computer settings should be made to facilitate written communication between and among the offices and the employees in each country.

Then, match a feature of Windows 2000 to each requirement:

- Deploying the appropriate localized version of Windows 2000 Professional in English, French, Chinese, and Russian will allow each employee working in each country to view the Windows UI in the appropriate language.

- Deploying the Multilanguage version of Windows 2000 Professional on the manager's computer will allow the manager to choose the language in which his or her UI is displayed.

- Regardless of the language being displayed in the UI, each employee will be able to communicate with other employees using locales.

- On each computer, install the following Language Groups: English (US), English (UK), French (France), Russian, and Chinese. The presence of these Language Groups will allow you to enable various locales.

- Enable the appropriate User locale to allow each user to display date, time, numbers, and currency according to his or her country.

- Install the appropriate Input locale for each user, and ensure that the input device or IME is mapped correctly. Verify that the non-Roman keyboard and the speech-to-text software work correctly, and enable the manager to switch Input locales quickly by installing the option in the taskbar.

You do not need to do anything extra to set the correct System locale. The default System locale is UNICODE-based, and will allow all users in each country to communicate.

MICROSOFT CERTIFIED SYSTEMS ENGINEER

10

Implementing, Managing, and Troubleshooting Network Protocols and Services

TEST YOURSELF OBJECTIVES

I n order for computers of all makes, models, languages, speeds, and file system types to communicate, there have to be rules for exchanging data. TCP/IP was born from this need, and configuring and troubleshooting this protocol became a very important skill. Tools like TRACERT, PING, ROUTE, ARP, and IPCONFIG are all used for troubleshooting TCP/IP configurations. Understanding TCP/IP also involves a thorough knowledge of DHCP, DNS, VPNs, WINS, DDNS, and gateways, just to name a few.

Dial-up networking is another aspect of data collaboration that includes communication for local and wide-area networks, as well as RAS and direct cable connection. A few of the protocols involved with dial-up networking are BAP, EAP, L2TP, PPTP, and PPP. Dial-up networking is one way to allow computers that are great distances from each other to communicate at minimal cost.

Some other offerings included in Windows 2000 are Bandwidth Allocation Protocol, PATHPING, and Offline Files. These enhance network efficiency and are new to Windows products. The ability to have files and folders available offline is extremely important to mobile computer users.

TEST YOURSELF OBJECTIVE 10.01

Configuring and Troubleshooting TCP/IP Protocol

TCP/IP is an industry-standard suite of protocols that is the dominant means of communication in Windows 2000. TCP/IP is defined in four layers: Application, Transport, Internet, and Network. These four layers and the rules associated with them allow all users to access the Internet or an intranet regardless of their computer's characteristics: managing, configuring, and troubleshooting TCP/IP may be heavily tested on the exam.

■ TCP/IP includes many useful tools to aid in troubleshooting. Among them are PING, IPCONFIG, TRACERT, PATHPING, ARP, ROUTE, NBSTAT, NSLOOKUP, and NETSTAT.

■ Windows 2000 Professional can obtain its TCP/IP information dynamically via DHCP. The IP address of the client, DNS server, WINS server, subnet mask, and the default gateway can all be automatically configured. DDNS also allows dynamic name registration to a DNS server.

■ Virtual private networks (VPNs) are a financially prudent way of interconnecting remote clients and networks. The security enhancements of Windows 2000 (IPSec and EAP) make this an even more viable alternative to other interconnecting technologies.

■ DNS name resolution is used to map IP addresses to host names. A HOSTS file can be used for the same purpose in smaller networks.

exam
ⓦatch

Be very comfortable with the following utilities and their uses. When a question on the exam asks to troubleshoot invalid cached entries, think ARP; if the question is about current TCP/IP values, DHCP leases, or DNS names, consider IPCONFIG. If you receive a question about NetBIOS over TCP/IP connections choose NBTSTAT, or current TCP/IP connections, NETSTAT. NETDIAG checks all current connections; NSLOOKUP is for DNS information. PATHPING is used for tracing lost data packets. PING is used for echo requests; ROUTE for the IP-Routing table, and TRACERT for tracing a path to a remote system. Expect scenario questions that will ask for the appropriate tool for solving given problems.

QUESTIONS

10.01: Configuring and Troubleshooting TCP/IP Protocol

Questions 1–4   This scenario should be used to answer questions 1, 2, 3, and 4.

Current Situation: Some clients on your network are having problems communicating with other computers on the network. The problems for each of these clients differ and are listed in the questions to follow. Consider each type of problem and locate the probable cause choosing the appropriate command line utility to use to isolate the problem.

1. John is a user in subnet 3 of your network, but is having problems connecting to subnet 1. He can connect to users on his own subnet easily. You believe that

this is a problem that involves the router, and you want to isolate the problem. Which of the following command line utilities will help the most?

A. PING 127.0.0.1

B. TRACERT

C. ARP

D. NETSTAT

2. Nathan has just configured the TCP/IP settings on his new computer, including a subnet mask, gateway, DHCP and DNS server, and IP address. Which tool can he use to verify he's typed all of this in correctly, before trying to connect to the network?

A. PING followed by the TCP/IP address of the DHCP Server

B. IPCONFIG /ALL

C. ROUTE

D. NBTSTAT

3. Thomas is having problems with his DNS server. He thinks he may have an incorrect IP address for the server listed on his computer. He knows the name of the DNS server. Which utility can you use to provide information about the IP address?

A. PATHPING

B. NSLOOKUP

C. ROUTE

D. NETSTAT

4. Terry is having problems with data on his network being delivered reliably. He has checked the physical connections on his network, and has tested the cable for flaws. Up to this point, he is unable to correct the problem. He is aware that there are problems with the mapping of IP addresses to their MAC sublayer addresses. What layer of the TCP/IP Protocol Suite should Terry focus on when trying to find a solution to this problem?

A. Application

B. Transport

C. Internet

D. Network Interface

5. You want to monitor and capture packets on your local network. You have installed Network Monitor and the Network Monitor driver on your Windows 2000 workstation. You need to capture packets that contain a certain data pattern. What can you specify when you set up this capture filter? (Choose all that apply.)

A. You can set up where this pattern occurs in the frame.

B. You can choose to capture only frames that contain a pattern of ASCII or hexadecimal text.

C. When a certain set of events occurs, you can specify that a certain program be run.

D. Network Monitor does not support the capture of data patterns.

6. You transfer a lot of sensitive data across your VPN. You've employed many encryption techniques, as well as techniques new to Windows 2000, like IPSec and TCP/IP filtering technologies. You've decided that the best way to secure the data transfer on your network is to make sure the data is encapsulated and that the entire IP datagram is encrypted, so you can securely transmit it across your public and private networks. Which of the following technologies offered by Windows 2000 Professional does this?

A. ESP Tunnel mode

B. ESP with AH

C. ESP Transport mode

D. ESP at the Transport layer

7. You have just typed in the URL www.microsoft.com into your Web browser, and your computer has begun the search for the closest DNS server on the network to find out what Microsoft's IP address is. This is the first step of DNS host name to IP address resolution and is called a forward lookup query. Put the other steps in this process in order, beginning with the next step in the process.

A. The IP address is found and is returned to the client.

B. A recursive query is made to a root DNS server, known as its forwarder. The result is sent back to the name server.

C. A recursive query is made to a com DNS server, known as its forwarder. The result is sent back to the name server.

D. The DNS server (name server) checks its cache and Zone database file to see if this name has been resolved recently, or if it has the mapping in its database.

E. A recursive query is made to the host DNS server. The result is sent back to the name server.

8. You want to set up your Windows 2000 Professional workstation to serve as a DNS host for your small network. Up to this point you have been using a HOSTS file for mapping names to IP addresses on a server, but the management of this is getting rather hectic as your network expands. How will you begin setting up your workstation to serve as a DNS host?

A. Install the DNS Service utilities from the Windows 2000 Professional CD-ROM.

B. Configure your network into two zones, giving the workstation authority for your namespace.

C. Upgrade the computer to Windows 2000 Server.

D. None of the above. The workstation already has the necessary files installed.

TEST YOURSELF OBJECTIVE 10.02

Connecting to Computers by Using Dial-Up Networking

Dial-up networking is used when you need to connect a computer to an ISP, the Internet, another computer, or a private network. The Dial-Up Networking Wizard assists in making this connection. Virtual private networks allow users to connect to networks across the Internet, thus resulting in lower total cost of ownership when compared to dedicated lines or other means of connection. Dial-up networking can also be used to set up dial-in capabilities for computers.

■ Most network connections can be made through the Network Connection Wizard. You can set up Internet, private networks (LAN, WAN), virtual private networks, incoming connections (RAS), and direct cable connections.

- Bandwidth Allocation Protocol (BAP) is new to Windows 2000 and is used to dynamically allocate dial-up resources as needed.

- The Extensible Authentication Protocol (EAP) is a standard mechanism that allows you to add additional authentication schemes.

- L2TP and PPTP are two protocols that enable the use of virtual private networks (VPNs). Along with IPSec and EAP, they establish secure connections to two remote networks.

- The encryption and authentication capabilities of PPP (Point-to-Point Protocol) make it a much better choice than SLIP.

exam
ⓦatch

Internet Connection Sharing allows multiple users to share an Internet connection without setting up separate ISP accounts for each user, or even having a modem installed on each computer. You may be called upon to know how and when this type of sharing can cause connectivity problems for the rest of your network. The following are no-no's when it comes to Internet Connection Sharing: If you are on a network that uses static IP addresses, has a Windows 2000 domain controller, or uses other DNS and DHCP servers and gateways, you should not attempt to use Internet Connection Sharing. This will create problems because it sets up a new static IP address for the computer with the physical link to the Internet, and doles out addresses to the clients that are sharing the connection. It tries to take the role of a DHCP server!

QUESTIONS

10.02: Connecting to Computers by Using Dial-Up Networking

9. You work for a large firm that employs a few people that telecommute or dial into the network while on the road. This hasn't previously been a problem, but with more and more network data transfers, the long-distance bills for these clients are getting out of hand. You have had your clients dial directly into the network instead of using an ISP or the Internet, for security reasons. After

upgrading to Windows 2000 Professional on the client machines, you've begun reading about PPTP and L2TP protocols. How can these protocols help your situation? (Choose all the apply.)

A. PPTP provides encapsulated packets, encrypting and tunneling the data.

B. In L2TP, IPSec provides the encryption, and L2TP provides the tunneling.

C. PPTP and L2P2 are only available on the server versions of Windows 2000. These technologies will not help the clients.

D. PPTP does not encapsulate the packets, but provides encrypting and tunneling the data.

10. **Current Situation:** You are setting up a small data server and you want to configure your Windows 2000 Professional computer to accept incoming calls. You will configure the inbound connections to be from dial-up guests. The users have local accounts on the workstation.

Required Result: Configure your computer to accept incoming dial-up calls from clients to your Windows 2000 Professional computer and function as a Remote Access Server.

Optional Desired Results:

1. Allow up to 20 concurrent connections.

2. Allow users to access your local area network that contains three other computers.

Proposed Solution: Use the Network Connection Wizard, choose the Accept Incoming Connection radio button, and continue. On the Devices for Incoming Connections page, configure port speed, flow control, compression, and data protocol. Configure the properties appropriate for your hardware, and then choose Allow the User to Set the Callback Number. When prompted for number of concurrent network connections, choose 20. Choose PPP as the protocol.

What result does the proposed solution produce?

A. The proposed solution produces the required results and both of the optional results.

B. The proposed solution produces the required results and only one of the optional results.

C. The proposed solution produces the required results and none of the optional results.

D. The proposed solution does not produce the required result.

11. You run a very large network with users dialing out to ISPs and clients dialing in via remote access technologies. You use token cards, smart cards, and one-time logons for guests and temporary workers. You are extremely concerned about the security of your network and presently use PPTP for security over phone lines. What other protocols can you use to beef up security on your network? (Choose all the apply.)

A. EAP

B. MD5-CHAP

C. TLS

D. RADIUS

12. You are a member of a small network that consists of seven users. You want to share an Internet connection since not many employees have a great need for access. Under Networking and Dial-up connections on the computer that has the connection, you have enabled Internet Connection Sharing, and since you are using a modem you have also checked Enable-on-Demand Calling. When users log on to access the Internet, however, the rest of the network loses connectivity. What could cause this reaction to Internet Sharing? (Choose all the apply.)

A. Your network users have static IP addresses.

B. The modem is not on Window's HCL.

C. TCP/IP is not installed on the client computers.

D. You are using DHCP.

13. You are trying to decide between PPTP and L2TP as protocols for your virtual private network. You need to use a protocol that has built-in encryption and can transmit over an IP-based network. You do not need header compression or tunnel authentication. Which protocol should you use?

A. Both protocols offer all of these things. Either one is fine.

B. PPTP.

C. L2TP.

D. Neither has the requirements you are looking for.

TEST YOURSELF OBJECTIVE 10.03

Connecting to Shared Resources on a Microsoft Network

Connecting to shared resources is the main purpose of a having a network. Users want to manipulate data, print, and email co-workers. They need to be able to access files and folders from a network server, or perhaps a shared file on another user's computer. Shares can be given permissions, and users can be given needed access to the shares. Caching can be used to make these files and folders available when the users are no longer connected to the network. Other aspects of Microsoft networking follow.

- New to Windows 2000 is the ability to cache files and folders on your local hard drive. The ability to have folders available for users when they are offline or disconnected from the network is especially useful for mobile users.

- Windows 2000 Professional will allow ten concurrent connections, while Windows 2000 Server has an unlimited amount.

- Knowing the terms that Microsoft uses to describe the different aspects of printing is integral to understanding its implementation.

- When configuring a client computer to connect to a network printer, be aware that printer drivers will automatically be installed on client computers running Windows 2000 and Windows NT. Other Microsoft operating systems need to have printer drivers installed manually. On other clients, you may need to have other services to allow printing.

- Caching makes it possible to have folders available for users when they are offline or disconnected from the network. This is especially useful for mobile computer users, as the data will be cached on their hard drives.

exam
⍢atch

You may be asked about who has the ability to create shared folders and assign permissions for them. Power Users, Administrators, and Server Operators are the only built-in groups that can share files and folders. Power Users can only share them on their machines, while Administrators and Server Operators can share files and folders remotely. Of course, questions will again arise concerning what share and NTFS permissions are, calculating effective permissions, and managing users and access to resources. Review Chapter 3 if you are not completely comfortable with these subjects. You can expect to see many questions regarding these topics.

QUESTIONS

10.03: Connecting to Shared Resources on a Microsoft Network

14. You are a member of a network that contains 200 users. Your department consists of 20 members who share files and folders when collaborating on large projects. You rarely share folders with anyone outside of this group. Recently you tried to share a folder with your coworkers on your Windows 2000 Professional workstation, and set up the sharing as shown below. What will happen after you assign permissions and click OK?

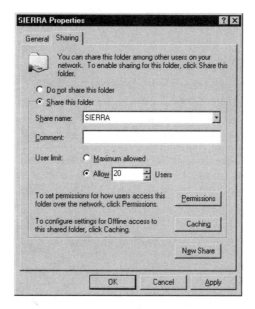

A. Nothing special will happen. The folder will be shared with all of your co-workers.

B. The folder will not be shared because you have selected an illegal number of users in the Allow Users option.

C. You will receive an error message requiring you to change the number of users to a number that is ten or less before continuing.

D. The number of shared users will change automatically to ten, and the folder will be shared without any other intervention.

E. You will be prompted that you have a FAT volume and will need to upgrade to NTFS to support more than ten users for a shared folder.

15. **Current Situation:** You have a large, diverse network that includes Windows 9*x* and 2000 workstations, clients that use NetWare, a few Macintoshes in the graphics department, and three Unix clients. You have chosen a new network print device to install, a Hewlett Packard LaserJet 4Si.

Required Result: Set up the print device to function as a network printer.

Optional Desired Results:

1. The Windows 9*x* and 2000 clients should be configured to use the printer.

2. The Netware, Macintoshes, and Unix clients should be configured to use the printer.

Proposed Solution: Use the Add Printer Wizard to install the printer. Choose Standard TCP/IP port when prompted for local or TCP/IP. Make sure the print device is turned on, connected, and configured on a print server. Type in the TCP/IP address of the printer, and when prompted, choose Finish. For the Windows-based clients, use the Add Printer Wizard. The drivers will be automatically installed. For all other clients, manually install the printer drivers. On the print server add File and Print Services for NetWare (FPNW), Services for Macintosh, and Line Printer Daemon for the Unix.

What result does the proposed solution produce?

A. The proposed solution produces the required results and both of the optional results.

B. The proposed solution produces the required results and only one of the optional results.

C. The proposed solution produces the required results and none of the optional results.

D. The proposed solution does not produce the required result.

16. Elizabeth is a member of the Power Users group in her Windows 2000 domain. She has successfully shared folders before, but now is having difficulty sharing

the folder that resides in her home folder on the main network server. Why is Elizabeth having problems with this?

A. Elizabeth needs at least the Read permission to share folders, and she must not have this permission.

B. Only Administrators and Server Operators can share folders in a domain. Elizabeth must have previously shared a folder when she was a member of a workgroup.

C. Power Users can only share folders on the computer on which their local account resides.

D. She should be able to share this folder since she is a member of the Power Users group. She should check her network connection or the network server for connectivity problems.

17. Jim, a junior network administrator for your corporation, has spent many weeks creating documents and templates necessary for users in his department to write proposals, invoices, and take inventory. He has shared this folder and told his co-workers the path to these new items. He accesses the folder after a week or so, to add some other templates he has created for his users, and is shocked to find the documents either missing, corrupt, or altered. What common mistakes might Jim have made when sharing these folders?

A. Jim did not remove the Everyone group when he first shared the folder.

B. Jim gave users in his department too high a level of access. Read may have been more appropriate.

C. Jim put these shared folders on a FAT volume. NTFS is a better choice.

D. All of the above.

18. Marsha is a member of three groups. These groups are Marketing, Accounting, and Sales. The shared folder "Audit" is on the network server. Marketing has NTFS and share permissions to read the file, Accounting has only the NTFS permission Full Control, and Sales has NTFS permission Read, and Share Permission Change. What are Marsha's effective permissions?

A. Change

B. Full Control

C. Read

D. Modify

LAB QUESTION

Objectives 10.01–10.03

You are in the initial planning stages of installing a new network. This network will consist of four domain controllers and 200 workstations, and all will run Windows 2000 products. You need to plan the configuration of TCP/IP so that the addresses are automatically handed out to the clients when requested. You also want the clients to automatically receive the subnet mask, default gateway, and DNS Server addresses. Some of the users on this network will access the network via Dial-Up Connections.

Shown below are some of the steps involved in the initial configuration of the TCP/IP properties on the servers, enabling DHCP on the clients, and configuring Dial-Up Connections. Follow the directions given in each section.

What are some of the characteristics of DHCP, and how does it work?

Note that the following characteristics listed are all true; try to think of more characteristics of DHCP that are not mentioned.

- Network servers can be DHCP servers.
- DHCP works by an administrator creating a pool of TCP/IP addresses for the clients to use (scope).
- The DHCP client, upon booting up, requests its IP address from a pool of addresses (its scope) defined on the DHCP server.
- The DHCP server offers its information, and if the client accepts the offer, the DHCP server leases the IP information to the client for a specified period of time.

What steps are involved in enabling Windows 2000 clients to use a DHCP Server?

Some steps to follow may be incorrect or missing. Find any mistakes and omissions.

1. Right-click My Network Places and select Properties from the content menu.

2. Right-click the Local Area Connection icon in the Network and Dial-Up Connections window. Click Properties.

3. In the Local Area Connection Properties dialog box, make sure that the check box is selected next to Client for Microsoft Networks. Select this entry and click Properties.

4. On the Properties General tab, make sure that DHCP is checked.

5. Click OK to close the Network and Dial-Up Connections window.

What steps are involved in establishing a Dial-Up Connection to a Private Network?

Some steps to follow may be incorrect or missing. Find any mistakes and omissions.

1. Right-click Network Neighborhood on your desktop, and choose Properties from the context menu.

2. Double-click New Dial-Up Connection. The New Dial-Up Connection Wizard starts. Click Next.

3. Select the Dial-Up to Private Network radio button, and click Next.

4. Enter the IP address of the computer or network you want to dial into, and click Next.

5. You now have a choice of who can use this connection: For All Users (of this computer), or Only for Myself. Choose the For All Users radio button, and click Next.

6. Type a friendly name for this connection in the dialog box.

7. Click Finish to complete setting up the connection.

QUICK ANSWER KEY

Objective 10.01

1.	B
2.	B
3.	B
4.	C
5.	A, B, and C
6.	A
7.	D, B, C, E, and A
8.	C

Objective 10.02

9.	A and B
10.	C
11.	A and B
12.	A and D
13.	B

Objective 10.03

14.	D
15.	D
16.	C
17.	D
18.	A

IN-DEPTH ANSWERS

10.01: Configuring and Troubleshooting TCP/IP Protocol

1. ☑ **B.** TRACERT allows you to trace the path from a computer to a specified IP address, and identify all of the hops in between. This tool is used when you feel there are router or subnet problems.

   ☒ **A** is incorrect because pinging the loopback address will not help because the user is able to connect to others on his subnet, meaning TCP/IP is installed correctly. ARP is used to map IP addresses to the MAC addresses and is not an appropriate solution here, thus **C** is incorrect. **D** is a tool that is used to display all connections and protocol statistics for TCP/IP and is not the best answer here.

2. ☑ **B.** IPCONFIG /ALL. This is the best choice here because IPCONFIG /ALL offers all of this information and more.

   ☒ **A** will not give the information required and is incorrect. **C** gives information to view or change routing tables and is also incorrect. **D** is used for troubleshooting NetBIOS name resolution and is not correct.

3. ☑ **B.** NSLOOKUP queries the DNS server and provides information about the host and its status. NSLOOKUP also gives information about host name and IP address.

   ☒ **A** is incorrect because PATHPING is a combination of the PING and TRACERT tools, and does not give us the needed information. ROUTE is used to display the current routing table, and allows modifications to the table; therefore **C** is incorrect. **D** is incorrect because NETSTAT is used for listing the current connections and protocol statistics for TCP/IP.

4. ☑ **C.** The Internet layer is where data is encapsulated. Included in this layer are IP, ARP, IGMP, and ICMP protocols.

☒ **A** is incorrect because the Application layer is used to provide network access for applications. **B** is incorrect since ARP is not a protocol at this layer. This layer is responsible for reliable data transmission, and includes TCP and UDP. **D** is incorrect since this is the lowest level of the layers, and is responsible for putting packets on the wire.

5. ☑ **A, B**, and **C** are correct choices. When using Network Monitor to filter and capture packets, all of the above can be configured.

☒ **D** is incorrect because you can use Network Monitor to capture data patterns.

6. ☑ **A.** ESP Tunnel mode encapsulates and encrypts the entire IP datagram so that you can securely transmit it across public and private internetworks. The IP datagram is encapsulated and then encrypted with ESP. It is then further encapsulated with a plain-text IP header and sent on its way. When it is received at the destination (as it is leaving the tunnel), the plain-text header is processed and discarded. The ESP packet is then authenticated, decrypted, and processed in the normal way.

☒ **B** is ESP with Authentication Header that permits the client and the server to validate each other before communication starts, and is incorrect. **C** and **D** are incorrect because they do not offer full encapsulation of the datagram.

7. ☑ **D, B, C, E, A** is the correct sequence of events for resolving a host name to an IP address. Although this scenario describes forward lookups, make sure you also understand the process for reverse lookups. Additionally, the name server caches the results for a short period of time in case the information is needed again.

8. ☑ **C.** The DNS service is only available on the Windows 2000 Server product CDs, not on Windows 2000 Professional.

☒ **A** is incorrect because the DNS service is not located on the Windows 2000 Professional CD. **B** is incorrect because giving the workstation authority over a certain zone will still not enable it to function as a DNS Server. **D** is incorrect because upgrading to Windows 2000 Server will enable the machine to function as a DNS Server, and Professional does not have the necessary files installed.

10.02: Connecting to Computers by Using Dial-Up Networking

9. ☑ **A** and **B** are correct. Both describe the characteristics of the two protocols.

☒ **C** is incorrect because these technologies are available to Windows 2000 Professional and allow secure communications between clients and servers. **D** is incorrect since packets are encapsulated in PPTP.

10. ☑ **C.** The directions given for creating a remote access server are accurate, and will enable clients to dial in to your computer. However, the last sentence that addresses prompting for number of concurrent connections is not. Windows 2000 Professional can only support three (3) concurrent connections at a time. These three connections can consist of one dialup, one serial, and one VPN. (Note that this is different from NT Workstation, which could only support 1 RAS connection.) Thus, the first optional result can only be met if the computer is upgraded to Windows 2000 Server. The second optional result is not met because you have not enabled (in TCP/IP Properties) Allow Callers to Access My Local Area Network. Without this box checked, users can call in but will not be able to access the other computers on the network.

☒ **A** and **B** are incorrect because the proposed result does not meet any of the optional results. **D** is wrong because the proposed result meets the required result.

11. ☑ Only **A** and **B** are protocols. EAP is a new protocol supported under Windows 2000 and is an extension to the PPP Protocol. It allows additional authentication schemes to be added. MD5-CHAP's function is to encrypt usernames and passwords.

☒ TLS, or Transport Level Security, provides support for smart cards and certificates, making **C** incorrect, and RADIUS is vendor-independent remote user authentication scheme. **C** and **D** are not protocols and are therefore incorrect.

12. ☑ **A** and **D** are correct. Both can cause users to lose connectivity to the network if Internet sharing is enabled. Internet sharing is for small networks that are not part of a domain and are not using DHCP.

☒ If either **B** or **C** were true, then the users would never have been connected to the Internet to begin with, which is clearly stated in the question.

13. ☑ **B.** PPTP offers all of these requirements and L2TP does not.

☒ L2TP does offer transmission over IP-based networks, but none of the others. This makes **A**, **C**, and **D** incorrect.

10.03: Connecting to Shared Resources on a Microsoft Network

14. ☑ **D.** If you try to share a folder with any number of users greater than ten, the number of users automatically changes back to ten without any message, warning, or other type of intervention.

☒ **A** is incorrect because the number of users will be automatically changed to ten, and will not be shared among the twenty co-workers. **B** is incorrect because the folder will be shared, but only for ten concurrent users. **C** is incorrect because you will not receive an error message; instead, the number will be changed automatically. **E** is incorrect because to share a folder with a FAT volume or NTFS, user limits remain at ten. To share with more than ten users, upgrade to a Windows Server product.

15. ☑ **D.** An important step was left out when installing the network printer. If the printer is directly connected to the network via an adapter card, such as Hewlett Packard LaserJet 4Si, you need to install the DLC protocol on the print server for the device. The first optional result is not met because Windows 9*x* printer drivers are not automatically installed. Windows NT and 2000 will be installed automatically, but the Windows 9*x* machines will need to be configured manually. The second optional result is met by the proposal to manually install drivers on these clients.

☒ **A**, **B**, and **C** are all incorrect as the proposed solution does not produce the required result, it produces only one of the optional results.

16. ☑ **C.** Power Users can share folders only on the computer on which their local account resides. Only Administrators and Server Operators can share to any computer in the domain. Elizabeth has previously shared folders from her local computer.

☒ **A** is incorrect. On an NTFS volume, you must have the Read permission on a folder to be able to share it, however this is not the main issue. **B** is incorrect because Power Users can share folders in a domain, but only on their local machine. **D** is incorrect for reasons already mentioned.

17. ☑ **D.** When sharing a folder, you should always remove the Everyone group right away; the default is that they have Full Control. This is not a Best Practice. Giving users only the level of access they need is also very important. It is always easier to add leniency than to place higher restrictions. Of course, NTFS is a better choice than FAT for security and sharing folders.

☒ **A**, **B**, and **C** are individually incorrect because all are possible mistakes Jim could have made.

18. ☑ **A.** The cumulative NTFS permissions are Full Control, and the cumulative share permissions are Change.

☒ The more restrictive of these two is Change. **B**, **C**, and **D** are all incorrect for this reason.

LAB ANSWER

Objectives 10.01–10.03

What are some of the characteristics of DHCP, and how does it work?

DHCP characteristics not mentioned:

- You should also make sure the DHCP server has a static address.

- The clients need to be running Windows 2000, NT 3.51 or later, Windows 95 or later, WFW3.11 with MS TCP/IP-32, MS Network Client v3 for MS-DOS (with the real-mode TCP/IP driver), or LAN Manager 2.2c (2.2c for OS/2 is not supported).

- If DHCP is not working properly, Windows 2000 offers APIPA to assign an IP address to itself.

What steps are involved in enabling Windows 2000 clients to use a DHCP Server?

The following steps are correct. (Corrections are in bold.)

1. Right-click My Network Places and select Properties from the context menu.

2. Right-click the Local Area Connection icon in the Network and Dial-Up Connections window. Click Properties.

3. In the Local Area Connection Properties dialog box, make sure that the check box is selected next to **Internet Protocol (TCP/IP)**. Select this entry and click Properties.

4. On the Properties General tab, make sure that **Obtain an IP Address Automatically** is checked.

5. Click OK to close the Network and Dial-Up Connections window.

What steps are involved in establishing a Dial-up Connection to a Private Network?

The following steps are correct. (Corrections are in bold.)

1. Right-click **My Network Places** on your desktop, and choose Properties from the context menu.

2. Double-click **Make New Connection**. The **Make New Connection** Wizard starts. Click Next.

3. Select the Dial-Up to Private Network radio button, and click Next.

4. Enter the **telephone number** of the computer or network you want to dial into, and click Next.

5. You now have a choice of who can use this connection: For All Users (of this computer), or Only for Myself. Choose the For All Users radio button, and click Next.

6. Type a friendly name for this connection in the dialog box. **You may also add a shortcut to your desktop by clicking the Add a Shortcut to My Desktop check box.**

7. Click Finish to complete setting up the connection.

11

Implementing, Monitoring, and Troubleshooting Security and User Accounts

I mplementing, monitoring, and troubleshooting security and user accounts is what makes a network efficient and productive or not. Without strong security measures in place to form a defense against hackers, unintentional user errors, or other mishaps, a network can fall apart pretty quickly. Security options available in Windows 2000 include encryption using EFS, private keys, and user profiles and policies. Audit policy settings allow administrators to record network activity and record it to a security log. Password policies force users to maintain appropriate password configurations, while account lockout policies disable numerous incorrect password attempts by hackers. Group policies allow an administrator to alter users' rights and permissions to network resources.

Local user profiles can also be set to save desktop settings made by a user on a workstation, and are stored locally on that computer. Roaming and mandatory profiles are available for configuration for mobile computer users. Default user profiles can also be created for specific groups of people like guests, temporary workers, or users who perform specific tasks.

TEST YOURSELF OBJECTIVE 11.01

Implementing, Configuring, Managing, and Troubleshooting Local Group Policy

Local group policy is the lowest level of security available for Windows 2000 products. These group policies can enforce rules, rights, permissions, and accessibility to resources for the local user on a system. These policies can include restrictions on passwords, logon attempts, account lockout settings, public key settings, security settings, and user rights. User rights include accessing the network, taking ownership of files or folders, and acting as part of the operating system. You modify local computer policy from the Group Policy Editor.

- Group policy settings alter users' rights, abilities, and powers.
- Audit policy sets auditing, which allows you to record activity to the security log.

■ Password policy can force users to create harder-to-guess passwords, and to change these passwords more often.

■ Account lockout policy sets the circumstances under which an account will lock out, refusing access even to the proper password, and sets the length of time a lockout lasts.

■ Higher level settings to group policy override local settings.

■ Every level is higher than the local level.

exam
ⓦatch
While experimenting with group policies, you'll find there are a number of rights that can be configured for security. Space limitations do not permit an in-depth description of each here. To see some of the rights that are available for configuration, choose Run | Gpedit.msc from the command line, then Computer Configuration | Windows Settings | Security Settings | Local Policies | User Rights Assignment or Security Settings. By right-clicking the policy and choosing Security, you can add users or groups.

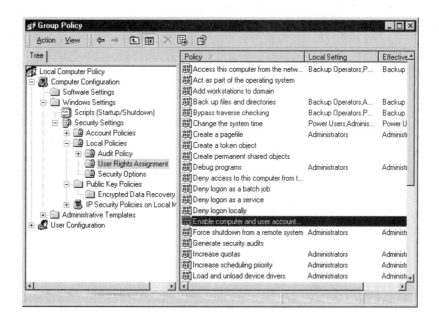

QUESTIONS

11.01: Implementing, Configuring, Managing, and Troubleshooting Local Group Policy

1. The Widget Factory has just had a developer create a Web site, and now has a URL for the company. From this Web site, customers can obtain information concerning pricing, delivery, and products, and there is an area for employees to obtain data. This part of the site is restricted from customers. You want to create a group policy where this restricted area of the Web site is the default URL for Internet Explorer for your employees. You also need to create policies that address content and Authenticode issues. Where do you create this policy?

   A. From each employee's computer, open Internet Explorer, Tools, and Internet Options to make the necessary configuration changes.

   B. From the Group Policy console, choose Local Computer Policy, User Configuration, Windows Settings, Internet Explorer Maintenance, URLs, and Security.

   C. From the Group Policy console, choose Local Computer Policy, Computer Configuration, Windows Settings, Internet Explorer Maintenance, URLs, and Security.

   D. From the Group Policy console, choose Local Computer Policy, User Configuration, Software Settings, Internet Explorer Maintenance, URLs, and Security.

2. After creating a complicated and secure local group policy for users in your small department; which includes password requirements, auditing logs, logon scripts, user rights assignments, and public key policies; you realize that the users do not have to abide by these policies. You think you've set it up correctly and added members appropriately, but for some reason none of the policies have taken effect. Why is this?

   A. Public key policies can only be configured on Windows 2000 Server machines, and you are running Windows 2000 Professional.

    B. Site-level policies are overriding your local policies.

    C. Domain-level policies are overriding your local policies.

    D. You need to ask the users to log off and log back on for the changes to take effect.

3. Celestina and Jim are administrators of St. Sophia's in a small suburb of Syracuse. They allow all users access to the church's computers whenever they need, and these users log on as guests. A shared folder on the hard drive contains information about cook-offs, meetings, bake sales, and other church events. They would like to audit access to this folder to see if anyone ever uses it, and if so, how often. The steps that are required to enable auditing of a folder are listed below. Put them in order starting with the first step.

    A. Choose to audit List Folder/Read Data, and click OK. Then choose Apply and OK.

    B. Select the Guest group, type in a name for this event in the Name box, and click OK.

    C. Right-click the shared folder and select Properties from the pull-down menu.

    D. Double-click Audit Object Access in the right-hand pane and check the Successes box.

    E. Click the Security tab, and Advanced. Select the Auditing tab. Click Add.

    F. Open the Audit Policy folder, inside Local Computer Policy | Computer Configuration | Windows Settings | Security Settings | Local Policies | Audit Policy.

    G. Use Windows Explorer to browse to the shared folder.

4. Following a lapse in security, you have had to make numerous changes to your group policy. You need to make sure these changes take effect immediately to reduce further damage to your system, and audit events that are occurring. Which of the following is the best way to have a group policy change take effect immediately?

    A. Set the group policy refresh rate to a very large interval.

    B. Reboot the computer.

    C. Set the group policy refresh rate to a very small interval.

    D. Type **secedit /refreshpolicy MACHINE_POLICY** at the command prompt.

TEST YOURSELF OBJECTIVE 11.02

Encrypting Data on a Hard Disk by Using EFS

Encrypting File System (EFS) is a way to secure data on NTFS drives in Windows 2000 Professional. EFS works by using public key technology. That is, a user who wishes to access a file on an NTFS volume must have the private key to that file to open it. The key allows the file to be decrypted, and those who do not have a key are denied access. All of this technology is invisible to the user.

- EFS is built-in encryption that comes with NTFS.

- You can either encrypt or compress with NTFS, but not both.

- Encrypted files can only be decrypted by the encrypting user, or a designated encryption recovery agent.

- You can take your private key with you by creating a roaming profile, or by exporting your certificate with a private key.

- When you encrypt a folder, Windows simply marks the folder and automatically encrypts any files placed inside the folder.

exam
ⓦatch

EFS is used to provide security on an NTFS volume. However, many programs create temporary files while data is being edited, and this can pose a security risk since that data may not always be encrypted. Of course, this issue has been addressed in Windows 2000 products. EFS uses folder-level security, so any temporary copies of files are stored in those folders, thus ensuring that the data remains encrypted. For further security, EFS is also an operating system kernel product that uses a nonpaged pool to store the encryption keys, ensuring that these keys are never copied to the paging file.

QUESTIONS

11.02: Encrypting Data on a Hard Disk by Using EFS

5. Mary works mainly at a workstation located in her office, but occasionally does specialty work and performs Internet downloads on a computer in another department. She does not want or need a roaming profile, as the network is already congested, but wants to be able to take her private key with her to access encrypted files when she is at the other computer. Is this possible, and if so, how? (Select all possible answers.)

    A. This is not possible. An administrator should make Mary's profile roaming so she can have the access she needs.

    B. Mary can carry a floppy disk to the other department that has her private key on it.

    C. Mary should save her private key to a network server, and when logged on to the other computer, should access the key from there.

    D. Add the Certificates snap-in to her console, and use the Certificate Export Wizard to export the key.

    Questions 6–8   This scenario should be used to answer questions 6, 7, and 8.

    Alice works for a government lab in San Jose creating and managing security policies and programs for large government offices around the country. Alice is creating an encrypted folder on an NTFS volume. This folder will be used for saving sensitive documents for a member of the Security Experts team. Answer the following questions concerning this folder and its contents.

6. The files that are saved to this encrypted folder have certain attributes by default. Which of the following describe the characteristics of the files that are saved in this folder?

    A. Encryption is 128-bit.

    B. The file encryption keys are stored in the DDF and DRF in the file header.

    C. The file encryption keys are symmetric keys.

    D. The file is encrypted in blocks, and each block of a file uses the same encryption key. Keys change with each file.

7. Two other security experts have arrived at the San Jose office. These two employees want to access files in the folder that Alice just created for the security experts in her office. They want to work on some projects together and collaborate on some of the files that are stored in the folder. How will Alice do this?

    A. Give the two new users Read permission to access the file.

    B. Give the two new users Full Control permission to access the file.

    C. Give the two new users Modify permission to access the file.

    D. Different individuals cannot access encrypted files.

8. The security expert is concerned that EFS doesn't encrypt data that is transferred over a network, but only encrypts data as it is saved, and while it is edited. He wants the data to be encrypted in transit. What do you tell him?

    A. SMB provides data encryption across network lines.

    B. Windows 2000 offers protocols like IPSec for encrypting data over the network.

    C. Data moves so quickly through the network, there is no danger involved in the data being unencrypted for such a short period of time.

    D. TCP/IP handles this task.

9. Patty is encrypting the file Sierra as shown below. What will this command accomplish when it is run from the command line?

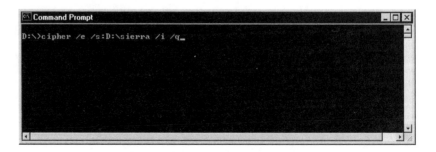

A. The file Sierra will be encrypted, and will continue even if errors occur. Patty will not be given any information during this process.

B. The file Sierra will be encrypted, and it will continue even if errors occur. Patty will be given only the most essential information during this process.

C. The file Sierra will be encrypted, and will run without user interaction.

D. Nothing but an error message will be generated; the syntax is incorrect.

10. **Current Situation:** You have a computer running Windows 2000 Professional which contains data that is critical to your network. You need to protect this data from harm, and have stored it on an NTFS volume, making sure that only administrators can obtain access to these files. Because of the amount of the data on the drive, you have chosen to compress the data first.

Required Result: The data must be encrypted, easy to manage, and difficult to gain unauthorized access to. Encryption must be invisible to administrators who access it.

Optional Desired Results:

1. All files and subfolders must be automatically encrypted, as well as backups of the data.

2. Files must remain encrypted if they are moved or renamed, and there should be no lapse in security from files being moved to temporary locations when they are being edited.

Proposed Solution: Log on as administrator. Implement EFS through Windows Explorer by right-clicking the folder that needs encryption. Enable encryption on that folder by clicking the Encrypt Contents to Secure Data check box, and clicking OK.

What result does the proposed solution produce?

A. The proposed solution produces the required results and both of the optional results.

B. The proposed solution produces the required results and only one of the optional results.

C. The proposed solution produces the required results and none of the optional results.

D. The proposed solution does not produce the required result.

TEST YOURSELF OBJECTIVE 11.03

Implementing, Configuring, Managing, and Troubleshooting Local User Accounts

Local user accounts allow users to log on to specific computers on a network and gain access to resources on that computer. Local user accounts are created on the computer that is to be accessed, and the information about that user is stored in the local security database of that computer. Creating and managing user accounts, computer accounts, local groups, and group members is also part of administering a network. This consists of adding and deleting users and groups, assigning and managing rights and privileges, and adding computers to a domain.

- New Users are created in Computer Management | Users | Groups.
- You have to be a member of the Domain Administrators group to create a computer account in a domain.
- Users get all the rights and permissions granted to them by their group membership.

exam
Watch

Make sure you know the difference between local user accounts, domain user accounts, and built-in user accounts. Local user accounts are created on the computer that is to be accessed, and the information about that user is stored in the local security database of that computer. Domain user accounts are used to allow access to network resources. Windows 2000 will authenticate the user and provide an access token that will identify that user at all of the computers and resources in the domain. Built-in groups are those groups that are automatically created when Windows 2000 is installed, and the two default groups are Administrator and Guest. For security reasons, it is always best to rename the administrator account immediately, and leave the guest account disabled.

QUESTIONS

11.03: Implementing, Configuring, Managing, and Troubleshooting Local User Accounts

11. A user on your network is complaining that it takes an inordinate amount of time to log on everyday. She doesn't notice slow network performance during the day, and other users do not complain of network congestion when they log on their computers in the morning. How can you solve this problem?

A. She is a member of too many groups and this is affecting the time it takes to be authenticated in the morning.

B. She is at the physical end of the network and should be moved closer to the server.

C. She has a large user profile that has to be downloaded every time she logs on a machine.

D. You can solve this problem by adding another domain controller and segmenting the network.

12. Kathryn is a member of three groups: Inventory, Cash Flow, and Assets. For the folder Taxes 2000, the Inventory group has the share permission Full Control and NTFS permission Read; the Cash Flow group has the share permission Read and NTFS permission Full Control; and the Assets group has share permission Change and NTFS permission Modify. What are Kathryn's effective permissions for the folder?

A. Full Control

B. Change

C. Read

D. Modify

13. You manage a team of database programmers who are going on a business trip next week. You have configured their laptops to connect to the server, in order

to access the shared files, and have enabled caching on these files and computers. After testing the computers you find that you can open the database files but cannot cache them. What is the problem?

A. You need to reboot the laptops for the changes to take effect.

B. You need to configure a group policy that enables .DB files to be cached.

C. You need to synchronize the laptops with the server.

D. You need to enable caching in group policy.

14. **Current Situation:** Your five-computer workgroup has a computer running Windows 2000 Professional. You have previously completed all workgroup-related tasks yourself, but would now like to delegate some of that responsibility among your employees. You want to use the built-in local groups on this machine to administer tasks on this computer. You will also need to make some changes to the built-in local groups.

Required Result: Allow Bill, who is the junior network administrator, rights to back up and restore data, and access this computer from the network. Bill should also be able to log on locally to your computer.

Optional Desired Results:

1. Joe shall take over the responsibilities of modifying local user accounts by accessing the computer, and managing the auditing and security log from his own computer in his office.

2. The guest account shall not only be disabled, but shall be removed for security reasons.

3. Jane shall accept the duties of profiling system performance.

Proposed Solution: Make Bill a member of the Backup Operators group and make no other specific changes to his account. Make Joe a member of the Power Users group and make no other changes to his account. Make Jane a member of the Everyone group and give her the right to Profile System Performance. Remove the guest account through MMC.

What result does the proposed solution produce?

A. The proposed solution produces the required results and all of the optional results.

B. The proposed solution produces the required results and only one of the optional results.

C. The proposed solution produces the required results and two of the optional results.

D. The proposed solution does not produce the required result.

TEST YOURSELF OBJECTIVE 11.04

Creating and Managing User Profiles

User Profiles are collections of users' settings, preferences, favorites, cookies, and desktops that allow the user to maintain consistency every time he or she logs on. If a computer is shared between users, each user can always log on and receive his or her own settings. A default profile is created at the time of installation, and can be modified to suit any user's needs. Roaming and mandatory profiles can be employed for networks and domains, so that users who travel can maintain consistency also. The default user profile is stored in the *system partition root* | Documents and Settings | *user logon name* folder.

- Local user profiles are used to save any personal desktop settings made by a user on a particular computer, and are stored locally on that computer.

- Roaming user profiles are used to save a user's settings to be used on any computer in the domain. These profiles are stored on a network file server.

- Mandatory profiles are read-only roaming profiles.

- Default user profiles can be created as a basis for users' settings.

- NTUSER.DAT in the user profile must be renamed to NTUSER.MAN to change a nonmandatory roaming profile to a mandatory profile.

exam
watch

A roaming user profile is used in a domain environment when a user works at more than one computer and wants to maintain desktop settings wherever he or she is working. Do not choose roaming user profiles if asked about it in a workgroup environment. The mandatory user profile is also considered a roaming profile, although the name is deceiving. By definition, a mandatory user profile is a read-only roaming user profile. This is also used in a domain environment. Mandatory user profiles can be established for specific users or groups of users and do not allow changes to the profile to be saved. Make sure you know the difference between the different types of profiles.

QUESTIONS

11.04: Creating and Managing User Profiles

15. Tim is an employee at a company called Travel2day. He manages four travel agencies in the area, which are all connected as one large network with four subnets. He has a roaming user profile that he can alter. He logged on yesterday, but his roaming user profile was unavailable. What happened when Tim logged on?

    A. He received an error stating that his profile was unavailable, and access to the network was denied.

    B. Because he had logged on to this computer before, he received a locally cached copy of the roaming profile.

    C. Because he had logged on to this computer before, he received a temporary profile created from the workstation's default user profile.

    D. He received the Windows Standard desktop and was granted access to the network.

16. **Current Situation:** You need to create a specialized User Profile for the CEO of your company. He needs to run a login script each time he logs on his computer and save his data to the network server. He also belongs to three groups and has three accounts in the Security, Management, and Sales Departments.

    Required Result: The CEO wants all changes that he makes while logged on one of these accounts to affect all three.

    Optional Desired Results:

    1. Set up a login script that will run the CEO's necessary programs at logon.

    2. Set up a home folder so the CEO can save all his data to the network server.

    Proposed Solution: When setting up the three accounts, make sure that the profile path for all of these accounts is the same. Set a path for a login script in the Profile tab of his user properties, and point to a file written in JavaScript that contains the necessary information. Use folder redirection to create a path for a home folder on the network server.

What result does the proposed solution produce?

A. The proposed solution produces the required results and both of the optional results.

B. The proposed solution produces the required results and only one of the optional results.

C. The proposed solution produces the required results and none of the optional results.

D. The proposed solution does not produce the required result.

17. You are planning to use group policy to restrict some users' access to resources and their ability to harm their systems unintentionally. Although these members belong to the Power Users group, you need to restrict their ability to remove a computer from a docking station, access this computer from a network, logon locally, and debug programs. Which of these is not granted to Power Users by default?

A. Logon locally.

B. Remove a computer from a docking station.

C. Debug programs.

D. Access this computer from a network.

18. Johnny has a roaming user profile that he uses to access network resources and maintain his settings when he travels from office-to-office, or site-to-site. Recently, you've been having some problems with Johnny, and need to restrict what he can and cannot do with his profile. You are planning on making his roaming user profile a mandatory profile. What is the best way to accomplish this?

A. Delete the profile from the network server and create a new one. Have Johnny log off and log back on to get the new profile.

B. In the \%systemroot% | Documents and Settings | <username> directory, delete the profile. Create a new mandatory profile on the network server and have Johnny log back on.

C. Move the profile that is located in the \%systemdrive%\Documents and Settings\<username> folder to the C:\Winnt\Shell New\<username> folder.

D. Change NTUSER.DAT in the user profile to NTUSER.MAN.

LAB QUESTION

Objectives 11.01–11.04

You have tried to create a secure and efficient network for your company, and have many security features in place, including NTFS volumes, NTFS permissions, firewalls, and an excellent backup schedule. Even with all of these securities in place, there are times when you think that unhappy employees, the cleaning crew, or outsiders are trying to hack into the system. You need to log events that apply to logon attempts, and create a stronger password policy for your users. You should also configure a lockout policy for users who do not log on the network in a predetermined number of attempts.

Decide what you should do first, then, on a computer installed with Windows 2000 Professional, work your way through the steps to do this. Write down the paths to the tools that allow configuration of these audit policies. Also, explain how to encrypt sensitive files with EFS.

QUICK ANSWER KEY

Objective 11.01

1. **B**
2. **B, C,** and **D**
3. **F, D, G, C, E, B,** and **A**
4. **D**

Objective 11.02

5. **B** and **D**
6. **B** and **C**
7. **D**
8. **B**
9. **B**
10. **D**

Objective 11.03

11. **C**
12. **A**
13 **B**
14. **B**

Objective 11.04

15. **B**
16. **A**
17. **C**
18. **D**

IN-DEPTH ANSWERS

11.01: Implementing, Configuring, Managing, and Troubleshooting Local Group Policy

1. ☑ **B** describes the correct place to configure a new group policy.

    ☒ **A** is incorrect because this will only create the settings on a local machine. **C** offers Computer Configuration instead of User Configuration, and is incorrect. **D** offers Software settings instead of Windows settings and is incorrect.

2. ☑ **B, C**, and **D** are correct. B is correct because site-level policies override local policies, C is correct because domain-level policies override local polices, and D is correct because a user must log off and log back on to enable new user policies.

    ☒ **A** is not correct because public key policies can be configured on Windows 2000 Professional machines.

3. ☑ The correct order of events is **F, D, G, C, E, B**, and **A**. Make sure you can do this before taking the exam! Microsoft promises more hands-on exercises to determine if candidates know how to use the software and not just answer questions.

4. ☑ **D.** By typing **secedit /refreshpolicy MACHINE_POLICY** at the command prompt, the changes will take effect immediately.

    ☒ **A** is incorrect because setting the refresh rate to a large interval would increase the time for changes to take place. **B** is unnecessary and not the best choice since rebooting the computer is unnecessary. **C** is a good idea and a way to decrease refresh rate, but typing the command is faster. Thus, D is the best answer.

11.02: Encrypting Data on a Hard Disk by Using EFS

5. ☑ **B** and **D** are correct. B is correct because Mary can carry a floppy disk with her private key on it to the other department. D is correct because Mary can access the Certificate Export Wizard from the Certificates snap-in.

☒ **A** is incorrect because carrying the profile with her is possible. **C** is not the best answer because a network connection may not always be present.

6. ☑ **B** and **C** are correct. B is correct because DDF and DRF are Data Decryption Field and Data Recovery Field in a file header, and C is correct because file encryption keys are symmetric.

☒ **A** is incorrect because the default encryption is 56-bit. **D** is incorrect because each block of data is encrypted with different keys, not each file.

7. ☑ **D.** Different individuals cannot access encrypted files.

☒ **A** is incorrect because the Read permission will not allow a user to access someone else's encrypted files. **B** is incorrect because the Full Control permission will not allow users to access others' encrypted files. **C** is incorrect, again, for the same reason.

8. ☑ **B.** IPSec (IP Security) is a protocol available to transmit data securely.

☒ SMB is Server Message Block, which is also a protocol, but it does not encrypt data; therefore, **A** is incorrect. **C** is incorrect because there is always a security issue involved when unencrypted data is transferred through a network, no matter how quickly it is done. **D** is incorrect because TCP/IP is not responsible for encrypting data.

9. ☑ **B.** The /i switch is used to perform the encryption even if errors occur, and the /q switch is used to report only the most essential information.

☒ **A** is incorrect because the switch /q will offer some information during encryption. **C** is incorrect because the /q switch does not mean "quiet" as in other utilities, and the issue of encrypting, even if errors occur, is not addressed. **D** is incorrect because the syntax is correct in this instance.

10. ☑ **D.** You cannot both compress and encrypt data at the same time. Since the data is being saved to a compressed drive, encryption will not be available. Both optional results are not met since the data has not been successfully encrypted.

    ☒ **A**, **B**, and **C** are incorrect as the required result is not met.

11.03: Implementing, Configuring, Managing, and Troubleshooting Local User Accounts

11. ☑ **C** is correct and is explained properly.

    ☒ Since no other users complain of slow logons or network congestion, it would seem unnecessary to add another domain controller, making **D** incorrect. Being at the physical end of the network would not affect her logon, making **B** incorrect; and **A** would also not cause a noticeable delay, making it an incorrect answer.

12. ☑ **A.** The least restrictive of the share permissions is Full Control, and the least restrictive of the NTFS permissions is Full Control. The most restrictive of those two is Full Control.

    ☒ **B** is incorrect because Change is not the effective permission. **C** is incorrect because Read is not the effective permission. **D** is incorrect because Modify is not the effective permission.

13 ☑ **B.** By default, files that end in .DB cannot be cached. This will need to be configured in a group policy for these users. Other extensions that cannot be cached by default are .SLM, .LBD, .MDB, .MDE, and .PST.

    ☒ **A** is unnecessary, and **C** will not help with an inability to cache offline files. **D** is incorrect because the administrator has enabled it already.

14. ☑ **B.** In order to answer this question correctly, you must know what each of the built-in groups can do by default. The Backup Operators group can back up and restore data, log on locally. Power Users and the Everyone group can access the computer from a network. Thus the required result is met. The first optional result is not met because the default rights of the Power Users group does not allow modifying local user accounts. Only the administrator can view security logs and perform auditing, unless you have given a user the specific

right to do so. The third optional result is met because the right to Profile System Performance is granted. The second optional result is not met because the guest account cannot be removed. (No built-in groups can be removed.)

☒ **A** and **C** are incorrect because the proposed solution meets one optional result. **D** is incorrect because the proposed solution meets the required result.

11.04: Implementing, Configuring, Managing, and Troubleshooting Local User Accounts

15. ☑ **B.** If a user has logged on locally to the computer, there exists a locally cached version of his or her profile. It may be a little outdated, but will suffice.

☒ **A** is incorrect because access to a network will not be denied if the user profile is not available. **C** is incorrect because the temporary profile is what he would have received had he *not* ever logged on the computer before. **D** is incorrect because he will not be given the Windows Standard desktop; he will be given his locally cached copy.

16. ☑ **A.** All of these things can be accomplished with the proposed solution. Three accounts can all use the same profile path, and therefore changes to one account will affect all three. JavaScript is a valid language for creating login scripts, and folder redirection is the correct term for creating home folder storage on a network server.

☒ **B** and **C** are incorrect. The proposed solution meets both optional results. **D** is incorrect. The proposed solution meets the required result.

17. ☑ **C.** Power Users are not granted rights to debug programs by default, only administrators are.

☒ **A** is incorrect because logging on locally is a right granted to Power Users by default. **B** is incorrect because Power Users can remove computers from docking stations. **D** is incorrect because Power Users already have the right to access the computer from a network.

18. ☑ **D** is how to change a roaming user profile to a mandatory profile.

☒ **A** is incorrect because deleting the profile from the network server and creating a new one is not necessary when the profile can be easily changed by changing NTUSER.DAT to NTUSER.MAN. **B** is incorrect, again, for the same reason as A. **C** is incorrect since moving the profile will not make the profile mandatory.

LAB ANSWER

Objectives 11.01–11.04

To enable Auditing on Account Logon attempt successes and failures, and on logon events successes and failures:

> Create an audit policy from Local Computer Policy | Computer Configuration| Windows Settings | Security Settings| Local Policies| Audit policies

To enable and configure an account lockout policy:

> Create an account lockout policy from Local Computer Policy | Computer Configuration | Windows Settings | Security Settings | Account Policies | Account Lockout Policy and enable account lockout after three failures.

To create a password policy:

> From Local Computer Policy | Computer Configuration | Windows Settings | Security Settings | Account Policies | Password Policy and enable Password, which must meet complexity requirements.

To encrypt the data with EFS:

> Explore to the folder you want to encrypt, and right-click the folder that needs encryption. Enable encryption on that folder by clicking the Encrypt Contents to Secure Data check box and clicking OK.

Practice Exam

Q & A

QUESTIONS

1. Jan would like to distribute an upgrade of Windows 2000 Professional to all of the employees in her company. She also needs to install office applications, a generic desktop, and power management settings. She is using RIPrep to begin these installations. Which of the following are true concerning RIPrep? (Select all that apply.)

   A. Client computers must have identical hardware configurations.

   B. The RIPrep Wizard enables the network administrator to distribute a standard desktop configuration that includes the operating system and the applications to a large number of client computers.

   C. RIPrep can replicate images of multiple disks with multiple partitions.

   D. All of the above are true.

2. Look at the illustration below. Three users have access to this computer, and all have usernames and passwords. Notice the group membership of each member. What exactly can user Mary Anne accomplish while using this computer?

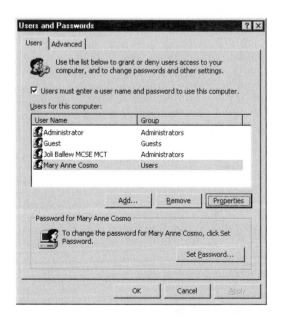

A. Mary Anne has complete and unrestricted access to this computer.

B. Mary Anne can modify the computer and install programs, but cannot read files that belong to other users.

C. Mary Anne can operate the computer and save files, but cannot install programs or make potentially damaging changes to the system files and settings.

D. Mary Anne can install programs, read files that belong to other users, save and delete files, and change desktop settings, but cannot manipulate users and passwords.

3. **Current Situation:** You have been an administrator for a small biotech company for two years. Recently, the company began expanding, and now you support 200 users instead of the 25 you started with when you configured the network. Initially, you went from computer to computer manually configuring the TCP/IP address and default gateway, with very few problems. With this larger network, however, and the influx of new employees, you are having a hard time keeping up.

Required Result: Simplify the management of network administration by eliminating the overhead associated with manually configuring the addresses on the network.

Optional Desired Results:

1. If the clients do not receive TCP/IP addresses from the network because the server is unavailable, allow the clients to assign IP addresses to themselves.

2. If the computers assign IP addresses to themselves, make sure that the clients will be able to communicate with other subnets of the network.

Proposed Solution: Configure a DC on your network to be a DHCP server. Enable TCP/IP on the clients and check the box Obtain an IP Address Automatically. Edit the following subkey in the registry:

HKEY_LOCAL_MACHINE\SYSTEM\CurrentControlSet\Services\Tcpip\ Parameters\Interfaces\Adapter

Change its value from 1 to 0.

What result does the proposed solution produce?

A. The proposed solution produces the required results and both of the optional results.

B. The proposed solution produces the required results and only one of the optional results.

C. The proposed solution produces the required results and none of the optional results.

D. The proposed solution does not produce the required result.

4. Your boss thinks that employees of the night staff have been trying to hack into his computer after he has gone home for the evening. He wants you to log events that occur on his computer that will assist him in finding out when and if this is happening. What can you do to about these illegal log-on attempts? (Choose all that apply.)

A. Log on as administrator, create an audit policy from Local Computer Policy | Computer Configuration | Windows Settings | Security Settings | Local Policies | Audit Policies, and choose to Enable Auditing on Account Log-on Attempt Successes and Failures, and Logon Events Successes and Failures.

B. Log on as administrator, create an account lockout policy from Local Computer Policy | Computer Configuration | Windows Settings | Security Settings | Account Policies | Account Lockout Policy, and Enable Account Lockout After Two Failures.

C. Log on as administrator, create a password policy from Local Computer Policy | Computer Configuration | Windows Settings | Security Settings | Account Policies | Password Policy, and enable Password Must Meet Complexity Requirements.

D. Log on as administrator, create an IP security policy from Local Computer Policy | Computer Configuration | Windows Settings | Security Settings | IP Security Policies on local machine.

5. Which of the following correctly identifies the troubleshooting logs and their matching descriptions?

A. **Setupact.log** This log file contains details about the device driver files that were copied during setup, and can be used to facilitate troubleshooting device installations. This file contains errors and warnings, along with a timestamp for each issue.

B. **Setuperr.log**   This action log file contains details about the files that are copied during setup.

C. **Setupapi.log**   This error log file contains details about errors that occurred during setup.

D. **Setuplog.txt**   This log file contains additional information about the device driver files that were copied during setup.

6. The last step, when using the Setup Manager Wizard, to create an unattended setup script is shown below. If you fill in all of the information as prompted, accept defaults, use the path C:\Deploy\Unattend.txt for the location and name of the answer file, and name the installation folder W2000Pro, what files are created?

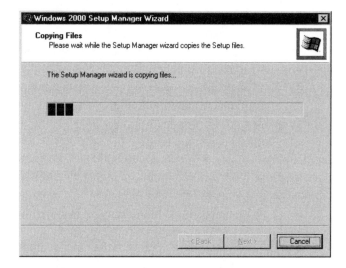

A. Unattend.bat, Unattend.txt, Unattend.udf

B. Unattend.bat, Unattend.txt, Unattend.udf, and C:\Win2000dist folder that is shared

C. Unattend.udf, and C:\Win2000dist folder that is shared

D. C:\Win2000dist folder that is shared

7. **Current Situation:** The Networking Department in your building runs a Web server for your company's Web site. It has two network interface cards installed and accesses both your intranet and the Internet. You use TCP/IP as your company's main protocol.

   Required Result: Allow people from outside the company to access this computer on NIC 1, and allow people inside the company to access this computer on NIC 2.

   Optional Desired Results:

   1. Configure the binding order so that it optimizes network performance.

   2. Employ security measures to keep hackers out of your internal network.

   Proposed Solution: Assign NIC 1 an external TCP/IP address, and assign NIC 2 an internal TCP/IP address. The two addresses must be different. Configure the binding order on NIC 1 as TCP/IP only, and the binding order on NIC 2 as NetBEUI first, and TCP/IP second. Set up a firewall or proxy server to assist in keeping your network secure.

   What result does the proposed solution produce?

   A. The proposed solution produces the required results and both of the optional results.

   B. The proposed solution produces the required results and only one of the optional results.

   C. The proposed solution produces the required results and none of the optional results.

   D. The proposed solution does not produce the required result.

8. The computers where you work have all been upgraded to Windows 2000. Your boss has decided to use Installer Packages to deploy applications throughout the network. He has told you to create a generic Installer Package

that can be used with any application that isn't written specifically for Windows 2000. How do you begin?

A. Install the Veritas Installer Lite software console by running the following file found on the Windows 2000 Professional CD:

D:\VALUEADD\3RDPARTY\MGMT\WINSTLE\SWIADMLE.MSI

B. Start the Windows Installer Package Wizard from Programs | Administrative Tools | Services.

C. Take a before snapshot of the system using WinINSTALL and VERITAS software Discover.

D. None of the above.

E. All of the above.

9. You need a dual-boot system in your office because your $6,000 plotter does not have a Windows 2000 driver available at this time, but you need to secure files and folders on that same computer with the NTFS file system. You've been told that you'll have to use the FAT or FAT32 file system on this computer in order to dual-boot between the two operating systems. What are your options?

A. There are no other options. To dual-boot with Windows 2000 and Windows 95, you must use the FAT or FAT32 file system.

B. Make both drives NTFS anyway, and use a boot disk when starting the computer. This will give you the security you need for the Professional partition, and allow you to dual-boot to Windows 95.

C. Partition your hard drive space into different logical drives and make one NTFS and another FAT32, with the system files on the NTFS drive.

D. Use the Partition Management feature, when installing Windows 2000, to configure your disks properly.

10. Mike wants to set up his Microsoft Management Console with the Disk Management snap-in as shown in the following screen shot. However, every time he tries to get to Disk Management, he ends up in the Computer

Management window. He wants to use the MMC to centralize his tasks. What is he doing wrong?

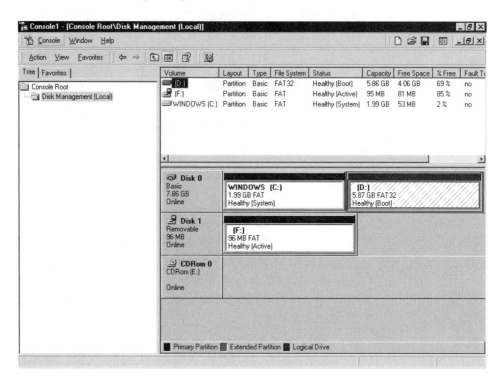

A. He is choosing Start | Programs | Administrative Tools | Computer Management instead of typing in **mmc** at the Run command, where he can then add the Disk Management snap-in.

B. He has right-clicked the My Computer icon and chosen Manage instead of typing **mmc** at the Run command, where he can then add the Disk Management snap-in.

C. If he wants to centralize his tasks in an individualized console, he'll need to use Windows 2000 Server instead of Professional.

D. A and B are correct.

11. **Current Situation:** Your company, Broadband Enterprises, has 250 Windows 2000 Professional workstations. Each of these workstations has at

least two users, one user that is logged on during the day, and one user that is logged on at night.

Required Result: Use Task Scheduler to run Disk Cleanup every Tuesday morning at 3:00A.M.

Optional Desired Results:

1. If the computer is asleep when this task is to be run, wake the computer to run it.

2. Record a log file of the activity of the Task Scheduler so it can be accessed later.

Proposed Solution: Use Task Scheduler to Add Scheduled Task. Choose Disk Cleanup when prompted to choose a task. Configure the time and date through the wizard. Accept the rest of the defaults and choose Finish.

What result does the proposed solution produce?

A. The proposed solution produces the required results and both of the optional results.

B. The proposed solution produces the required results and only one of the optional results.

C. The proposed solution produces the required results and none of the optional results.

D. The proposed solution does not produce the required result.

12. If your disk is brand-new, or if you have deleted all the partitions on the disk, you will need to create at least one partition in which to install Windows 2000 Professional. Which of the following statements is true concerning partitioning a hard disk? (Choose all the apply.)

A. You can use the fdisk utility from an MS-DOS boot disk; however, you will be limited to the 2GB-partition size supported by MS-DOS.

B. You can let Windows 2000 Professional create the partitions automatically during setup.

C. You can choose the Advanced button option during setup. This will let you chose the partition on which to install Windows 2000 Professional.

D. The partition to which Windows 2000 Professional will be installed must be a minimum of 350MB.

13. Your secretary needs to access a shared folder on your computer. This folder contains information she will need to use on a daily basis. You tell her to map a network drive and connect to the share on your PC, but she explains that she does not know how to do this. What is the simplest and most accurate way to explain this to her? (Choose two.)

A. Use Windows Explorer to find the file, then right-click it. Enable sharing and caching for offline use.

B. Use Windows Explorer to find the file, right-click it, and choose Sharing. Select Map Network Drive from the Sharing dialog box and choose a drive letter.

C. Open Windows Explorer and choose Tools/Map Network Drive. Select a drive letter you wish to use for the shared resource. Type the UNC path to the resource.

D. Type in the following command at the command prompt:

NET USE Drive_Letter:\\computername\sharename

14. You are having problems with your CD-ROM drive and want to install an updated driver for it. You do not have this driver on a disk and cannot find it on the Internet. In Device Manager you see this option and check it. What is this and how does it work?

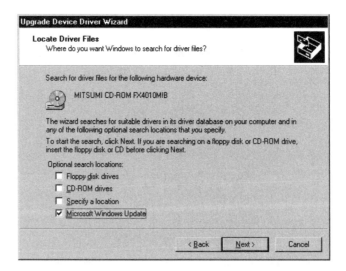

A. Choosing Next will connect you to Microsoft's Web site where you can fill out a Driver Update Request Form. When the driver is available, you will receive an email with downloading instructions.

B. If you are connected to the Internet, this will search Microsoft's updated list of drivers located at http://windowsupdate.microsoft.com.

C. If you are connected to the Internet, you will be directed to the manufacturer's Web site, where you will be able to download the new driver.

D. You will be prompted to insert the newest service pack into your CD-ROM. The files will be in the I386\DRIVER\CAB folder.

15. Tracy has set a local computer policy for Joe's computer at work. She has removed the My Documents icon from the desktop because she wants Joe to save to the network server. She has also removed the Internet Explorer icon so Joe can't surf the Internet when he should be working. Tracy has made sure that there are no policies in place that will override these local settings, however, she sees that Joe is still saving to My Documents and surfing the net on his computer. What is most likely the problem?

A. Even though the icons are removed from the desktop, Joe can still access these items off the network server.

B. Even though these icons are removed from the desktop, Joe can still access these items from Windows Explorer.

C. Joe knows the administrator name and password and has logged on using these credentials.

D. Joe changed the policies from the Group Policy snap-in or has disabled the restrictions.

16. Phil wants to map a network drive so that every time he logs on, this connection is automatically made. He currently connects to this drive using My Network Places and browsing to the appropriate folder. Select all of the ways he can map a network drive and logon automatically, from the choices below.

A. Choose Start | Run and type **\\computer_name** and double-click the shared folder you wish to connect to. Choose Reconnect at Logon when prompted to select logon options.

    B. Double-click My Network Places and browse to the folder you wish to connect to. Right-click the shared folder, and check the box Reconnect at Logon.

    C. Using the Map Network Drive Wizard, type the UNC path to the shared folder you wish to map to, and check the box Reconnect at Logon.

    D. Using Explorer, browse to the shared folder. Under Tools | Folder Options, choose Reconnect at Logon.

17. **Current Situation:** As an administrator for employees in the Programming Department of a large research and development firm, you are assigned the task of giving the programmers the access they need to do their jobs, while also maintaining a high level of security. These programmers need some special rights to create applications and work effectively at their computers. The programmers are members of the Power Users group.

    Required Result: The programmers must be able to debug programs, change system time, create page files, and modify firmware environmental variables.

    Optional Desired Results:

    1. There must be a password policy in effect that addresses complexity, length, and encryption.

    2. There must be an audit policy in place to record logs concerning object access and system events by the programmers.

    Proposed Solution: Create a local group policy for the programmers. From Local Computer Policy | Computer Configuration | Windows Settings | Security Settings | Local Policies | User Rights Assessment, enable debug programs, create page files, and modify firmware environment variables. From Account Policies in Computer Policy, set a password policy that enables length requirements of 12 letters or more; passwords must meet complexity requirements; and store passwords using reversible encryption. From Audit Policy under User Configuration, audit the success and failure of object access and system events.

    What result does the proposed solution produce?

    A. The proposed solution produces the required results and both of the optional results.

B. The proposed solution produces the required results and only one of the optional results.

C. The proposed solution produces the required results and none of the optional results.

D. The proposed solution does not produce the required result.

18. Tim wants to set a schedule for backing up his data onto magnetic tape. His network is in high demand weekdays and Sunday afternoons. Weeknights have some traffic, but not a whole lot. What would be a good schedule for Tim to use to back up his company's data?

   A. Perform Normal backups each night and Incremental backups on Saturday.

   B. Perform Normal backups each Saturday and Differential backups each weeknight.

   C. Perform only Incremental and Differential backups, switching each day. On Saturday do a Copy backup.

   D. Do Normal backups each weeknight and a Copy backup every Saturday.

19. Rachel works at home creating logos and corporate designs for companies all over the world. She uses Windows 2000 Professional, on a FAT32 system, and several proprietary graphics applications, to create the proposals. She usually faxes or emails her designs to their destinations, but has recently been asked by a client to print to their Internet printer. She uses the Add Printer Wizard, chooses to add an Internet printer, and types in the URL. She is unable to connect to the Internet Printer. What could be wrong?

   A. The syntax should be http://Printers/printer_share_name/.printer.

   B. The syntax should be http://print_server_name/Printers/printer_share_name/.printer.

   C. She cannot add an Internet printer unless she is using the NTFS file system.

   D. She doesn't need a URL or the Add Printer Wizard. She needs to add a Network Place. After adding the location of the Internet printer, she will be able to print successfully.

20. Jim is installing multiple monitors to his existing computer system. After returning from the store, Jim's wife noticed he bought ten adapters and ten monitors. She gets a chuckle out of this. Why is Jim's wife laughing at him?

    A. Windows 2000 only supports multiple adapters up to eight.

    B. To use multiple monitors in Windows 2000 Professional you must also have multiple processors installed. Jim does not.

    C. Jim purchased too many monitors and adapters.

    D. Jim's computer is formatted FAT32 and multiple monitors are not supported unless he converts to NTFS.

21. **Current Situation:** You have created an Installer Package for an application that is to be deployed throughout your network. It is stored as an MSI file on your network server. Most of your users are either temporary workers, or only do data processing. They are not familiar with many aspects of computing.

    Required Result: Deploy the MSI file and install the required application without having the users set it up themselves.

    Optional Desired Results:

    1. Do not give the users a choice to install or not.

    2. Allow the application to be installed under a user's profile wherever a user logs on.

    Proposed Solution: Use group policy to deploy the application. Choose to Assign to Computers.

    What result does the proposed solution produce?

    A. The proposed solution produces the required results and both of the optional results.

    B. The proposed solution produces the required results and only one of the optional results.

    C. The proposed solution produces the required results and none of the optional results.

    D. The proposed solution does not produce the required result.

22. Tim has a roaming user profile for times he is on the road, but at the home office he wants to maintain a local user profile. This profile will have printer drivers, specialized programs, and database files. Can Tim create a local user profile and change between his roaming user profile and his local user profile when he is in his home office?

    A. No, the roaming user profile will always override any local settings since it resides on the server.

    B. No, the roaming user profile will always override any local settings since it was created and implemented by the network administrator.

    C. Yes, he can switch between the two using the User Profiles tab of System Properties, and choosing Change Type.

    D. Yes, he can switch between the two using the Users and Passwords icon in Control Panel. Choose Profiles, then Change Type.

23. Jackie has numerous compressed files on her computer and needs to move some of these compressed files to other folders. Some of these folders are on the same partition, but others are not. She is concerned that once the files are moved, they will no longer be compressed. You need to explain to Jackie the rules about moving compressed files. Which one of the following explains this correctly?

    A. A move will always retain its attributes regardless of where you move the data.

    B. A move will always retain the compression attribute regardless of where you move the data, unless you move it to a different partition or an encrypted folder.

    C. A move will always retain its attributes regardless of where you move the data, unless you move it to a different partition.

    D. A move will always retain its attributes regardless of where you move the data, unless you move the data to an encrypted folder.

24. Before deploying a service pack throughout your enterprise, you should test it first. Which of the following is the best way to test a new service pack?

    A. Use the Update.exe file with the /slip switch, and deploy the new service pack throughout the company for all new installations. If this works well, deploy throughout the network.

    B. Create test environments for each computer configuration in your enterprise. Make sure the test computers have the same hardware, are running the same software, and performing the same operations as the computers in the enterprise. If this works well, deploy throughout the network.

    C. Test the new service pack on one client machine that resembles the majority of the computers in your network. If this works, deploy throughout the network.

    D. Test the new service pack on the domain controllers in your network. If they work on the domain controllers, then they will work on the workstations.

25. **Current Situation:** Your company has an employee that only has use of three fingers on his left hand due to a recent motorcycle accident. His right hand did not suffer any debilitating injuries, but is weak and shaky.

    Required Result: Reconfigure this user's computer to address the shakiness of his right hand.

    Optional Desired Results:

    1. Configure the keyboard so that this employee will never have to press two keys at a time when trying to type; so that it toggles the ALT and CTRL keys.

    2. Make sure the mouse moves to the default options in dialog boxes.

    Proposed Solution: Turn on and configure Sticky Keys. Turn on and configure Filter Keys.

    What results does the proposed solution produce?

    A. The proposed solution produces the required results and both of the optional results.

    B. The proposed solution produces the required results and only one of the optional results.

    C. The proposed solution produces the required results and none of the optional results.

    D. The proposed solution does not produce the required result.

26. Your company uses three ISDN links to allow its users access to the Internet. Some days the demand for bandwidth is high, but on other days, demand is low. You would like to dynamically add or drop links based on necessity.

Which protocol allows you to do this in Windows 2000, and where do you configure it?

A. BAP and BACP can be used and are configured through the PPP tab of RAS policies.

B. PPP is used and is configured in the BAP tab of RAS policies.

C. PPTP can be used and is configured in RAS policies.

D. BAP and BACP can be used and are configured through Networking and Dial-up Connections in Control Panel.

27. You've been working for a start-up company for some time now, and your personal computer on the network is formatted as NTFS. The company is going out of business and you'd like to change from NTFS back to FAT32, and use the computer at home as a stand-alone server. How will you proceed?

A. Type **CONVERT** [*drive:*] **/NTFS:FAT32** [*/v*] at the command prompt.

B. Back up all the data on the drive, and reformat the drive as FAT32 in Disk Manager. Then restore the data.

C. Type **CONVERT** [*drive:*] **/NTFS:FS32** at the command prompt.

D. You cannot do this conversion successfully. Even if you back up the data on the drive, reformat as FAT32, and restore the data, the new FAT32 physical disk will not recognize the NTFS data.

28. James is a member of the Seasonal Workers group and is using a computer running Windows 2000 Professional. His disk was configured as a basic disk when it was installed and is a simple volume that contains only space from a single disk that is 10GB. James was playing around one day (when he should have been working) and configured his computer to use dynamic disks. He thought he might get in trouble for this and chose to revert back to a basic disk configuration immediately. Do you think James got caught for his antics? (Choose all possible correct answers.)

A. No. James got away with it completely.

B. Yes. James was caught and fired immediately

C. Probably not, no one ever checks the event logs.

D. Yes, James got caught. The network administrator was also reprimanded for failing to assign appropriate permissions to the Seasonal Workers group.

29. Kathy is trying to enable the use of Offline Files and Folders so she can do some work over the weekend at home. She has checked the appropriate boxes, run the Offline Files Wizard, and is currently accessing a large file from her office. Everything seems to be going well, but suddenly the application fails and she gets an error message concerning the amount of storage she has available. What is wrong and how can it be fixed?

   A. She doesn't have enough memory in her computer to use offline file caching. She should add more RAM.

   B. She didn't configure the options in the Offline Files Wizard correctly.

   C. She does not have enough disk space allocated for these files. The option for Amount of disk space to use for temporary offline files should be increased.

   D. Her computer is not configured as NTFS.

30. Linda has a laptop computer that is usually docked at her office workstation. She is going on a business trip next week and would like to configure a profile that she can use while she is away. Shown below is her current profile. What is the first thing she will need to do to create a profile for her computer when it is not docked?

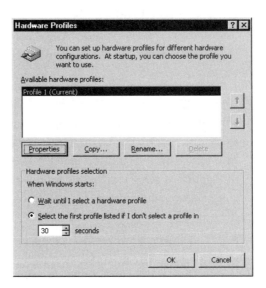

   A. Click Properties; change the profile to suit the needs of Profile 2, then save as Profile 2 when prompted.

B. Click Copy to create a copy of this profile to modify.

C. Click Rename; change the name to Profile 2, and make the necessary modifications.

D. Select Wait Until I Select a Hardware Profile, click OK, and reboot the computer. When the computer starts up, choose Create New Profile from the menu and configure as needed.

31. John has done his very best to ensure that his rollout using Remote Installation Service will go smoothly. He has the RIS server up and running, the DHCP authorized to service RIS clients in the Active Directory, and an IP address scope created in the DHCP server for RIS clients. John's clients, however, cannot contact the RIS server. What is most likely the problem? (Choose all that apply.)

A. The IP address scope on the DHCP server has not been activated.

B. The RIS server has not been configured to forward BootP broadcasts.

C. The clients' network adapters are not supported by the RIS service.

D. All of the above.

E. A and C only.

32. **Current Situation:** Maria is a member of the Printing Department. She is also a member of three groups: Technical, Sales, and Printing. The groups Technical and Printing need access to the shared help file located in the directory C:\Printing\Printers\Help on an NTFS volume.

Required Result: Maria's effective permissions must allow her access to Read and Execute the file C:\Printing\Printers\Help.

Optional Desired Results:

1. Maria should be able to edit and make changes to the file because she is a member of the Technical group.

2. The members of the Sales group should not be allowed access to the file.

Proposed Solution: Because the Technical group edits and makes changes to the Help file, give them the permission to Modify the file. Give the Printing group Read Access to the Help file. Finally, give all members of the Sales group the Deny permission since they do not need to have access to this file.

What result does the proposed solution produce?

A. The proposed solution produces the required results and both of the optional results.

B. The proposed solution produces the required results and only one of the optional results.

C. The proposed solution produces the required results and none of the optional results.

D. The proposed solution does not produce the required result.

33. Bob has an older computer that uses ASCII as its character set and is running Windows 3.1. He wants to collaborate with his younger brother who has a newer computer system that uses the UNICODE character set. They want to work together to create plans for a new sprinkler system they are installing. Will Bob and his brother be able to collaborate, and if so, will there be problems?

A. They will not be able to collaborate. Bob's computer uses a 7-bit character set, and his brother's uses a 16-bit character set. They need to be the same.

B. They will be able to collaborate. Even though Bob's computer uses a 7-bit character set, and his brother's uses a 16-bit character set, they do not need to be the same, and there will not be any problems.

C. They will be able to collaborate. Bob's computer uses an 8-bit character set, and his brother's uses a 16-bit character set. They do not need to be the same, and there will not be any problems.

D. They will be able to collaborate, but there may be interoperability problems between the two systems.

34. The illustration on the following page shows the Computer Management window, and Local Users and Groups are open. Notice that Groups is chosen.

What steps were involved in creating a new group, Sample Test Group, and then adding users to it? (Select all correct choices.)

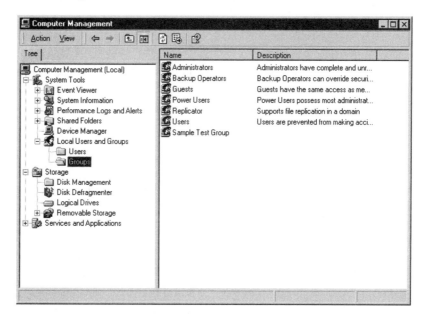

A. Right-click in the right pane, and select New Group from the choices. Select a group name, click Add, and select users.

B. Right-click in the left pane on the highlighted word Groups, and select New Group from the choices. Select a group name, click Add, and select users.

C. From the menu bar, choose Action | New Group from the choices. Select a group name, click Add, and select users.

D. Double-click the highlighted word "Groups," and select New Group from the choices. Select a group name, click Add, and select users.

35. Casey is in charge of all of the printers for his company and is currently installing a local printer that has bi-directional capabilities. He has configured a port monitor for this printer, but the printer is not yet working properly. What else does Casey need to configure to complete setup of this printer?

A. The printer needs a TCP/IP address to work correctly.

B. The printer needs a dedicated print server.

    C. The drivers need to be added and configured.

    D. The language monitor is not set up properly.

36. What is the best way to create a network share for installation files for a network/unattended installation?

    A. Log on to the distribution server as administrator, create a folder to share, and copy the contents of the i386 folder to it. Share the folder. Create a OEM folder under this folder, and copy any drivers necessary for installation to it.

    B. Log on to the distribution server as administrator, create a folder to share, and copy the contents of the Windows 2000 Professional CD to it. Share the folder. Create a OEM folder under this folder, and copy any drivers necessary for installation to it.

    C. Log on to the distribution server as administrator, share the CD-ROM drive, place the Windows 2000 Professional CD in the drive, and tell users to begin installation.

    D. Log on to the distribution server as administrator, create a folder to share, and copy the contents of the i386 folder to it. Share the folder.

37. John is a mobile computer user and caches offline files regularly. He usually works on small projects for the research department, but has recently been promoted to the programming department. The projects he will be working on now will be much larger than before. Should John make any configuration changes to his laptop concerning the use of offline files and caching, and if so, what?

    A. John should access the Folder Options dialog box from Windows Explorer's Tools menu, and raise the default cache size of 10 percent to 20 percent.

    B. John should access the Folder Options dialog box from Windows Explorer's Tools menu, and raise the default cache size of 25 percent to 50 percent.

    C. John should access the caching options dialog box from Windows Explorer's Tools menu, and raise the default cache size of 10 percent to 30 percent.

    D. There is no need to change the cache size; the size will be enlarged or reduced dynamically based on need.

38. **Current Situation:** The company DigiWalk has just purchased a new computer for its Computer Drafting Department. The applications used in this department are CPU-intensive and this computer has four processors on board.

    Required Result: Configure this computer using the available multiple processors.

    Optional Desired Results:

    1. Configure this computer to join the network.

    2. Make sure that the highest level of security is enabled when installing Windows 2000 Professional.

    Proposed Solution: Install Windows 2000 Professional on this computer and choose the NTFS file system. Install the driver for the multiple processors in Device Manager using the Update Device Driver Wizard. Install the NIC when installing the operating system, and configure the network connections after installation is complete.

    What result does the proposed solution produce?

    A. The proposed solution produces the required results and all of the optional results.

    B. The proposed solution produces the required results and only one of the optional results.

    C. The proposed solution produces the required results and none of the optional results.

    D. The proposed solution does not produce the required result.

39. Jason has trouble using the keyboard and had been using MouseKeys at his last job. He wants you to configure this for him here, also. How can you configure MouseKeys, and what does it do for Jason?

    A. MouseKeys allows you to substitute keyboard inputs for mouse handling, and can be enabled at Control Panel | Mouse icon.

    B. MouseKeys was used in Windows NT, but was dropped for 2000. It is not available.

    C. MouseKeys allows you to substitute keyboard inputs for mouse handling, and can be enabled at Accessibility Options | Mouse tab.

    D. MouseKeys allows you to substitute mouse inputs for keyboard handling, and can be enabled at Accessibility Options | Mouse tab.

40. You are planning to deploy Windows 2000 Professional throughout your enterprise. You have 50 machines running Windows NT 4.0, 35 running Windows 98, 15 running Windows 95, 1 running Windows NT 3.5, and 1 running Windows 3.1. What steps are necessary to upgrade these machines?

    A. No upgrade path—install Windows 2000 Professional on all the machines and reinstall the applications.

    B. Upgrade all machines directly to Windows 2000 Professional.

    C. Upgrade all machines directly to Windows 2000 Professional, except for the Windows 3.1 computer. For this machine, install a clean copy of Windows 2000 Professional and reinstall all the applications.

    D. Upgrade all machines to Windows 2000 Professional except for the Windows NT 3.5 and Windows 3.1. For Windows 3.1, install a clean copy, and for Windows NT 3.5, upgrade to 3.51 or 4.0, then to Windows 2000 Professional.

41. You plan to install Windows 2000 Professional on a number of computers that all have identical hardware configurations. You want to create a disk image of an installation so you can install these computers in the least amount of time possible. Your boss told you to use the sysprep.exe utility to do this. Where will you find this utility, and how should you use it?

    A. Insert the Windows 2000 Server CD, and look under Support | Tools | Sysprep.cab.

    B. Insert the Windows 2000 Professional CD, and look under Support | Tools | Deploy.cab.

    C. The Sysprep utility is installed with Windows 2000 Professional and can be found in C:\Program Files\Accessories\Sysprep, where "C:\" represents the drive letter of the operating system. Double-click the icon to begin the application.

    D. You can download it from Microsoft's Web site only if you are a member of the Microsoft Open License Program.

42. Kenneth and Kuan are members of a workgroup and use shares to provide permissions to their local resources. When Kenneth accesses Kuan's files over the network, he has read-only access to the folder. However, when Kenneth

logs on Kuan's computer where the folder is stored, he has Full Control. Why is this? (Choose two.)

A. Because Kenneth is logged on at Kuan's computer, he gets the least restrictive of the two share permissions.

B. Share permissions have no local significance; they only apply to users who attach to your PC over the network.

C. If someone is logged on your PC locally, the share will have no effect; unlike NTFS permissions, which always apply.

D. Kuan's computer is running Windows for Workgroups, and share permissions are not available.

43. You have decided to use the FAT file system for your stand-alone Windows 2000 Professional because it is not connected to a network, there are no security issues or shared printers, and you do not need to compress or encrypt files or folders. Which one of the following is *not* a reason to choose FAT32 over FAT16?

A. FAT32 supports larger drive or partition sizes, smaller file clusters, and has some additional performance-optimization features.

B. FAT16 file system can grow to 8GB in size; FAT64 supports 32GB.

C. FAT16 uses a 16-bit allocation scheme and FAT32 uses a 32-bit scheme

D. FAT16 is supported by Windows 95/98, Windows NT, and Windows 2000; FAT 32 is supported by Windows 95/98 and 2000, but not by NT.

44. Theresa has a folder and a subfolder that she needs to encrypt, and she also wants to force the encryption operation on subfolders that are already encrypted. She knows these files are skipped by default. She will do this at a command line prompt using the Cipher command. Which of the following offers the correct syntax for these operations?

A. cipher /e /s /f :folder_name

B. cipher /e /f /s:folder_name

C. cipher /e /s:folder_name /f

D. cipher /f /e /s:folder_name

45. You are a client on a Windows 2000 network and run Windows 2000 Professional on your machine. You are having problems communicating with others on your network. Pinging the loopback address works fine, but pinging

the IP address assigned to your network card fails, as well as pinging a host on the local subnet. Your settings are shown in the illustration below. What is wrong?

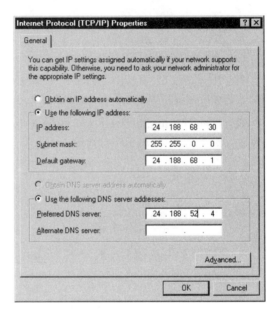

A. The IP address is incorrect.

B. The Subnet Mask is incorrect.

C. The Default Gateway is incorrect.

D. The DNS Server is incorrect.

46. Tim administers a small network that has recently grown dramatically. He used to be able to monitor his users, making sure they were backing up their data daily or weekly, and these users could share files and folders via floppies or workgroup shares. Now that the network has grown, he needs to change the users' configurations to meet the needs of a larger network. What should Tim do?

A. Use Folder Replication to save a copy of all users' data onto the network server.

B. Use Folder Redirection to have users save their work on the network server.

C. Use RIS to manage the data on the users' workstations.

D. Set Security Configurations to High Secure on the clients' computers.

47. Your boss is using one application almost exclusively and wants this application to have a higher priority when accessing system resources than other programs on his computer. After explaining the pros and cons of making these changes, he wants you to go ahead and change the priority anyway. In what ways can you do this? (Choose two.)

    A. Type **START** [*program name*] **/high** at the command prompt.

    B. Type **START /high** [*program name*] at the command prompt.

    C. Open Task Manager, right-click the process, and then Set Priority.

    D. Open Task Manager, highlight the process in question, and choose Tools | Set Priority from the menu bar.

48. Mary has a laptop and wants to configure an infrared device and a PCMCIA adapter. She has obtained the drivers for these devices from the manufacturer. After booting up the computer, Windows 2000 notices the PCMCIA adapter as Plug and Play and installs it. However, the infrared device is not recognized. What are Mary's options?

    A. From Control Panel, choose to Add/Remove Hardware. When prompted, insert the manufacturer's driver disk for the infrared device to install.

    B. Windows 2000 does not support infrared devices on laptops.

    C. Windows 2000 only supports USB interface infrared devices. Exchange this infrared device with one that has a USB interface.

    D. Install this device from the Network icon in the Control Panel.

49. You have a generic video adapter in your computer that came with the system when you purchased it three years ago. You've upgraded to Windows 2000 Professional and would like to take advantage of the display settings available. You have purchased a new adapter and installed it in the PCI slot that contained the generic adapter. You turn on your computer and the screen goes blank after Windows 2000 boots up. What should you do? (Choose two.)

    A. Reboot your computer using the device driver disk that came with the new adapter.

    B. This video adapter is not supported on the HCL. Replace it with one that is.

    C. Restart the computer and choose Last Known Good Configuration.

    D. Restart the computer and press F8 to boot in VGA mode.

50. Jonathan is a member of the International Marketing Department at your company. He deals with clients in Great Britain and France on a daily basis. He wants to configure his Regional Options settings to use metric instead of the standard U.S. system of measurement. Under which tab could Jonathan make these configuration changes, and does he need to change his locale in the screen shot below, before he can make that change?

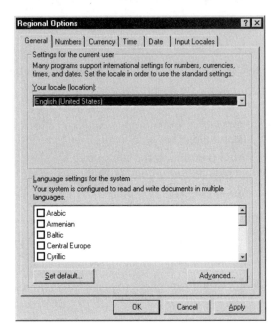

A. Jonathan will need to change his locale to English (United Kingdom) to use metric as the system of measurement.

B. Jonathan will need to change his local to French (Canada) to use metric as the system of measurement.

C. Jonathan can change the setting under the Numbers tab without changing the locale settings.

D. Jonathan can change the setting under the Currency tab without changing the locale settings.

ANSWERS

1. ☑ **B.** RIPrep enables the administrator to simplify deployment of Windows 2000 by enabling distribution of standard desktop configurations.

   ☒ **A** is incorrect because the hardware configurations can be different as long as the HAL is the same. **C** is incorrect because one of the limitations of RIPrep is that it can replicate images only of a single disk with a single partition.

2. ☑ **C.** The Users group is the most restrictive of the three available under the Properties tab in this screen shot.

   ☒ **A** represents the Administrators group, **B** represents the Power Users (Standard) group, and **D** is not a choice for group membership under this utility.

3. ☑ **C.** By configuring a DC to be a DHCP server, and enabling TCP/IP on the client computers, you can ease the pain of manually entering addresses to client computers. A new feature of Windows 2000 is Automatic IP Addressing, or APIPA. It is automatically enabled by default. By changing the registry key as suggested, you will disable this utility, making the first optional result incorrect. The second optional result is incorrect not only because making the change to the registry has disabled APIPA, but also because APIPA only works on the subnet where the local computer is located. Therefore, neither of the optional results is met.

   ☒ **A** and **B** are incorrect because neither of the optional results is met. **D** is incorrect because the required result is produced.

4. ☑ **A, B,** and **C** are correct; they are all good ways to approach the problem your boss is having. **A** is correct because auditing logon successes and failures will allow you to decide how often log-on attempts take place and who is successful. **B** is correct because enabling account lockout after two failures ensures security of the network from multiple log-on attempts. **C** is correct because complex passwords will make it more difficult for someone to break into the computer.

☒ **D** is incorrect because IP security is used to determine how your computer will communicate with another, and is not a factor in this scenario.

5. ☑ **C.** Setupapi.log is the log file that contains details about the device driver files that were copied during setup, and can be used to facilitate troubleshooting device installations. This file contains errors and warnings, along with a timestamp for each issue.

☒ **A** is incorrect because Setupact.log is the action log file that contains details about the files that are copied during setup. **B** is also wrong, as Setuperr.log is the error log file that contains details about errors that occurred during setup. **D** is incorrect because Setuplog.txt is the log file that contains additional information about the device driver files that were copied during setup.

6. ☑ **B.** These three files and one shared folder are created automatically after the Setup Manager has been executed.

☒ **A, C**, and **D** are incorrect because they each do not list *all* the created files.

7. ☑ **B.** By configuring the NICs to use two different TCP/IP addresses you are meeting the required result. The second optional result is met because you will set up a firewall of some sort to keep out the hackers. The first optional result is not met because the protocols for NIC 2 are NetBeui first and TCP/IP last. It should be the other way around because TCP/IP is the intranet's main protocol.

☒ **A** and **C** are incorrect because one of the optional results is met. **D** is incorrect because the proposed solution produced the required result.

8. ☑ **D.** A generic Installer Package cannot be created for multiple applications. This is because this utility works by taking a snapshot of the system both before and after an application is installed, and creating the Installer Package based on the net changes detected.

☒ **A, B**, and **C** are incorrect for this reason, although A and C represent valid steps for single applications. There is no Windows Installer Package Wizard, but there is a WinINSTALL Discover Wizard. **E** is incorrect because none of the answer options provided is correct.

9. ☑ **C.** You can put some drives in FAT and some drives in NTFS, with the secure files on NTFS and still maintain a dual-boot scenario.

☒ **A** is incorrect because the two file systems can coexist on different partitions. **B** is incorrect because at least one partition must be FAT or FAT32. **D** is incorrect because there is no Partition Management application.

10. ☑ **D.** Either one of these answers will take Mike to the Computer Management window. If Mike wants to use MMC to centralize his tasks, he'll have to run MMC and individualize his console by adding the Disk Management snap-in.

☒ **C** is incorrect because these applications are available in the Professional version.

11. ☑ **B.** This is the correct answer, but the optional results are not intuitive in this question. The required result is met by using the Task Manager to schedule the task mentioned. The first optional result is not met by accepting the defaults. You will have to make a point to check the box that says Wake the Computer to Run This Task, or it will not. The second optional result is met because a log file is automatically written to the file SchedLog.txt and stored in the SystemRoot folder.

☒ **A** and **C** are incorrect, as one of the optional results is met. **D** is incorrect because the proposed solution produced the required result.

12. ☑ **A, B,** and **C** are correct. Fdisk can be used to form partitions prior to installation, and you can set the partitions during the installation of Windows 2000 Professional by choosing the advanced option during setup. In a clean install, Windows will automatically select an appropriate disk partition unless you click the advanced option during setup and specify otherwise.

☒ **D** is incorrect because the requirement is 650MB.

13. ☑ **C** and **D** are correct. They are both acceptable ways to map a network drive.

☒ **A** is incorrect because the secretary cannot create a share on your computer for a folder she'd like to access, and **B** is incorrect because there is no choice to Map a Network Drive from the Sharing dialog box.

14. ☑ **B.** The Windows Update will take you to the site listed where you can search for an updated driver for the device.

☒ **A** and **C** are incorrect because the Windows Update will take you to Microsoft's Web site that contains drivers. There is no such thing as a Driver Update Request Form, and you will not be redirected to another manufacturer's site. **D** is incorrect because the Update looks for files on the Internet.

15. ☑ **B.** All the "disable something from the menu" items and the "remove icons from the desktop" policy items don't actually make it impossible for the

user to access programs. For example, if you remove the My Documents icon from the desktop, users can still get to their My Documents folder by navigating Windows Explorer to the correct pathway. If you remove Networks and Dial-up Access from the Settings submenu, users can still right-click My Network and Dial-up Properties. And, of course, if users know how, they can run applications through the command-line interface.

☒ **A** is incorrect because the My Documents folder is local to Joe's machine, and he may or may not have access to an Internet connection from there. **C** is a possibility, but not likely. **D** is incorrect because Joe is unable to undo the administrators' work in the local policy settings.

16. ☑ **C.** The Map Network Drive Wizard gives the option of reconnecting each time you log on your network.

☒ **A** is incorrect because Start | Run is not a valid way to map a network drive, and does not offer any reconnect at logon option boxes. **B** is incorrect because double-clicking My Network Places will show the computers on your network, but will not allow you to map network drives to shares. **D** is incorrect because Tools | Folder Options does not offer the Reconnect at Logon box, or configuration of network shares.

17. ☑ **B.** The proposed solution offers everything that is needed to meet the required result. Changing the system time is not offered in the proposed solution because the programmers are members of the Power Users group and have that right already. The second optional result is not met because the configuration has to be made under Computer Configuration, not User Configuration.

☒ **A** and **C** are incorrect because one of the optional results is met. **D** is incorrect because the proposed solution produced the required result.

18. ☑ **B.** This is a good strategy for Tim and is the correct answer. Normal backups take the longest and should be done when there is little or no network traffic. Differential backups will back up all selected files that have changed since the last Normal or Incremental backup, but will not mark them as backed up. This allows for a faster recovery time if needed.

☒ **A** is incorrect because a Normal backup each night is more than is necessary, and will waste time and money. **C** is incorrect because there should be at least one Full (normal) backup each week. **D** is incorrect, again, because Normal backups each night are overkill.

19. ☑ **B.** To add an Internet printer, use the Add Printer Wizard, choose Internet Printer, and type in the URL. If Rachel did this and it did not work, most likely the syntax or path to the printer was incorrect.

 ☒ **A** is not the correct syntax. **C** is incorrect because the file system is not an issue when adding an Internet printer. **D** is incorrect because adding a network place will not install an Internet printer. It only adds a link where you can store documents on the Internet, to a share folder, or an FTP site.

20. ☑ **C.** Jim only needed to purchase nine adapters and monitors because he is adding to his existing computer system. Windows 2000 only supports up to ten monitors for multiple displays.

 ☒ **A** is incorrect because Windows can support up to ten monitors for multiple display. **B** is incorrect because the computer does not have to be configured with multiple processors to enable multiple monitors. **D** is incorrect because a computer can be FAT, FAT32, or NTFS and use multiple monitors.

21. ☑ **B.** By using group policy to deploy the file and application, it can be installed without the users having to set it up manually, like they would if it were left on the network server. By choosing Assign to Computers, the users will not have a choice of installing the application, it will be done automatically, thus the first optional result is met. The second optional result is not met because this is a characteristic of Assign to Users, not Assign to Computers.

 ☒ **A** and **C** are incorrect because one of the optional results is met. **D** is incorrect because the proposed solution produced the required result.

22. ☑ **C.** A user can switch between a roaming and local profile at any time.

 ☒ **A** is incorrect because the roaming user profile will not always override the local settings since the user can choose between the two. **B** is incorrect for the same reason **A** is, and the fact that the administrator assigned the profile is not an issue here. **D** is incorrect because it represents the wrong applet in Control Panel.

23. ☑ **B.** A move will always retain the compression attribute regardless of where you move the data, unless you move it to a different partition or an encrypted folder.

 ☒ **A, C,** and **D** do not correctly describe what happens to compressed files when they are moved.

24. ☑ **B.** Testing a new service pack on computers configured exactly like the ones in your enterprise will allow you to see that the service pack will work properly.

 ☒ **A** is incorrect because the Update.exe file is used to deploy service packs, and this does not address the issue of testing them. **C** and **D** are incorrect because testing must be done on all the different machine configurations to identify problems that may occur only on specific machines.

25. ☑ **B**. Sticky Keys addresses the first optional result and will allow the user to toggle between ALT or CTRL and the required key, instead of having to press them both at the same time. Filter Keys addresses the required result, and makes allowances for disabilities that include shaky hands and repeated keystrokes. In order for the second optional result to be met, you would have to enable this under Mouse Pointers | Motion at the Mouse icon in Control Panel.

 ☒ **A** and **C** are incorrect because one of the optional results is met. **D** is incorrect because the proposed solution produced the required result.

26. ☑ **A.** BAP and BACP stand for Bandwidth Allocation Protocol and Bandwidth Allocation Control Protocol, and are used in Windows 2000 to dynamically add or drop links based on need.

 ☒ **B** is incorrect. The statement in this choice is backward and therefore incorrect. **C** does not offer bandwidth allocation utilities, and **D** is incorrect because BAP is not configured under Networking and Dial-up Connections.

27. ☑ **B.** You cannot convert from NTFS to FAT or FAT32 without losing the data on the drive. You can, however, convert FAT or FAT32 to NTFS.

☒   **A** and **C** resemble the correct syntax to convert FAT or FAT32 to NTFS, which is CONVERT [*drive:*] /FS:NTFS, and are incorrect choices. **D** is incorrect because conversion can be done and restoring data is possible.

28.   ☑   **B** or **D** are correct. It is impossible to revert back from dynamic to basic disk configuration without losing data, unless all the data was backed up before hand. There is no mention of this in our scenario. The network administrator should have disabled the Seasonal Workers group from this type of access, and was probably reprimanded.

☒   **A** and **C** are incorrect because someone would have noticed the data loss.

29.   ☑   **C.** You can change the amount of disk space allocated for these files. This setting defaults to 10 percent of the drive.

☒   **A** is incorrect because the files are not loaded into RAM; they are saved in the computer's boot partition. **B** is incorrect because the application had started to download the files already, and must have been set up appropriately. **D** is not an issue and is incorrect.

30.   ☑   **B.** Click Copy, and give the new profile a name. Next, make the necessary changes under Properties. Restart the computer and use the new profile, making changes in Device Manager.

☒   **A**, **C**, and **D** are incorrect second steps for creating a new profile and will not work.

31.   ☑   **D.** All of the choices are necessary for clients to successfully use the RIS server.

☒   **A**, **B**, and **C** are incorrect individually because all of these are necessary. **E** is incorrect because B is also correct.

32.   ☑   **D.** Maria is a member of all three groups. Because the Deny permission is given to all members of the Sales group, Maria will have the Deny permission associated with her accesses. Even though she is allowed permission to Modify in the Technical group, and Read in the Printing group, Deny still overrides those permissions. The second optional result was met, because the Sales group was given the Deny permission to the file.

☒   **A**, **B**, and **C** are incorrect because the proposed solution does not product the required result.

33.   ☑   **D.** Documents that use another character set still need to be translated into UNICODE in order to be read by the user. This may cause interoperability issues.

☒ **A** and **B** are incorrect for the reasons provided previously. **C** is incorrect because ASCII is a 7-bit character set with 128 characters.

34. ☑ **A**, **B**, and **C** are correct. **A** is correct because right-clicking in the right-hand pane brings up a pop-up menu that offers New Group. **B** is correct because right-clicking highlighted Groups will offer a menu for New Group. **C** is correct because a new group can be added from the Action menu on the toolbar.

☒ **D** is not correct because you cannot access the New Group option this way.

35. ☑ **C** and **D** are correct. Every printer requires that a print driver be installed. A print driver is the software that serves as the interface between the general print instructions generated by an application and contained in a print job, and the specific inputs required by a particular model of printer from a particular manufacturer. A language monitor is necessary if the printer has bi-directional communications capability. The language monitor can pick up the error messages sent by the printer to the computer, and send them to the spooler.

☒ **A** is incorrect because this is a local printer, and a TCP/IP address is not necessary for the printer to work properly. **B** is incorrect because the printer can work without a print server.

36. ☑ **A.** This is the *best* way to create a network share for installation files for a network/unattended installation. A folder must be created and shared that contains the installation files from the CD-ROM, and an OEM folder should be added to hold drivers necessary for successful installation.

☒ **B** is not the best solution because the entire CD does not need to be copied to the distribution server. **C** is not the best solution because the files from the CD have not been copied to the distribution server, and distributions would be slow. **D** is incorrect because it does not address issues that relate to needed drivers.

37. ☑ **A.** The default cache size of offline file and folder storage is 10 percent, and this may need to be raised. This is done through Explorer | Tools | Folder Options.

☒ **B** gives the wrong default cache size as 25 percent, and is incorrect. **C** describes the caching options dialog box in the Tools menu and is not a valid option. **D** is not true because the cache size should be configured manually.

38. ☑ **D.** Windows 2000 Professional only supports up to two processors. In order to use the four processors mentioned here, Windows 2000 Server would

have to be installed. Thus, the required result is not met. The two optional results would be met if the installation was successful, because NTFS provides a high level of security and the NIC is installed and configured as part of the proposed solution.

☒ **A**, **B**, and **C** are incorrect as the proposed solution does not meet the required result.

39. ☑ **C.** The MouseKeys option allows you to substitute keyboard inputs for mouse handling, and can be enabled at Accessibility Options | Mouse tab.

☒ **A** is incorrect because this feature is not available under the Mouse icon; it is under Accessibilities options. **B** is incorrect because MouseKeys is available in 2000. **D** is incorrect because the words mouse and keyboard are used backwards.

40. ☑ **D.** It addresses the correct upgrade path for each operating system.

☒ **A** is incorrect because Windows 2000 Professional can perform an upgrade on any machine running Windows 95 or higher, and Windows NT 3.51 or higher. **B** is incorrect because the Windows NT 3.5 and Windows 3.1 machines cannot be upgraded in this manner. **C** is incorrect because the Windows NT 3.5 machine will need to be upgraded to Windows NT 3.51 or 4.0, before Windows 2000 Professional can be installed as an upgrade.

41. ☑ **B.** The Sysprep utility is found on the Windows 2000 Professional CD.

☒ **A** is incorrect for this reason, and **C** is incorrect because the utility is not found in the Accessories folder. **D** can be correct, but is not the best choice because an Internet connection may not be readily available.

42. ☑ **B** and **C** are correct. Share permissions only work when the resource is being accessed through the network, and do not apply at the computer where the file is located.

☒ **A** and **D** are incorrect for this reason.

43. ☑ **B.** FAT16 file system can grow to 4GB in size; FAT32 supports 32GB.

☒ **A**, **C**, and **D** are all true statements concerning FAT16 and FAT32, and, generally, reasons you should choose FAT32 over FAT16.

44. ☑ **C.** Here is the full syntax and all of the options: cipher [/e | /d] [/s:folder name} [/a] [/i] [/f] [/q] [/h] [/k] [file_name].

☒ **A** is incorrect because the /f switch is listed in an incorrect location. **B** is incorrect because the /f switch is again listed incorrectly. **D** is incorrect because the /e switch should be listed first, and the /f switch should be listed last.

45. ☑ **B.** Class A addresses run from 1 to 126.x.y.z, and have a default subnet mask of 255.0.0.0. Either the IP address is wrong or the subnet mask is.

☒ **A** is incorrect. Because the Default Gateway and the DNS server all begin with 24, it is unlikely it is the IP address. **C** and **D** are incorrect for the same reason.

46. ☑ **B.** To centrally manage users' work and data, have them save to the network server instead of their own local hard drives. By default, user profiles save to the My Documents folder.

☒ **A** is incorrect because Folder Replication is an incorrect term. **C** is incorrect because RIS is Remote Installation Services, and will not help here. **D** is incorrect because High Secure will not assist in the location of users' stored files.

47. ☑ **B** and **C** are correct. Both can be used to change the priority of a program or process.

☒ **A** offers incorrect syntax, and **D** is not an option under Task Manager.

48. ☑ **A.** Infrared devices are supported in Windows 2000 and on laptops and can be installed using the Add/Remove Hardware Wizard.

☒ **B** and **C** are incorrect for this reason. **D** is incorrect because installations of new hardware cannot be made form the Network icon in the Control Panel.

49. ☑ **C** and **D** are correct. They are both viable options available when you have display adapter problems, Microsoft does not recommend Last Known Good for video problems, so C would not be the *best* choice.

☒ **A** is incorrect because the driver that came with the adapter is not a boot disk. **B** is incorrect because it just might work if you can install or reinstall the driver using F8 and advanced options.

50. ☑ **C.** Although the default setting for system of measurement is U.S. Standard, metric can be chosen as an alternative while still using the English (United States) locale.

☒ **A**, **B**, and **D** are all the incorrect tabs.

Glossary

A TO *Z*

account lockout policy   The account lockout policy dictates the behavior for locking and unlocking user accounts. There are three configurable parameters: account lockout threshold determines how many times users can attempt to log on before their accounts are locked. This can range from low (five attempts) to high (one or two attempts). The account lockout duration parameter controls how long an account is locked after the account lockout threshold parameter is triggered.

ACPI   *See* Advanced Configuration and Power Interface.

Active Directory (AD)   The Active Directory is implemented on Windows 2000 domain controllers, and the directory can be accessed from Windows 2000 Professional as an Active Directory client. The Active Directory arranges objects—including computer information, user and group information, shared folders, printers, and other resources—in a hierarchical structure, in which domains can be joined into trees (groups of domains that share a contiguous namespace). Trees can be joined into forests (groups of domain trees that share a common schema, configuration, and global catalog).

Active Directory Service   This service provides the means for locating the Remote Installation Services (RIS) servers and the client computers on the network. The RIS server must have access to the Active Directory.

Add Printer Wizard   All clients running a version of the Windows operating system (Windows 2000, Windows NT, Windows 98, and Windows 95) can use the Add Printer Wizard to create a printer entry on the client. This Add Printer Wizard can create and share a printer on a print server. The Windows 2000 version of the Add Printer Wizard has more options than the wizard in other versions of Windows, but many of the same methods can be used to get the printer set up on the client.

administration   The word *administer* is generally used as a synonym for *manage,* which in turn means to exert control. One of the many enhancements to Windows 2000—both the Professional and Server incarnations—is the ability Microsoft has given administrators to apply the degree of control desired, in a flexible and granular manner.

Advanced Configuration and Power Interface (ACPI)   ACPI combines Plug-and-Play (PnP) capability with Power Management, and places these functions under complete control of the operating system.

Advanced Power Management (APM)   An Intel/Microsoft application program interface (API) allowing programs to indicate their requirements for power to regulate the speed of components.

alerts   Alerts allow some action to be performed when a performance counter reaches a particular threshold. A common action is to log the event in the application event log. You can also send a network message to a specified computer. You can have the alert start a performance log to start logging when the alert occurs. And finally, you can configure the alert to start a program.

analysis   Analysis is the process of comparison, contrast, diagnosis, diagramming, discrimination, and/or drawing conclusions.

answer file   An answer file is a file containing the information you would normally have to key in during the setup process. Answer files help automate the installation process as all the queries presented to you during installation are answered by the answer files. With careful planning, you can prepare answers that eliminate the possibility of incorrect answers typed in by the person performing the installation, thus reducing the chances of setup failure. You can use the Setup Manager wizard to create a customized answer file. This technique minimizes the chances of committing syntax-related errors while manually creating or editing the sample answer files.

APIPA   *See* Automatic Private Internet Protocol Addressing.

APM   *See* Advanced Power Management.

AppleTalk   The AppleTalk protocol suite was developed by Apple Computer for use in its Macintosh line of personal computers. AppleTalk is a local area networking system that was developed by Apple Computer Inc. AppleTalk networks can run over a variety of networks that include Ethernet, FDDI, and Token Ring as well as Apple's proprietary media system LocalTalk. Macintosh computers are very popular in the education and art industries, so familiarity with the way they communicate using their native protocol is very useful.

AppleTalk printing device   Another type of remote printer is the AppleTalk printing device. Like a Transmission Control Protocol/Internet Protocol (TCP/IP) printer, an AppleTalk printer can be connected directly to an AppleTalk network or shared across the network through an AppleShare print server. Like the TCP/IP printers, a large number of modern, high-capacity PostScript printers can be configured to communicate with an AppleTalk network as well as a TCP/IP network. In fact, many Hewlett-Packard LaserJet printers have JetDirect cards that will speak to TCP/IP and AppleTalk at the same time.

application   A program designed to perform a specific function directly for the user or for another application program. An application would be, for example, word processors, database programs, graphics/drawing programs, Web browsers, email programs.

application service provider (ASP)   ASPs are companies that manage applications and provide organizations with application hosting services. Analysts expect the ASP market will be a six billion-dollar industry by the year 2001. The application-hosting model offers organizations the option of outsourcing application support and maintenance.

ASP   *See* application service provider.

auditing   Windows 2000 gives the ability to audit security-related events, track access to objects and use of user rights, and detect attempted and successful access (authorized and unauthorized) to the network. Auditing is not enabled by default, but once enabled, a security log is generated that provides information in regard to specific activities performed on the computer.

Automatic Private Internet Protocol Addressing (APIPA)   APIPA, or Automatic Client Configuration, is a new feature initially available in Windows 98. The feature has been extended to Windows 2000 and allows Dynamic Host Control Protocol (DHCP) client computers to self-configure their IP addressing information in the event a DHCP server is not available when the computer issues a DHCPDISCOVER message. It also allows self-configuration when it senses that it has been moved from a previous network via Windows 2000 media sensing capabilities.

backup domain controller (BDC)   A backup file or copy of the primary domain controller (PDC). Periodically, the BDC is synchronized with the PDC.

backup logs   Windows Backup generates a backup log file for every backup job. These files are the best place to review the backup process in case some problem is encountered by the program. The backup log is a text file that records all the events during the backup process.

basic input/output system (BIOS)   A set of programs encoded in ROM on IBM PC-compatible computers programs handle startup operations such as Power On Self Test (POST) and low-level control for hardware such as disk drives, keyboards, etc.

BDC   *See* backup domain controller.

BIOS   *See* basic input/output system.

boot   The process of loading an operating system into the computer's memory (RAM) so those applications can be run on it.

boot ROM   A boot ROM is a chip on the network adapter that helps the computer boot from the network. Such a computer need not have a previously installed operating system. The BIOS of the computer that has a PXE-based boot ROM must be configured to boot from the network. Windows 2000 Server RIS supports PXE ROM versions 99 or later.

bottleneck   A bottleneck in computer terms is also a component of the system as a whole that restricts the system from operating at its peak. When a bottleneck occurs, the component that is a bottleneck will have a high rate of usage and other components will have a low rate of usage. A lack of memory is a common cause of bottleneck when your computer doesn't have enough memory for the applications and services that are running.

CA   *See* certificate authority.

CAL   *See* Client Access License.

CAPI   *See* CryptoAPI.

Centralized model   This model consolidates administrative control of group policies. A single team of administrators is responsible for managing all Group Policy Objects (GPOs) no matter where they are. This is usually applied by giving all the top-level organizational unit (OU) administrators full control to all GPOs no matter where they are located. They give each second-level OU administrator Read permission only to each GPO. You can also decentralize other resources or keep all resources centralized, depending on the environment.

certificate authority (CA) An authority/organization that produces digital certificates with its available public key. A certificate authority (CA) is a public key certificate issuer (for example, Verisign). To use a public key certificate, you must trust the issuer (CA). This means that you have faith in the CA's authentication policies. The CA is used for doing things such as authorizing certification authenticity, revoking expired certificates, and responding to certification requests. Windows 2000 offers an alternative to a third-party CA. You can become a CA within your own Intranet. Thus, you can manage your own certificates rather than relying on a third-party certification authority.

certificate service Provides security and authentication support, including secure email, Web-based authentication, and smart card authentication.

Change permission You can use this permission to allow users the ability to change permissions on files and folders without giving them the Full Control permission. You can use this permission to give a user or group access to modify permissions on file or folder objects without giving them the ability to have complete control over the object.

Cipher command The Cipher command is another way to encrypt and decrypt data. You can use it from the command line, and it has many switches that you can use to define exactly what you want to have done. The Cipher.exe command syntax is simply CIPHER, followed by the switches that you would like to use, followed by the path and directory/file name. The most common switches are the /E switch (encrypts the specified directories) and the /D switch (decrypts the specified directories). You can also use wildcards with the Cipher command. For example, C:\>cipher /e /s *win* will encrypt all files and folders with "win" in the name and all files within them.

CIW *See* Client Installation Wizard.

Client Access License (CAL) The CAL allows clients to access the Windows 2000's network services, shared folders, and printers. There are two types of CAL modes: Per Seat and Per Server. It is important to understand the difference between these two modes. When you use the Per Seat mode, each computer that accesses the server must have a CAL. The Per Server mode requires a CAL for each connection to the server. This is a subtle but significant difference. The licensing modes are the same as under Windows NT 4.0.

Client Installation Wizard (CIW) When a client computer boots using either the Remote Boot Disk or the PXE-based boot ROM, it tries to establish a connection to the Remote Installation Services (RIS) server. If the RIS server is pre-configured to service the RIS clients, it helps the client get an Internet Protocol (IP) address from the Dynamic Host Control Protocol (DHCP) service. The CIW is then downloaded from the RIS server. This wizard has four installation options. The options that are presented to the user depend on the group policy set in the Active Directory. A user may get all four options, or may not get any of the options when starting an automatic setup.

cloning   *See* disk imaging/cloning.

comprehension   The process of distinguishing between situations, discussing, estimation, explaining, indicating, paraphrasing, and giving examples.

computer account   A computer account is an account that is created by a domain administrator and uniquely identifies the computer on the domain. A newly created account is used so that a computer may be brought into a Windows 2000 Domain.

configuration   Configuration of an operating system involves specifying settings that will govern how the system behaves.

Container object   Container objects can contain other objects. A special type of Container object you can create in the Active Directory is the organizational unit (OU).

containers   Containers are used to describe any group of related items, whether they are objects, containers, domains, or an entire network.

Control Panel Accessibility options   These are options that include StickyKeys, FilterKeys, ToggleKeys, SoundSentry, ShowSounds, High Contrast, MouseKeys, and SerialKeys.

cooperative multitasking   An environment in which an application relinquishes its use of the computer's Central Processing Unit (CPU) so that another application can use the CPU.

Copy backup   This type of backup simply copies the selected files. It neither looks for any markers set on the files nor does it clear them. The Copy backup does not affect the other Incremental or Differential backup jobs and can be performed along with the other types of backup jobs.

counter logs   Counter logs are maintained in a similar fashion as they were in Windows NT 4.0, but the procedure for configuring the counter logs is a bit different.

Trace logs are much easier to configure in Windows 2000 because you now can set them up from the console, rather than having to edit the registry as you had to do in Windows NT 4.0.

CryptoAPI (CAPI) CryptoAPI (CAPI) architecture is a collection of tasks that permit applications to digitally sign or encrypt data while providing security for the user's private key data.

Daily backup This type of backup does not use any markers to back up selected files and folders. The files that have changed during the day are backed up every day at a specified time. This backup will not affect other backup schedules.

data backup A backup and disaster protection plan is an essential part of a network administrator's duties. Windows 2000 provides a built-in the Backup utility used to back up data to tape or file, or to create an emergency repair disk (ERD). An ERD can be used to repair a computer with damaged system files.

data compression Windows 2000 offers the capability of compressing data on a file-level basis, so long as the files and folders are located on an NT File System (NTFS) formatted partition or volume. Compression saves disk space; however, NTFS compression cannot be used in conjunction with file encryption.

Data Link Control (DLC) DLC is a nonroutable protocol used for connecting to IBM mainframes and some network-connected laser printers.

DC *See* domain controller.

Debugging mode This is the most advanced startup option of all. To use this option you will need to connect another computer to the problematic computer through a serial cable. With proper configuration, the debug information is sent to the second computer.

Decentralized model This model is appropriate for companies that rely on delegated levels of administration. They decentralize the management of Group Policy Objects (GPOs), which distributes the workload to a number of domains. To apply this model, simply give all organizational unit (OU) administrators full control of their respective GPOs.

dedicated server A dedicated printer server is a Windows 2000 server whose only role is to provide printing services. The server does not provide directory space for users other than storage for spooled print jobs. It does not provide authentication services, does not host database services, does not act as a Domain Name System (DNS) server, and so on. A dedicated print server can host several hundred printers and print queues, however. Though it may not be obvious, the printing process does have an impact on the performance of the server providing the printing services. An environment with a large number of printers or print jobs should strongly consider using at least one dedicated print server.

defragmentation   The task of finding fragmented files and moving them into contiguous space is called defragmentation.

Deny permission   Unlike the Allow permission, the Deny permission overrides all other permissions set for a file or folder. If a user is a member of one group with a Deny Write permission for a folder and is a member of another group with an Allow Full Control permission, the user will be unable to perform any of the Write permission tasks allowed because it has been denied. The Deny permission should be used with extreme caution, as it can actually lock out all users, even administrators, from a file or folder. The proper way to remove a permission from a user or group on a file or folder is to uncheck the Allow permission for that user or group, not to check the Deny permission.

Dfs   *See* Distributed File System.

DHCP   *See* Dynamic Host Control Protocol.

Differential backup   The Differential backup checks and performs a backup of only those files that are marked. It does not clear the markers after the back up, which means that any consecutive Differential backups will back up the marked files again. When you need to restore from a Differential backup, you will need the most current Full backup and the Differential backup performed after that.

digital subscriber line (DSL)   There are many variants of digital subscriber line (xDSL). All versions utilize the existing copper loop between a home and the local telco's Central Office (CO). Doing so allows them to be deployed rapidly and inexpensively. However, all DSL variants suffer from attenuation, and speeds drop as the loop length increases. Asymmetrical DSL (ADSL) and Symmetrical DSL (SDSL) may be deployed only within 17,500 feet of a CO, and Integrated Services Digital Network emulation over DSL (IDSL) will work only up to 30,500 feet. All DSL variants use Asynchronous Transfer mode (ATM) as the Data-Link layer.

Direct Memory Access (DMA)   DMA is a microprocessor capable of transferring data between memory units without the aid of the Central Processing Unit (CPU). Occasionally, built-in circuitry can do this same function.

directory   A directory is a database that contains information about objects and their attributes.

directory service   The directory service is the component that organizes the objects into a logical and accessible structure, and provides for a means of searching and locating objects within the directory. The directory service includes the entire directory and the method of storing it on the network.

Directory Services Restore mode   This startup mode is available on Windows 2000 Server domain controller computers only. This mode can be used to restore the SYSVOL directory and Active Directory on the domain controller.

discover   A Dynamic Host Control Protocol (DHCP) client begins the lease process with a DHCPDISCOVER message. The client broadcasts this message after loading a minimal Transmission Control Protocol/Internet Protocol (TCP/IP) environment. The client does not know the address of the DHCP server, so it sends the message using a TCP/IP broadcast, with 0.0.0.0 as the source address and 255.255.255.255 as the destination address. The DHCPDISCOVER message contains the clients network hardware address, its computer name, a list of DHCP options the client supports, and a message ID that will be used in all messages between the client and server to identify the particular request.

disk compression   This compression allows you to compress folders, subfolders, and files to increase the amount of file storage, but slow down access to the files.

Disk Defragmenter   Disk Defragmenter can analyze your volumes and make a recommendation as to whether or not you should defragment it. It will also give you a graphical display showing you the fragmented files, contiguous files, system files and free space. Disk Defragmenter does not always completely defragment free space; instead, it often moves it into just a few contiguous areas of the disk, which will still improve performance. Making the free space one contiguous space would have little added benefit.

disk imaging/cloning   The deployment of a new operating system is one of the most challenging and time-consuming tasks that a network administrator has to perform. The disk duplication methods are particularly useful when you need to deploy Windows 2000 Professional on a large number of computers. This is also known as disk imaging or cloning. These tools make the rollout fast and easy.

Disk Quota   Windows 2000 comes with a Disk Quota feature that allows you to control users' disk consumption on a per user/per partition basis. To begin setting disk quotas for your users, right-click any partition in either Windows Explorer or the My Computer object. Click Properties and then click the Quota tab. Also, a disk quota allows you to limit the amount of disk space used by each user.

Distributed File System (Dfs)   The Windows 2000 Distributed File System provides a method to centralize the organization of the shared resources on your network. In the past, shared resources were most often accessed via the Network Neighborhood applet, and users would have to wade through a number of domains and servers in order to access the shared folder or printer that they sought. Network users also had to remember where the obscure bit of information was stored, including both a cryptic server name and share name. The Distributed File System (Dfs) allows you to simplify the organization of your network resources by placing them in central shares accessed via a single server. Also, the Dfs allows you to create a central share point for shared resources located through the organization on a number of different servers.

Distribution Server   This is a server on which the Windows 2000 installation files reside. When you install the operating system over the network, the client machine does not need a CD-ROM drive. The first requirement for network installation is a Distribution Server that contains the installation files. The distribution server can be any computer on the network to which the clients have access.

DLC   *See* Data Link Control.

DMA   *See* Direct Memory Access.

DNS   *See* Domain Name System.

domain   A collection of connected areas. Routing domains provide full connectivity to all end systems within them. Also, a domain is a collection of accounts and network resources that are grouped together using a single domain name and security boundary.

domain controller (DC)   Domain controllers validate logons, participate in replication of logon scripts and policies, and synchronize the user account database. This means that domain controllers have an extra amount of work to perform. Since the Terminal Server already requires such heavy resources, it is not a good idea to burden a Terminal Server with the extra work of being a domain controller. Also, all user accounts, permissions, and other network details are all stored in a centralized database on the domain controllers.

domain local groups   Domain local groups are used for granting access rights to resources such as file systems or printers that are located on any computer in the domain where common access permissions are required. The advantage of domain local groups being used to protect resources in that a member of the domain local group can come from both inside the same domain and from outside as well.

Domain Name System (DNS)   Because the actual unique Internet Protocol (IP) address of a Web server is in the form of a number difficult for humans to work with, text labels separated by dots (domain names) are used instead. DNS is responsible for mapping these domain names to the actual Internet Protocol (IP) numbers in a process called resolution. Sometimes called a Domain Name Server.

domain restructure   Domain restructure, or domain consolidation, is the method of changing the structure of your domains. Restructuring your domains can allow you to take advantage of the new features of Windows 2000, such as greater scalability. Windows 2000 does not have the same limitation as the Security Accounts Manager (SAM) account database in Windows NT. Without this limitation, you can merge domains into one larger domain. Using Windows 2000 organizational units (OUs), you have finer granularity in delegating administrative tasks.

domain tree   A domain tree is a hierarchical collection of the child and parent domains within a network. The domains in a domain tree have contiguous namespaces. Domain trees in a domain forest do not share common security rights, but can access one another through the global catalog.

Driver Signing   One of the most frustrating things about Windows operating systems is that any software vendors can overwrite critical system level files with their own versions. Sometimes the vendor's version of a system level file is buggy or flawed, and it prevents the operating system from functioning correctly, or in the worst case, prevents it from starting at all. Windows 2000 uses a procedure called Driver Signing that allows the operating system to recognize functional, high-quality files approved by

Microsoft. With this seal of approval, you should be confident that installing applications containing signed files will not disable your computer. Windows 98 was the first Microsoft operating system to use digital signatures, but Windows 2000 marks the first Microsoft operating system based on NT technology to do this.

DSL   *See* digital subscriber line.

dynamic disks   Dynamic disks introduce conceptual as well as technical changes from traditional basic disk structure. Partitions are now called volumes, and these can be created or changed without losing existing data on the disk. Recall that when using basic disks, you must first create primary partitions (up to a maximum of four), then extended partitions (a maximum of one) with logical drives. Dynamic disks allow you to create volume after volume, with no limit on the number or type that can exist on a single disk; you are limited only by the capacity of the disk itself.

Dynamic Host Configuration Protocol (DHCP)   A software utility that is designed to assign Internet Protocol (IP) addresses to clients and their stations logging onto a Transmission Control Protocol/Internet Protocol (TCP/IP) and eliminates manual IP address assignments.

EAP   *See* Extensible Authentication Protocol.

EFS   *See* Encrypting File System.

Encrypting File System (EFS)   Unlike Windows NT 4.0, Windows 2000 provides the Encrypting File System (EFS) that allows you to encrypt and decrypt data on a file-by-file basis without the need for third-party software, as long as it is stored on an NTFS formatted partition or volume. If data packets are intercepted when sent over the network, the data will not be readable. EFS is based on public key cryptography.

encryption   Scrambling of data so as to be unreadable; therefore, an unauthorized person cannot decipher the data.

Ethernet   A networking protocol and shared media (or switched) local area network (LAN) access method linking up to 1K nodes in a bus topology.

evaluation   Evaluation is the process of assessing, summarizing, weighing, deciding, and applying standards.

extended partitions   Although extended partitions cannot be used to host operating systems, they can store other types of data and provide an excellent way to create more drives above the four-partition limit. Extended partitions do not represent one drive; rather, they can be subdivided into as many logical drives as there are letters in the alphabet. Therefore, one extended partition can contain several logical drives, each of which appears as a separate drive letter to the user.

Extensible Authentication Protocol (EAP)   EAP allows the administrator to "plug in" different authentication security providers outside of those included with Windows 2000. EAP allows your organization to take advantage of new authentication technologies including "smart card" logon and Certificate-based authentication.

FAT   *See* file allocation table.

fault tolerance   Fault tolerance is high-system availability with enough resources to accommodate unexpected failure. Fault tolerance is also the design of a computer to maintain its system's performance when some internal hardware problems occur. This is done through the use of backup systems.

FEK   *See* File Encryption Key.

file allocation table (FAT)   A FAT is an area on a disk that indicates the arrangement of files in the sectors. Because of the multi-user nature of Terminal Server, it is strongly recommended that the NTFS file system be used rather than the FAT file system. FAT does not offer file and directory security, whereas with NTFS you can limit access to subdirectories and files to certain users or groups of users.

file allocation table 16 (FAT16)   The earlier version of the FAT file system implemented in MS-DOS is known as FAT16, to differentiate it from the improved FAT32.

file allocation table 32 (FAT32)   FAT32 is the default file system for Windows 95 OSR2 and Windows 98. The FAT32 file system was first implemented in Windows 95 OSR2, and was supported by Windows 98 and now Windows 2000. While FAT16 cannot support partitions larger than 4GB in Windows 2000, FAT32 can support partitions up to 2TB (Terabytes) in size. However, for performance reasons, the creation of FAT32 partitions is limited to 32GB in Windows 2000. The second major benefit of FAT32 in comparison to FAT16 is that it supports a significantly smaller cluster size—as low as 4K for partitions up to 8GB. This results in more efficient use of disk space, with a 15 to 30 percent utilization improvement in comparison to FAT16.

File Encryption Key (FEK) A random key called a File Encryption Key (FEK) is used to encrypt each file and is then itself encrypted using the user's public key. At least two FEKs are created for every encrypted file. One FEK is created with the user's public key, and one is created with the public key of each recovery agent. There could be more than one recovery agent certificate used to encrypt each file, resulting in more than two FEKs. The user's public key can decrypt FEKs created with the public key.

File Transfer Protocol (FTP) An Internet protocol allowing the exchange of files. A program enables the user to contact another computer on the Internet and exchange files.

FireWire Also known as IEEE 1394. An Apple/Texas Instruments high-speed serial bus allowing up to 63 devices to connect; this bus supports hot swapping and isochronous data transfer.

forest A forest is a grouping of one or more domain trees that do not share a common namespace but do share a common schema, configuration, and global catalog; in fact, it forms a noncontiguous (or discontiguous) namespace. The users in one tree do not have global access to resources in other trees, but trusts can be created that allow users to access resources in another tree.

forward lookup query A forward lookup query occurs when a computer needs to get the Internet Protocol (IP) address for a computer with an Internet name. The local computer sends a query to a local Domain Name System (DNS) name server, which resolves the name or passes the request on to another server for resolution.

FQDN *See* fully qualified domain name.

FTP *See* File Transfer Protocol.

fully qualified domain name (FQDN) A full site name of a system rather than just its host name. The FQDN of each child domain is made up of the combination of its own name and the FQDN of the parent domain. The FQDN includes the host name and the domain membership of that computer.

gateway   In networking, gateway refers to a router or a computer functioning as one, the "way out" of the network or subnet, to get to another network. You also use gateways for software that connects a system using one protocol to a system using a different protocol, such as the Systems Network Architecture (SNA) software (allows a local area network (LAN) to connect to an IBM mainframe). You can also use Gateway Services for NetWare used to provide a way for Microsoft clients to go through a Windows NT or Windows 2000 server to access files on a Novell file server.

global groups   Global groups are used for combining users who share a common access profile based on job function or business role. Typically organizations use global groups for all groups in which membership is expected to change frequently. These groups can have as members only user accounts defined in the same domain as the global group.

globally unique identifier (GUID)   The globally unique identifier (GUID) is a unique numerical identification created at the time the object is created. An analogy would be a person's social security number, which is assigned once and never changes, even if the person changes his or her name, or moves.

GPC   *See* Group Policy Container.

GPO   *See* Group Policy Object.

GPT   *See* Group Policy Template.

graphical user interface (GUI)   An overall and consistent system for the interactive and visual program that interacts (or interfaces) with the user. GUI can involve pull-down menus, dialog boxes, on-screen graphics, and a variety of icons.

group policy   Group policy provides for change management and desktop control on the Windows 2000 platform. You are familiar with the control you had in Windows NT 4.0 using system policies. Group policy is similar to system policies but allows you a much higher level of granular configuration management over your network. Some of the confusion comes from the change of names applied to different groups in Windows 2000. You can apply group policy to sites, domains, and organizational units. Each of these represents a group of objects, so group policy is applied to the group of objects contained in each of these entities. Group policy cannot be directly applied to security groups that are similar to the groups you are used to working with in Windows NT 4.0. However, by using group policy filtering, you can successfully apply group policy to individual security groups.

Group Policy Container (GPC)   The Active Directory object Group Policy Containers (GPCs) store the information for the Folder Redirection snap-in and the Software Deployment snap-in. GPCs do not apply to local group policies. They contain component lists and status information, which indicate whether Group Policy Objects (GPOs) are enabled or disabled. They also contain version information, which insures that the information is synchronized with the Group Policy Template (GPT) information. GPCs also contain the class store in which GPO group policy extensions have settings.

Group Policy Object (GPO)   After you create a group policy, it is stored in a Group Policy Object (GPO) and applied to the site, domain, or organizational unit (OU). GPOs are used to keep the group policy information; essentially, it is a collection of policies. You can apply single or multiple GPOs to each site, domain or OU. Group policies are not inherited across domains, and users must have Read permission for the GPO that you want to have applied to them. This way, you can filter the scope of GPOs by adjusting who has read access to each GPO.

Group Policy Template (GPT)   The subset of folders created on each domain controller that store Group Policy Object (GPO) information for specific GPOs are called Group Policy Templates (GPTs). GPTs are stored in the SysVol (System Volume) folder, on the domain controller. GPTs store data for Software Policies, Scripts, Desktop File and Folder Management, Software Deployment, and Security settings. GPTs can be defined in computer or user configurations. Consequently, they take effect either when the computer starts or when the user logs on.

GUI   *See* graphical user interface.

GUID   *See* globally unique identifier.

HAL   *See* Hardware Abstraction Layer.

Hardware Abstraction Layer (HAL)   The Windows NT's translation layer existing between the hardware, kernel, and input/output (I/O) system.

Hardware Compatibility List (HCL)   The Hardware Compatibility List is published by Microsoft for each of its operating systems, and is updated on a monthly basis. There is a copy of the HCL on the Windows 2000 Professional CD, located in the Support folder and named Hcl.txt.

hardware profile   A hardware profile is a set of instructions that tells your computer how to boot the system properly, based on the setup of your hardware. Hardware profiles are most commonly used with laptops. This is because laptops are frequently used in at least two different settings: stand-alone and in a docking station on a network. For example, when the laptop is being used at a docking station, it requires a network adapter. However, when the laptop is used away from the network, it does not. The hardware profile dialog manages these configuration changes. If a profile is created for each situation, the user will automatically be presented these choices on Windows startup.

HCL   *See* Hardware Compatibility List.

HKEY_CLASSES_ROOT   Contains information used for software configuration and object linking and embedding (OLE), as well as file association information.

HKEY_CURRENT_CONFIG   Holds data about the current hardware profile that is in use.

HKEY_CURRENT_USER   Has information about the user who is currently logged on.

HKEY_LOCAL_MACHINE   Stores information about the hardware, software, system devices, and security information for the local computer.

HKEY_USERS   Holds information and settings for the environments of all users of the computer.

HTML   *See* HyperText Markup Language.

HTTP   *See* HyperText Transfer Protocol.

HyperText Markup Language (HTML)   The format used to create documents viewed on the World Wide Web (WWW) by the use of tags (codes) embedded within the text.

HyperText Transfer Protocol (HTTP)   HTTP is an Internet standard supporting World Wide Web (WWW) exchanges. By creating the definitions of Universal Resource Locators (URLs) and their retrieval usage throughout the Internet.

IAS   *See* Internet Authentication Services.

ICS   *See* Internet Connection Sharing.

IDE   *See* Integrated Drive Electronics.

IIS   *See* Internet Information Service.

Incremental backup   This backup process is similar to the Differential backup, but it clears the markers from the selected files after the process. Because it clears the markers, an Incremental backup will not back up any files that have not changed since the last Incremental backup. This type of backup is fast during the backup but is very slow while restoring the files. You will need the last Full backup and all of the subsequent Incremental backups to fully restore data. The positive side of this backup type is that it is fast and consumes very little media space.

indexing service   Provides indexing functions for documents stored on disk, allowing users to search for specific document text or properties.

Industry Standard Architecture (ISA)   A PC's expansion bus used for peripherals plug-in boards.

Integrated Drive Electronics (IDE) drive   An IDE drive is a hard disk drive for processors containing most controller circuitry within the drive. IDE drives combine Enhanced System Device Interface (ESDI) speed with small computer system interface (SCSI) hard drive interface intelligence.

Integrated Services Digital Network (ISDN)   Integrated Services indicates the provider offers voice and data services over the same medium. Digital Network is a reminder that ISDN was born out of the digital nature of the intercarrier and intracarrier networks. ISDN runs across the same copper wiring that carries regular telephone service. Before attenuation and noise cause the signal to be unintelligible, an ISDN circuit can run a maximum of 18,000 feet. A repeater doubles this distance to 36,000 feet.

Internet Authentication Services (IAS)   IAS performs authentication, authorization, and accounting of dial-up and virtual private network (VPN) users. IAS supports the Remote Access Dial-In User Service (RADIUS) protocol.

Internet Connection Sharing (ICS)   ICS can be thought of as a less robust version of Network Address Translation (NAT lite). ICS uses the same address translation technology. ICS is a simpler version of NAT useful for connecting a few computers on a small local area network (LAN) to the Internet or useful for a remote server through a single phone line and account.

Internet Information Service (IIS)   Windows NT Web browser software that supports Secure Sockets Layer (SSL) security protocol from Netscape. IIS provides support for Web site creation, configuration, and management, along with Network News Transfer Protocol (NNTP), File Transfer Protocol (FTP), and Simple Mail Transfer Protocol (SMTP).

Internet Packet Exchange (IPX)   Novell NetWare's built-in networking protocol for local area network (LAN) communication derived from the Xerox Network System protocol. IPX moves data between a server and/or workstation programs from different network nodes. Sometimes called an Internetwork Packet Exchange.

Internet Protocol Security (IPSec)   IPSec is a new feature included in Windows 2000 and provides for encryption of data as it travels between two computers, protecting it from modification and interpretation if anyone were to see it on the network.

Internet service provider (ISP)   The organization allowing users to connect to its computers and then to the Internet. ISPs provider the software to connect and sometimes a portal site and/or internal browsing capability.

interrupt request (IRQ)   An electronic signal that is sent to the computer's processor requiring the processor's attention. Also, a computer instruction designed to interrupt a program for an input/output (I/O).

IPSec   *See* Internet Protocol Security.

IPX   *See* Internet Packet Exchange.

IRQ   *See* interrupt request.

ISA   *See* Industry Standard Architecture.

ISDN   *See* Integrated Services Digital Network.

ISP   *See* Internet service provider.

Kerberos   Kerberos guards against username and password safety vulnerability by using tickets (temporary electronic credentials) to authenticate. Tickets have a limited life span and can be used in place of usernames and passwords (if the software supports this). Kerberos encrypts the password into the ticket. It uses a trusted server called the Kerberos Distribution Center (KDC) to handle authentication requests. Kerberos speeds up network processes by integrating security and rights across network domains and also eliminates workstations' need to authenticate themselves repeatedly at every domain they access. Kerberos security also makes maneuvering around networks simple using multiple platforms such as Unix or NetWare easier.

knowledge   Knowledge is the very lowest level of learning. It is, of course, important that a network administrator have this knowledge. Knowledge involves the processes of defining, location, recall, recognition, stating, matching, labeling, and identification.

L2TP   *See* Layer Two Tunneling Protocol.

Last Known Good Configuration   This mode starts the system using the configuration that was saved in the registry during the last system shutdown. This startup option is useful when you have changed some configuration parameters and the system fails to boot. When you use this mode to start the system, all changes that were made after the last successful logon are lost. Use this option when you suspect that some incorrect configuration changes are causing the system startup failure. This mode does not help if any of the installed drivers have been corrupted or any driver files are deleted by mistake.

Layer Two Tunneling Protocol (L2TP)   L2TP offers better security through the use of IPSec and creates virtual private networks (VPNs). Windows 2000 uses L2TP to provide tunneling services over Internet Protocol Security (IPSec)–based communications. L2TP tunnels can be set up to traverse data across intervening networks that are not part of the VPN being created. L2TP is used to send information across intervening and nonsecure networks.

LDAP   *See* Lightweight Directory Access Protocol.

legend   The legend displays information about the counters that are being measured. It is the set of columns at the bottom of System Monitor.

Lightweight Directory Access Protocol (LDAP)   A simplified Directory Access Protocol (DAP) accessing a computer's directory listing. LDAP is able to access to X.500 directories.

Line Printer Daemon (LPD)   LPD is the server process that advertises printer queues and accepts incoming print submissions, which are then routed to the print device.

Line Printer Remote (LPR)   LPR is a process that spools a print job to a remote print spool that is advertised by the Line Printer Daemon (LPD).

local policy   A group policy stored locally on a Windows 2000 member server or a Windows 2000 professional computer is called a local policy. The local policy is used to set up the configuration settings for each computer and for each user. Local policies are stored in the \%systemroot%\system32\grouppolicy folder on the local computer. Local policies include the auditing policy, user rights and privilege assignment, and various security options.

local printer   A print device that is directly attached, via a parallel or serial cable, to the computer that is providing the printing services. For a Windows 2000 Professional workstation, a local printer is one that is connected to the workstation. For a Windows 2000 Server, a local printer is one that is connected to the server. Drivers for the print device must reside on the computer that connects to the printer.

local user profiles (local profiles)   Local user profiles are kept on one local computer hard drive. When a user initially logs on to a computer, a local profile is created for them in the \%systemdrive%\Documents and Settings\<username> folder. When users log off the computer, the changes that they made while they were logged on will be saved to their local profile on that client computer. This way, subsequent logons to that computer will bring up their personal settings. When users log on to a different computer, they will not receive these settings, as they are local to the computer in which they made the changes. Therefore, each user that logs on to that computer receives individual desktop settings. Local profiles are ideal for users who only use one computer. For users that require access to multiple computers, the roaming profile would be the better choice.

LogicalDisk object   The LogicalDisk object measures the transfer of data for a logical drive (i.e., C or D) or storage volumes. You can use the PhysicalDisk object to determine which hard disk is causing the bottleneck. Then, to narrow the cause of the bottleneck, you can use the LogicalDisk object to determine which, if any, partition is the specific cause of the bottleneck. By default, the PhysicalDisk object is enabled and the LogicalDisk object is disabled on Windows 2000 Server.

LPD   *See* Line Printer Daemon.

LPR   *See* Line Printer Remote.

mandatory roaming profiles   Mandatory roaming profiles are mandatory user profiles the user cannot change. They are usually created to define desktop configuration settings for groups of users in order to simplify administration and support. Users can make changes to their desktop settings while they are logged on, but these changes will not be saved to the profile, as mandatory profiles are read-only. The next time they log on, their desktop will be set back to the original mandatory profile settings.

Master File Table (MFT)   The MFT stores the information needed by the operating system to retrieve files from the volume. Part of the MFT is stored at the beginning of the volume and cannot be moved. Also, if the volume contains a large number of directories, it can prevent the free space from being defragmented.

master image   After configuring one computer with the operating system and all the applications, Sysprep is run to create an image of the hard disk. This computer serves as the master or model computer that will have the complete setup of the operating system, application software, and any service packs. This hard disk image is the master image and is copied to a CD or put on a network share for distribution to many computers. Any third-party disk-imaging tool can then be used to replicate the image to other identical computers.

MCSE   *See* Microsoft Certified Systems Engineer.

Message Queuing Services   Provides a communication infrastructure and a development tool for creating distributed messaging applications. Such applications can communicate across heterogeneous networks and with computers that might be offline. Message queuing provides guaranteed message delivery, efficient routing, security, transactional support, and priority-based messaging.

MFT   *See* Master File Table.

Microsoft Certified Systems Engineer (MCSE)   An engineer who is a technical specialist in advanced Microsoft products, specifically NT Server and NT Workstation.

Microsoft Management Console (MMC)   The MMC provides a standardized interface for using administrative tools and utilities. The management applications contained in an MMC are called snap-ins, and custom MMCs hold the snap-ins required to perform specific tasks. Custom consoles can be saved as files with the .msc file extension. The MMC was first introduced with NT Option Pack. Using the MMC leverages the familiarity you have with the other snap-ins available within MMC, such as SQL Server 7 and Internet Information Server 4. With the MMC, all your administrative tasks can be done in one place.

Mini-Setup Wizard   The purpose of this wizard is to add some user-specific parameters on the destination computer. These parameters include: end-user license agreement (EULA); product key (serial number); username, company name, and administrator password; network configuration; domain or workgroup name; and, date and time zone selection.

mirror set   In a mirror set, all data on a selected partition or drive are automatically duplicated onto another physical disk. The main purpose of a mirror set is to provide fault tolerance in the event of missing or corrupt data. If one disk fails or contains corrupt files, the data is simply retrieved and rebuilt from the other disk.

mirrored volume   Like basic disks, dynamic disks can also be mirrored and are called mirrored volumes. A continuous and automatic backup of all data in a mirrored volume is saved to a separate disk to provide fault tolerance in the event of a disk failure or corrupt file. Note that you cannot mirror a spanned or striped volume.

mirroring   Also called RAID1. RAID1 consists of two drives that are identical matches, or mirrors, of each other. If one drive fails, you have another drive to boot up and keep the server going.

Mixed mode   When in Mixed mode, the domain still uses master replication with a Windows 2000 PDC. The Windows NT backup domain controllers (BDCs) replicate from the Windows 2000 server, as did the Windows NT primary domain controller (PDC). When you are operating in Mixed mode, some Windows 2000 functionality will not be available. You will not be able to use group nesting or transitive trusts. Mixed mode is the default mode.

MMC   *See* Microsoft Management Console.

NAT   *See* Network Address Translation.

Native mode   Native mode allows only Windows 2000 domain controllers to operate in the domain. When all domain controllers for the domain are upgraded to Windows 2000 Server, you can switch to Native mode. This allows you to use transitive trusts and the group-nesting features of Windows 2000. When switching to Native mode, ensure you no longer need to operate in Mixed mode because you cannot switch back to Mixed mode once you are in Native mode.

NDS   *See* NetWare Directory Service.

NetBEUI   *See* Network Basic Input/Output System Extended User Interface.

NetBIOS   *See* Network Basic Input/Output System.

NetWare Directory Service (NDS)   NDS (created by Novell) has a hierarchical information database allowing the user to log on to a network with NDS capable of calculating the user's access rights.

Network Address Translation (NAT)   With NAT, you can allow internal users to have access to important external resources while still preventing unauthorized access from the outside world.

Network Basic Input/Output System (NetBIOS)   A program in Microsoft's operating system that links personal computers to a local area network (LAN).

Network Basic Input/Output System Extended User Interface (NetBEUI)   The transport layer for the Disk Operating System (DOS) networking protocol called Network Basic Input/Output System (NetBIOS).

network   Two or more computers connected together by cable or wireless media for the purpose of sharing data, hardware peripherals, and other resources.

network interface card (NIC)   A board with encoding and decoding circuitry and a receptacle for a network cable connection that, bypassing the serial ports and operating through the internal bus, allows computers to be connected at higher speeds to media for communications between stations.

network printer   A print device that has a built-in network interface or connects directly to a dedicated network interface. Both workstations and servers can be configured to print directly to the network printer, and the network printer controls its own printer queue, determining which jobs from which clients will print in which order. Printing clients have no direct control over the printer queue and cannot see other print jobs being submitted to the printer. Administration of a network printer is difficult. Drivers for the print device must reside on the computer that connects to the printer.

NIC   *See* network interface card.

nondedicated server   A nondedicated print server is a Windows 2000 server that hosts printing services in addition to other services. A domain controller, database server, or Domain Name System (DNS) server can provide printing services as well, but should be used only for a smaller number of printers or for printers that are not heavily used. Anyone setting up a nondedicated print server should monitor the performance of the printing process and the other tasks running on the server and be prepared to modify the server configuration if the performance drops below acceptable levels.

nonmandatory roaming profiles   Roaming user profiles are stored on the network file server and are the perfect solution for users who have access to multiple computers. This way their profile is accessible no matter where they log on in the domain. When users log on to a computer within their domain, their roaming profile will be copied from the network server to the client computer and the settings will be applied to the computer while they are logged on. Subsequent logins will compare the roaming profile files to the local profile files. The file server then copies only any files that have been altered since the user last logged on locally, significantly decreasing the time required to logon. When the user logs off, any changes that the user made on the local computer will be copied back to the profile on the network file server.

Normal backup   This is the most common type and is also known as a Full backup. The Normal backup operation backs up all files and folders that are selected irrespective of the archive attributes of the files. This provides the easiest way to restore the files and folders but is expensive in terms of the time it takes to complete the backup job and the storage space it consumes. The restore process from a Normal backup is less complex because you do not have to use multiple tape sets to completely restore data.

NT File System (NTFS)   The NT File System (with file names up to 255 characters) is a system created to aid the computer and its components in recovering from hard disk crashes.

NTFS   *See* NT File System.

NWLink IPX/SPX/NetBIOS Compatible Transport Protocol (NWLink)
Microsoft's implementation of Novell's Internet Packet eXchange/Sequenced Packet eXchange (IPX/SPX) protocol stack, required for connecting to NetWare servers prior to version 5. NWLink can also be used on small networks that use only Windows 2000 and other Microsoft client software. NWLink is a Network Driver Interface Specification (NDIS) compliant, native 32-bit protocol. The NWLink protocol supports Windows sockets and NetBIOS.

ODBC   *See* Open Database Connectivity.

offer   After the Dynamic Host Control Protocol (DHCP) server receives the DHCPDISCOVER message, it looks at the request to see if the client configuration request is valid. If so, it sends back a DHCPOFFER message with the client's network hardware address, an IP address, a subnet mask, the length of time the lease is valid, and the IP address of the server that provided the DHCP information. This message is also a Transmission Control Protocol/Internet Protocol (TCP/IP) broadcast, as the client does not yet have an Internet Protocol (IP) address. The server then reserves the address it sent to the client so that it is not offered to another client making a request. If there are more than one DHCP servers on the network, all servers respond to the DHCPDISCOVER message with a DHCPOFFER message.

Open Database Connectivity (ODBC)   A database programming interface that allows applications a way to access network databases.

Open Systems Interconnection (OSI) model   This is a model of breaking networking tasks into layers. Each layer is responsible for a specific set of functionality. There are performance objects available in System Monitor for analyzing network performance.

organizational unit (OU)   OUs in Windows 2000 are objects that are containers for other objects, such as users, groups, or other organizational units. Objects cannot be placed in another domain's OUs. The whole purpose of an OU is to have a hierarchical structure to organize your network objects. You can assign a group policy to an OU. Generally, the OU will follow a structure from your company. It may be a location, if you have multiple locations. It can even be a department-level organization. Also, OUs are units used to organize objects within a domain. These objects can include user accounts, groups, computers, printers, and even other OUs. The hierarchy of OUs is independent of other domains.

OSI   *See* Open Systems Interconnection model.

OU   *See* organizational unit.

paging   When enough memory is not available for the running applications, pages of memory can be swapped from physical memory to the hard disk too much and slow the system down. This is also known as paging because pages of memory are swapped at a time. Windows 2000 separates memory into 4KB pages of memory to help prevent fragmentation of memory. Swapping can even get bad enough that you can hear your hard disk running constantly.

paging file   A file on the hard disk (or spanning multiple disks) that stores some of the program code that is normally in the computer's RAM. This is called virtual memory, and allows the programs to function as if the computer had more memory than is physically installed.

password policy   A password policy regulates how your users must establish and manage their passwords. This includes password complexity requirements and how often passwords must change. There are several settings that can be used to implement a successful password policy. You can enforce password uniqueness so those users cannot simply switch back and forth between a few easy-to-remember passwords. This can be set to low, medium, or high security. With low security, the system remembers the user's last 1 to 8 passwords (it is your choice as administrator to decide how many); with medium, it remembers the last 9 to 16 passwords; with high, it remembers the last 17 to 24 passwords.

PCMCIA   *See* Personal Computer Memory Card Interface Adapter.

PDC   *See* primary domain controller.

peer-to-peer network   A workgroup is also referred to as a peer-to-peer network, because all the computers connected together and communicating with one another are created equal. That is, there is no central computer that manages security and controls access to the network.

performance logging   Performance logging has many features. The data collected are stored in a comma-delimited or tab-delimited format, which allows for exportation to spreadsheet and database applications for a variety of tasks such as charting and reports. The data can also be viewed as collected. You can configure the logging by specifying start and stop times, the name of the log files, and the maximum size of the log. You can start and stop the logging of data manually or create a schedule for logging. You can even specify a program to run automatically when logging stops. You can also create trace logs. Trace logs track events that occur rather than measuring performance counters.

permissions inheritance   By default, all permissions set for a folder are inherited by the files in the folder, the subfolders in the folder, and the contents of the subfolders. When the permissions on a folder are viewed in the Security tab of the file or folder Permissions window, inherited permissions are indicated with a gray check box.

Personal Computer Memory Card Interface Adapter (PCMCIA)   An interface standard for plug-in cards for portable computers; devices meeting the standard (for example, fax cards, modems) are theoretically interchangeable.

physical memory   Physical memory is the actual random access memory (RAM) on the computer. When the physical memory becomes full, the operating system can also use space on the hard disk as virtual memory. When memory becomes full, rather than locking up the computer, the operating system stores unused data on the hard disk in a page file (also called paging or swap file). Data are swapped back and forth between the hard disk and physical memory as needed for running applications. If memory is needed that is in virtual memory, it is swapped back into physical memory.

PhysicalDisk object   The PhysicalDisk object measures the transfer of data for the entire hard disk. You can use the PhysicalDisk object to determine which hard disk is causing the bottleneck. By default, the PhysicalDisk object is enabled and the LogicalDisk object is disabled on Windows 2000 Server.

Plug and Play (PnP)   A standard requiring add-in hardware to carry the software to configure itself in a given way supported by Microsoft Windows 95. Plug and Play can make peripheral configuration software, jumper settings, and Dual In-line Package (DIP) switches unnecessary. PnP allows the operating system to load device drivers automatically and assign system resources dynamically to computer components and peripherals. Windows 2000 moves away from this older technology with its use of Kernel mode and User-mode PnP architecture. PnP autodetects, configures, and installs the necessary drivers in order to minimize user interaction with hardware configuration. Users no longer have to tinker with IRQ and I/O settings.

PnP   *See* Plug and Play.

Point-to-Point Protocol (PPP)   A serial communication protocol most commonly used to connect a personal computer to an Internet Service Provider (ISP). PPP is the successor to Serial Line Internet Protocol (SLIP) and may be used over both synchronous and asynchronous circuits. Also, PPP is a full-duplex, connectionless protocol that supports many different types of links. The advantages of PPP made it de facto standard for dial-up connections.

Point-to-Point Tunneling Protocol (PPTP)   One of two standards for dial-up telephone connection of computers to the Internet, with better data negotiation, compression, and error corrections than the other Serial Line Internet Protocol (SLIP), but costing more to transmit data and unnecessary when both sending and receiving modems can handle some of the procedures.

policy inheritance   Group policies have an order of inheritance in which the policies are applied. Local policies are applied first, then group policies are applied to the site, then the domain, and finally the organizational unit (OU). Policies applied first are overwritten by policies applied later. Therefore, group policies applied to a site overwrite the local policies and so on. When there are multiple Group Policy Objects (GPOs) for a site, domain, or OU, the order in which they appear in the Properties list applies. This policy inheritance order works well for small companies, but a more complex inheritance strategy may be essential for larger corporations.

ports   A channel of a device that can support single point-to-point connections is known as a port. Devices can be single port, as in a modem.

Power options   Power options are dependent on the particular hardware. Power options include Standby and Hibernation modes. Standby mode turns off the monitor and hard disks to save power. Hibernation mode turns off the monitor and disks, saves everything in memory to disk, turns off the computer, and then restores the desktop to the state in which you left it when the computer is turned on.

PPP   *See* Point-to-Point Protocol.

PPTP   *See* Point-to-Point Tunneling Protocol.

Preboot Execution Environment (PXE)   The PXE is a new Dynamic Host Control Protocol (DHCP)–based technology used to help client computers boot from the network. The Windows 2000 Remote Installation Service (RIS) uses the PXE technology along with the existing Transmission Control Protocol/Internet Protocol (TCP/IP) network infrastructure to implement the RIS-based deployment of Windows 2000 Professional. The client computer that has the PXE-based ROM uses its Basic Input/Output System (BIOS) to contact an existing RIS server and get an Internet Protocol (IP) address from the DHCP server running on the network. The RIS server then initializes the installation process on the client computer.

preemptive multitasking   An environment in which timesharing controls the programs in use by exploiting a scheduled time usage of the computer's Central Processing Unit (CPU).

primary domain controller (PDC)   Performs NT security management for its local domain. The PDC is periodically synchronized to its copy, the backup domain controller (BDC). Only one PDC can exist in a domain. In an NT 4.0 single domain model, any user having a valid domain user account and password in the user accounts database of the PDC has the ability to log onto any computer that is a member of the domain, including MetaFrame servers.

Primary Domain Name System (DNS) server   The Primary DNS server maintains the master copy of the DNS database for the zone. This copy of the database is the only one that can be modified, and any changes made to its database are distributed to secondary servers in the zone during a zone transfer process. The server can cache resolution requests locally, so a lookup query does not have to be sent across the network for a duplicate request. The primary server contains the address mappings for the Internet root DNS servers. Primary servers can also act as secondary servers for other zones.

primary partitions   Primary partitions are typically used to create bootable drives. Each primary partition represents one drive letter, up to a maximum of four on a single hard disk. One primary partition must be marked as active in order to boot the system, and most operating systems must be loaded on a primary partition to work.

print device   The hardware that actually does the printing. A print device is one of two types as defined in Windows 2000: local or network-interface. A local print device connects directly to the print server with a serial or parallel interface. A network-interface print device connects to the printer across the network and must have its own network interface or be connected to an external network adapter.

print driver   A software program used by Windows 2000 and other computer programs to connect with printers and plotters. It translates information sent to it into commands that the print device can understand.

print server   A print server is a computer that manages printing on the network. A print server can be a dedicated computer hosting multiple printers, or it can run as one of many processes on a nondedicated computer.

Printer permission   Printer permission is established through the Security tab in the printer's Properties dialog box. The security settings for printer objects are similar to the security settings for folder shares.

protocols   Protocols are sets of rules that computers use to communicate with one another. Protocols usually work together in stacks, so called because in a layered networking model, they operate at different layers or levels. These protocols govern the logic, formatting, and timing of information exchange between layers.

publishing resources   Resources, such as folders and printers, which are available to be shared on the network, can be published to the Active Directory. The resources are published to the directory and can be located by users, who can query the directory based on the resource's properties (for example, to locate all color printers).

PXE   *See* Preboot Execution Environment.

QoS   *See* Quality of Service.

Quality of Service (QoS) Admission Control   Admission control allows you to control how applications are allotted network bandwidth. You can give important applications more bandwidth, less important applications less bandwidth.

RAID   *See* redundant array of inexpensive disks.

RAS   *See* Remote Access Service.

RDP   *See* Remote Desktop Protocol.

recovery agent   The recovery agent restores the encrypted file on a secure computer with its private recovery keys. The agent decrypts it using the cipher command line and then returns the plain text file to the user. The recovery agent goes to the computer with the encrypted file, loads the recovery certificate and private key, and performs the recovery. It is not as safe as the first option because the recovery agent's private key may remain on the user's computer.

Recovery console   The Recovery console is a new command-line interpreter feature in Windows 2000 that helps in system maintenance activities and resolving system problems. This program is separate from the Windows 2000 command prompt.

redundant array of inexpensive disks (RAID)   Although mirroring and duplexing are forms of RAID, most people think of RAID as involving more than two drives. The most common form of RAID is RAID5, which is the striping of data across three or more drives, providing fault tolerance if one drive fails. For the best disk performance, consider using a SCSI RAID (redundant array of independent disks) controller. RAID controllers automatically place data on multiple disk drives and can increase disk performance. Using the software implementation of RAID provided by NT would increase performance if designed properly, but the best performance is always realized through hardware RAID controllers.

redundant array of inexpensive disks 5 (RAID5) volume   A RAID5 volume on a dynamic drive provides disk striping with parity, and is similar to a basic stripe set with parity. This disk configuration provides both increased storage capacity and fault tolerance. Data in a dynamic RAI5 volume are interleaved across three or more disks (up to 32 disks), and parity information is included to rebuild lost data in the event of an individual disk failure. Like a spanned or striped volume, a RAID5 volume cannot be mirrored.

registry   The registry is the hierarchical database that stores operating system and application configuration information. It was introduced in Windows 9*x* and NT and replaced much of the functionality of the old initialization, system, and command files used in the early versions of Windows (.INI, .SYS, and .COM extensions). The registry is also a Microsoft Windows program allowing the user to choose options for configuration and applications to set them; it replaces confusing text-based .INI files.

remote   The word "remote" can take on a number of different meanings depending on the context. In the case of an individual computer, the computer you are sitting in front of is sometimes referred to as being "local" while any other computer is considered "remote." In this context any machine but your own is considered a remote computer. In discussions related to network configuration and design, "remote" may refer to segments and machines that are on the far side of a router. In this context, all machines on your physical segment are considered "local" and machines located on other physical segments are referred to as remote.

remote access policy   Remote access policies allow you to create demand-dial connections to use specific authentication and encryption methods. In Windows NT versions 3.5x and Windows NT 4.0, authorization was much simpler. The administrator simply granted dial-in permission to the user. The callback options were configured on a per-user basis.

Remote Access Service (RAS)   Remote Access Service is a built-in feature of the Microsoft NT operating system. It allows users to establish a connection to an NT network over a standard phone line. Remote Access allows users to access files on a network or transfer files from a remote PC, over a Dial-up Networking connection. The performance of transferring files over a dial-up connection is very similar to the performance you would get if you were downloading a file from the Internet.

Remote Desktop Protocol (RDP)   Remote Desktop Protocol (RDP) is the application protocol between the client and the server. It informs the server of the keystrokes and mouse movement of the client and returns to the client the Windows 2000 graphical display from the server. RDP is a multi-channel, standard protocol that provides various levels of compression so that it can adapt to different connection speeds and encryption levels from 40 to 128 bit. Transmission Control Protocol/Internet Protocol (TCP/IP) carries the messages, and RDP is the language in which the messages are written. Both are needed to use Microsoft's implementation of Terminal Services.

Remote Installation Preparation (RIPrep)   RIPrep is a disk duplication tool included with Windows 2000 Server. It is an ideal tool for creating images of fully prepared client computers. These images are the customized images made from the base operating system, local installation of applications such as Microsoft Office, and customized configurations.

Remote Installation Preparation (RIPrep) Wizard   The RIPrep wizard enables the network administrator to distribute to a large number of client computers a standard desktop configuration that includes the operating system and the applications. This not only helps in maintaining a uniform standard across the enterprise; it also cuts the costs and time involved in a large-scale rollout of Windows 2000 Professional.

Remote Installation Services (RIS)   The RIS, part of Windows 2000 Server, allows client computers to install Windows 2000 Professional from a Windows 2000 Server with the service installed. The Remote Installation Services (RIS) facilitates installation of Windows 2000 Professional remotely on a large number of computers with similar or dissimilar hardware configurations. This not only reduces the installation time but also helps keep deployment costs low. Also, the Windows 2000 Remote Installation Services allow you a way to create an image of Windows 2000 Professional you can use to install Windows 2000 Professional on your network client systems. This image actually consists of the installation files from the Windows 2000 Professional CD-ROM.

remote local printer   A print device connected directly to a print server but accessed by another print server or by workstations. The queue for the print device exists on the server, and the print server controls job priority, print order, and queue administration. Client computers submit print jobs to the server and can observe the queue to monitor the printing process on the server. Drivers for the print device are loaded onto the client computer from the print server.

remote network printer   A network printer connected to a print server that is accessed by client workstations or other print servers. Like the remote local printer, the printer queue is controlled by the print server, meaning that the client computers submit their print jobs to the print server, rather than to the print device directly. This allows for server administration and monitoring of the printer queues. Drivers for the print device are loaded onto the client computers from the print server.

request   After the client receives the DHCPOFFER message and accepts the Internet Protocol (IP) address, it sends a DHCPREQUEST message out to all Dynamic Host Control Protocol (DHCP) servers indicating that it has accepted an offer. The message contains the IP address of the DHCP server that made the accepted offer, and all other DHCP servers release the addresses they had offered back into their available address pool.

reverse lookup query   A reverse lookup query resolves an Internet Protocol (IP) address to a Domain Name System (DNS) name, and can be used for a variety of reasons. The process is different, though, because it makes use of a special domain called in-addr.arpa. This domain is also hierarchical, but is based on IP addresses and not names. The sub-domains are organized by the *reverse* order of the IP address. For instance, the domain 16.254.169.in-addr.arpa contains the addresses in the 169.254.16.* range; the 120.129.in-addr.arpa domain contains the addresses for the 129.120.*.* range.

RIPrep   *See* Remote Installation Preparation.

rollback strategy   As with any upgrade, problems can sometimes require going back to the previous state. This possibility also applies to upgrading your domain to Windows 2000. You need to create a plan to roll back your network to its previous state if the upgrade to Windows 2000 fails. When upgrading the domain controllers, do not upgrade the backup domain controller (BDC) that has the current directory database. Make sure the BDC is synchronized with the primary domain controller (PDC), and then take it offline. Leave the BDC as is until the upgrade is successful. If you run into problems during the upgrade, you can bring the BDC back online, promote it to the PDC, and recover the Windows NT state. If this process is successful, you can upgrade the BDC to Windows 2000.

Routing and Remote Access Service (RRAS)   Within Windows NT, a software routing and remote access capability combining packet filtering, Open Shortest Path First (OSPF) support, etc.

RRAS   *See* Routing and Remote Access.

Safe mode   Safe mode starts Windows 2000 using only some basic files and device drivers. These devices include monitor, keyboard, mouse, basic VGA video, CD-ROM, and mass storage devices. The system starts only those system services that are necessary to load the operating system. Networking is not started in this mode. The Windows background screen is black in this mode, and the screen resolution is 640 by 480 pixels with 16 colors.

Safe Mode with Command Prompt   This option starts the operating system in a Safe mode using some basic files only. The Windows 2000 command prompt is shown instead of the usual Windows desktop.

Safe Mode with Networking   This mode is similar to Safe mode, but networking devices, drivers, and protocols are loaded. You may choose this mode when you are sure that the problem in the system is not due to any networking component.

SAM   *See* Security Accounts Manager.

scripted method   This method for Windows 2000 Professional installation uses an answer file to specify various configuration parameters. This is used to eliminate user interaction during installation, thereby automating the installation process. Answers to most of the questions asked by the setup process are specified in the answer file. Besides this, the scripted method can be used for clean installations and upgrades.

SCSI   *See* small computer system interface.

Secondary Domain Name System (DNS) server   Secondary DNS servers provide fault tolerance and load balancing for DNS zones. Secondary servers contain a read-only copy of the zone database that it receives from the primary server during a zone transfer. A secondary server will respond to a DNS request if the primary server fails to respond because of an error or a heavy load. Since secondary servers can resolve DNS queries, they are also considered authoritative within a domain, and can help with load balancing on the network. Secondary servers can be placed in remote locations on the network and configured to respond to DNS queries from local computers, potentially reducing query traffic across longer network distances. While there can be only one primary server in a zone, multiple secondary servers can be set up for redundancy and load balancing.

Security Accounts Manager (SAM)   The Security Accounts Manager (SAM) is the portion of the Windows NT Server registry that stores user account information and group membership. Attributes that are specific to Terminal Server can be added to user accounts. This adds a small amount of information to each user's entry in the domain's SAM.

security groups   The Windows 2000 security groups allow you to assign the same security permissions to large numbers of users in one operation. This ensures consistent security permissions across all members of a group. Using security groups to assign permissions means the access control on resources remains fairly static and easy to control and audit. Users who need access are added or removed from the appropriate security groups as needed, and the access control lists change infrequently.

security templates   Windows 2000 comes with several predefined security templates. These templates address several security scenarios. Security templates come in two basic categories: default and incremental. The default or basic templates are applied by the operating system when a clean install has been performed. They are not applied if an upgrade installation has been done. The incremental templates should be applied after the basic security templates have been applied. There are four types of incremental templates: compatible, secure, high secure, and dedicated domain controller.

segment   In discussions of Transmission Control Protocol/Internet Protocol (TCP/IP), segment often refers to the group of computers located on one side of a router, or sometimes a group of computers within the same collision domain. In TCP/IP terminology, "segment" can also be used to describe the chunk of data sent by TCP over the network (roughly equivalent to the usage of "packet" or "frame").

Sequenced Packet Exchange (SPX)   The communications protocol (from NetWare) used to control network message transport.

server   The word "server" can take on a variety of different meanings. A server can be a physical computer. Such as "Check out that Server over in the Accounting Department". A server can also represent a particular software package. For example, Microsoft Exchange 2000 is a mail and groupware server application. Often server applications are just referred to as "servers," as in "Check out what the problem is with the mail server." The term "server" is also used to refer to any computer that is currently sharing its resources on the network. In this context, all computers, whether Windows 3x or Windows 2000, can be servers on a network.

service pack   A service pack typically contains bug fixes, security fixes, systems administration tools, drivers, and additional components. Microsoft recommends installing the latest service packs as they are released. In addition, as a new feature in Windows 2000, you do not have to reinstall components after installing a service pack, as you did with Windows NT. You can also see what service pack is currently installed on a computer by running the WINVER utility program. WINVER brings up the About Windows dialog box. It displays the version of Windows and the version of the service pack you are running.

Setup Manager   The Setup Manager is the best tool to use when you have no idea of the answer file syntax or when you do not want to get into the time-consuming task of creating or modifying the sample answer file. When you choose to use the Setup Manager for unattended installations, you need to do a lot of planning beforehand. It is understood that you will not be using Setup Manager for automating installations on one or two computers; that would be a waste of effort. Setup Manager is useful for mass deployments only.

SETUPACT.LOG   The Action log file contains details about the files that are copied during setup.

SETUPAPI.LOG   This log file contains details about the device driver files that were copied during setup. This log can be used to facilitate troubleshooting device installations. The file contains errors and warnings along with a time stamp for each issue.

SETUPCL.EXE   The function of the SETUPCL.EXE file is to run the Mini-Setup Wizard and to regenerate the security IDs on the master and destination computers. The Mini-Setup Wizard starts on the master computer when it is booted for the first time after running Sysprep.

SETUPERR.LOG   The Error log file contains details about errors that occurred during setup.

SETUPLOG.TXT   This log file contains additional information about the device driver files that were copied during setup.

shared folders   Sharing folders so that other users can access their contents across the network is easy in Windows 2000, as easy as right-clicking the folder name in Windows Explorer, selecting the Sharing tab, and choosing Share This Folder. An entire drive and all the folders on that drive can be shared in the same way.

Shared Folders Permission   As only folders, not files, can be shared, Shared Folder Permission is a small subset of standard NT File System (NTFS) permissions for a folder. However, securing access to a folder through share permissions can be more restrictive or more liberal than standard NTFS folder permissions. Shared folder permission is applied in the same manner as NTFS permissions.

shared printers   The process for sharing a printer attached to your local computer is similar to that for sharing a folder or drive. If the users who will access your printer will do so from machines that don't run the Windows 2000 operating system, you will need to install drivers for the other operating system(s).

shared resource   A shared resource is a device, data, or program that is made available to network users. This can include folders, files, printers, and even Internet connections.

simple volume   A simple volume is a volume created on a dynamic disk that is not fault tolerant, and includes space from only one physical disk. A simple volume is just that—it is a single volume that does not span more than one physical disk, and does not provide improved drive performance, extra capacity or fault tolerance. One physical disk can contain a single, large simple volume, or several smaller ones. Each simple volume is assigned a separate drive letter. The number of simple volumes on a disk is limited only by the capacity of the disk and the number of available letters in the alphabet.

Single-Instance-Store (SIS) Volume　When you have more than one image on the Remote Installation Services (RIS) server, each holding Windows 2000 Professional files, there will be duplicate copies of hundreds of files. This may consume a significant hard drive space on the RIS server. To overcome this problem, Microsoft introduced a new feature called the Single-Instance-Store, which helps in deleting all the duplicate files, thus saving on hard drive space.

SIS　*See* Single-Instance-Store.

Site Server Internet Locator Server (ILS) Service　This service supports Internet Protocol (IP) telephony applications, publishes IP multicast conferences on a network, and can also publish user IP address mappings for H.323 IP telephony. Telephony applications, such as NetMeeting and Phone Dialer in Windows Accessories, use Site Server ILS Service to display user names and conferences with published addresses. Site Server ILS Service depends on Internet Information Services (IIS).

small computer system interface (SCSI)　A complete expansion bus interface that accepts such devices as a hard disk, CD-ROM, disk drivers, printers, or scanners.

SMP　*See* Symmetric Multiprocessing.

SMS　*See* Systems Management Server.

SNA　*See* Systems Network Architecture.

spanned volume　A spanned volume is similar to a volume set in NT 4.0. It contains space from multiple disks (up to 32), and provides a way to combine small "chunks" of disk space into one unit, seen by the operating system as a single volume. It is not fault tolerant. When a dynamic volume includes the space on more than one physical hard drive, it is called a spanned volume. Spanned volumes can be used to increase drive capacity, or to make use of the leftover space on up to 32 existing disks. Like those in a basic storage volume set, the portions of a spanned volume are all linked together and share a single drive letter.

SPX   *See* Sequenced Packet Exchange.

stack   A data structure in which the first items inserted are the last ones removed, unlike control structure programs that use the Last In First Out (LIFO) structure.

static Internet Protocol (IP) address   A static IP address allows users to use a domain name that can be translated into an IP address. The static IP address allows the server to always have the same IP address, so the domain name always translates to the correct IP address. If the address was assigned dynamically and occasionally changed, users might not be able to access the server across the Internet using the domain name.

stripe set   The term "striping" refers to the interleaving of data across separate physical disks. Each file is broken into small blocks, and each block is evenly and alternately saved to the disks in the stripe set. In a two-disk stripe set, the first block of data is saved to the first disk, the second block is saved to the second disk, and the third block is saved to the first disk, and so on. The two disks are treated as a single drive, and are given a single drive letter.

stripe set with parity   A stripe set with parity requires at least three hard disks, and provides both increased storage capacity and fault tolerance. In a stripe set with parity, data is interleaved across three or more disks and includes parity (error checking) information about the data. As long as only one disk in the set fails, the parity information can be used to reconstruct the lost data. If the parity information itself is lost, it can be reconstructed from the original data.

striped volume   Like a stripe set in NT 4.0, a striped volume is the dynamic storage equivalent of a basic stripe set and combines free space from up to 32 physical disks into one volume by writing data across the disks in stripes. This increases performance but does not provide fault tolerance. A striped volume improves drive performance and increases drive capacity. Because each data block is written only once, striped volumes do not provide fault tolerance.

striping   Striping is when the data are striped across the drives and there is parity information along with the data. The parity information is based on a mathematical formula that comes up with the parity based on the data on the other drives.

subnetting   Using several data paths to reduce traffic on a network and avoid problems if a single path should fail; usually configured as a dedicated Ethernet subnetwork between two systems based on two network interface cards (NICs).

Symmetric Multiprocessing (SMP)   SMP is a system in which all processors are treated as equals, and any thread can be run on any available processor. Windows 2000 also supports processor affinity, in which a process or thread can specify which set of processors it should run on. Application Programming Interfaces (APIs) must be defined in the application.

synthesis   The process of design, formulation, integration, prediction, proposal, generalization, and show relationships.

Sysprep.inf   Sysprep.inf is an answer file. When you want to automate the Mini-Setup Wizard by providing predetermined answers to all setup questions, you must use this file. This file needs to be placed in the %Systemroot%\Sysprep folder or on a floppy disk. When the Mini-Setup Wizard is run on the computer on which the image is being distributed, it takes answers from the Sysprep.inf file without prompting the user for any input.

System Monitor   The System Monitor is part of this Administrative Tools utility, and allows you to collect and view data about current memory usage, disk, processor utilization, network activity, and other system activity. The System Monitor replaces the Performance Monitor used in Windows NT. System Monitor allows you to collect information about your hardware's performance as well as network utilization. System Monitor can be used to measure different aspects of a computer's performance. It can be used on your own computer or other computers on the network.

system policy   Group policies have mostly replace system policies since group policies extend the functionality of system policies. A few situations still exist in which system policies are valuable. The system policy editor is used to provide user and computer configuration settings in the Windows NT registry database. The system policy editor is still used for the management of Windows 9x and Windows NT server and workstations and stand-alone computers using Windows 2000.

System Preparation (Sysprep)   Sysprep provides an excellent means of saving installation time and reducing installation costs. Sysprep is the best tool to copy the image of a computer to other computers that have identical hardware configurations. It is also helpful in standardizing the desktop environment throughout the organization. Since one Sysprep image cannot be used on computers with identical hardware and software applications, you can create multiple images when you have more than one standard. It is still the best option where the number of computers is in hundreds or thousands and you wish to implement uniform policies in the organization.

Systems Management Server (SMS)   This Windows NT software analyzes and monitors network usage and various network functions.

Systems Network Architecture (SNA)   Systems Network Architecture (SNA) was developed by IBM in the mainframe computer era (1974, to be precise) as a way of getting its various products to communicate with each other for distributed processing. SNA is a line of products designed to make other products cooperate. In your career of designing network solutions, you should expect to run into SNA from time to time because many of the bigger companies (i.e., banks, healthcare institutions, government offices) bought IBM equipment and will be reluctant to part with their investment. SNA is a proprietary protocol that runs over SDLC exclusively, although it may be transported within other protocols, such as X.25 and Token Ring. It is designed as a hierarchy and consists of a collection of machines called nodes.

Take Ownership permission   This permission can be given to allow a user to take ownership of a file or folder object. Every file and folder on an NT File System (NTFS) drive has an owner, usually the account that created the object. However, there are times when ownership of a file needs to be changed, perhaps because of a change in team membership or a set of new responsibilities for a user.

Task-based model   This model is appropriate for companies in which administrative duties are functionally divided. This means that this model divides the management of Group Policy Objects (GPOs) by certain tasks. To apply this model, the administrators that handle security-related tasks will also be responsible for managing all policy objects that affect security. The second set of administrators that normally deploy the companies' business applications will be responsible for all the GPOs that affect installation and maintenance.

TCP/IP   *See* Transmission Control Protocol/Internet Protocol.

Terminal Services   In application server mode, Terminal Services provides the ability to run client applications on the server, while "thin client" software acts as a terminal emulator on the client. Each user sees an individual session, displayed as a Windows 2000 desktop. The server manages each session, independent of any other client session. If you install Terminal Services as an application server, you must also install Terminal Services Licensing (not necessarily on the same computer). However, temporary licenses can be issued for clients that allow you to use Terminal servers for up to 90 days. In remote administration mode, you can use Terminal Services to log on remotely and manage Windows 2000 systems from virtually anywhere on your network (instead of being limited to working locally on a server). Remote administration mode allows for two concurrent connections from a given server and minimizes impact on server performance. Remote administration mode does not require you to install Terminal Services Licensing.

TFTP *See* Trivial File Transfer Protocol.

token ring A local area network (LAN) specification that was developed by IBM in the 1980s for PC-based networks and classified by the (Institute of Electrical and Electronics Engineers) IEEE as 802.5. It specifies a star topology physically and a ring topology logically. It runs at either 4 Mbps or 16 Mbps, but all nodes on the ring must run at the same speed.

Transmission Control Protocol/Internet Protocol (TCP/IP) A set of communications standards created by the U.S. Department of Defense (DoD) in the 1970s that has now become an accepted way to connect different types of computers in networks because the standards now support so many programs.

trees Trees are groups of domains that share a contiguous namespace. They allow you to create a hierarchical grouping of domains that share a common contiguous namespace. This hierarchy allows global sharing of resources among domains in the tree. All the domains in a tree share information and resources with a single directory, and there is only one directory per tree. However, each domain manages its own subset of the directory that contains the user accounts for that domain. So, when a user logs into a domain, the user has global access to all resources that are part of the tree, providing the user has the proper permissions.

Trivial File Transfer Protocol (TFTP) A simplified version of the File Transfer Protocol (FTP), associated with the Transmission Control Protocol/Internet Protocol (TCP/IP) family, that does not provide password protection or a user directory.

trust The users in one tree do not have global access to resources in other trees, but trusts can be created that allow users to access resources in another tree. A trust allows all the trees to share resources and have common administrative functions. Such sharing capability allows the trees to operate independently of each other, with separate namespaces, yet still be able to communicate and share resources through trusts.

trust relationship   A trust relationship is a connection between domains in which users who have accounts in and log on to one domain can then access resources in other domains, provided they have proper access permissions.

UDF   *See* Unique Database File.

UDP   *See* User Datagram Protocol.

Unattended method   The Unattended method for Windows 2000 Server installation uses the answer file to specify various configuration parameters. This method eliminates user interaction during installation, thereby automating the installation process and reducing the chances of input errors. Answers to most of the questions asked by the setup process are specified in the answer file. In addition, the scripted method can be used for clean installations and upgrades.

UNATTEND.TXT   The creation of customized UNATTEND.TXT answer files is the simplest form of providing answers to setup queries and unattended installation of Windows 2000. This can either be done using the Setup Manager or by editing the sample UNATTEND.TXT file using Notepad or the MS-DOS text editor. The UNATTEND.TXT file does not provide any means of creating an image of the computer.

UNATTEND.UDF   This file is the Unique Database File, which provides customized settings for each computer using the automated installation.

UNC   *See* universal naming convention.

UNICODE   UNICODE is a 16-bit character encoding standard developed by the Unicode Consortium between 1988 and 1991 that uses two bytes to represent each character and enables almost all of the written languages of the world to be represented using a single character set.

uninterruptible power supply (UPS)   A battery that can supply power to a computer system if the power fails. It charges while the computer is on and, if the power fails, provides power for a certain amount of time allowing the user to shut down the computer properly to preserve data

Unique Database File (UDF)   When you use the WINNT32.EXE command with the /unattend option, you can also specify a Unique Database File (UDF), which has a .UDB extension. This file forces Setup to use certain values from the UDF file, thus overriding the values given in the answer file. This is particularly useful when you want to specify multiple users during the setup.

universal groups   Universal groups are used in larger, multi-domain organizations, in which there is a need to grant access to similar groups of accounts defined in multiple domains. It is better to use global groups as members of universal groups to reduce overall replication traffic from changes to universal group membership. Users can be added and removed from the corresponding global groups with their account domains, and a small number of global groups are the direct members of the universal group. universal groups are used only in multiple domain trees or forests. A Windows 2000 domain must be in native mode to use universal groups.

Universal Serial Bus (USB)   A low-speed hardware interface (supports MPEG video) with a maximum bandwidth up to 1.5 MBps (megabytes per second).

universal naming convention (UNC)   A UNC is an identification standard of servers and other network resources.

UPS   *See* uninterruptible power supply.

USB   *See* Universal Serial Bus.

user account   The information that defines a particular user on a network, which includes the username, password, group memberships, and rights and permissions assigned to the user.

User Datagram Protocol (UDP)   A Transmission Control Protocol/Internet Protocol (TCP/IP) normally bundled with an Internet Protocol (IP) layer software that describes how messages received reached application programs within the destination computer.

value bar   The value bar is positioned below the graph area. It displays data for the selected sample, the last sample value, the average of the counter samples, the maximum and minimum of the samples, and the duration of time the samples have been taken over.

virtual private network (VPN)   VPNs reduce service costs and long distance/ usage fees, lighten infrastructure investments, and simplify wide area network (WAN) operations over time. To determine just how cost-effective a VPN solution could be in connecting remote offices, use the VPN Calculator located on Cisco's Web site at www.cisco.com.

volume set   The term "volume" indicates a single drive letter. One physical hard disk can contain several volumes, one for each primary partition or logical drive. However, the opposite is also true. You can create a single volume that spans more than one physical disk. This is a good option when you require a volume that exceeds the capacity of a single physical disk. You can also create a volume set when you want to make use of leftover space on several disks by piecing them together as one volume.

VPN   *See* virtual private network.

WDM   *See* Windows32 Drive Model.

Windows 2000   Microsoft's latest incarnation of the corporate operating system was originally called NT 5, but the name was changed to Windows 2000 between the second and third beta versions—perhaps to underscore the fact that this is truly a *new* version of the operating system, not merely an upgrade to NT.

Windows 2000 Control Panel   The Control Panel in Windows 2000 functions similarly to the Control Panel in Windows 9x and NT, except that "under the hood" there are now two locations that information is stored, which is modified by the Control Panel applets. The Control Panel in previous operating systems was a graphical interface for editing registry information.

Windows 3x   Windows 3x changed everything. It was a 16-bit operating system with a user interface that resembled the look and feel of IBM's (at that time not yet released) OS/2, with 3D buttons and the ability to run multiple programs simultaneously, using a method called cooperative multitasking. Windows 3x also provided virtual memory, the ability to use hard disk space to "fool" the applications into behaving as if they had more RAM than was physically installed in the machine.

Windows 9x   In August of 1995, Microsoft released its long-awaited upgrade of Windows, Windows 95. For the first time, Windows could be installed on a machine that didn't already have MS-DOS installed. Many improvements were made: the new 32-bit functionality (although still retaining some 16-bit code for backward compatibility); preemptive multitasking (a more efficient way to run multiple programs in which the operating system controls use of the processor, and the crash of one application does not bring down the others that are currently running); and support for filenames longer than the DOS-based eight-character limit.

Windows Backup   Windows Backup is a built-in Backup and Restore utility, which has many more features than the backup tool provided in Windows NT 4.0. It supports all five types of backup: Normal, Copy, Differential, Incremental, and Daily. Windows Backup allows you to perform the backup operation manually or you may schedule it to run at a later time in unattended mode. Included with the operating system, it is a tool that is flexible and easy to use.

Windows Internet Naming Service (WINS)   WINS provides name resolution for clients running Windows NT and earlier versions of Microsoft operating systems. With name resolution, users can access servers by name, instead of having to use Internet Protocol (IP) addresses that are difficult to recognize and remember. WINS is used to map NetBIOS computer names to IP addresses. This allows users to access other computers on the network by computer name. WINS servers should be assigned a static IP address, which allows clients to be able to find the WINS servers. Clients cannot find a WINS server by name because they need to know where the WINS server is in order to translate the name into an IP address.

Windows Internet Naming Service (WINS) Name Registration   Each WINS client has one or more WINS servers identified in the network configuration on the computer, either through static assignment or through DHCP configuration. When the client boots and connects to the network, it registers its name and IP address with the WINS server by sending a registration request directly to the server. This is not a broadcast message, since the client has the address of the server. If the server is available and the name is not already registered, the server responds with a successful registration message, which contains the amount of time the name will be registered to the client, the time-to-live (TTL). Then the server stores the name and address combination in its local database.

Windows Internet Naming Service (WINS) Name Release   When a WINS client shuts down properly, it will send a name release request to the WINS server. This releases the name from the WINS server's database so that another client can use the name if necessary. The release request contains the WINS name and address of the client. If the server cannot find the name, it sends a negative release response to the client. If the server finds the matching name and address in its database, it releases the name and marks the record as inactive. If the name is found but the address does not match, the server ignores the request.

Windows Internet Naming Service (WINS) Name Renewal   As with Dynamic Host Control Protocol (DHCP), WINS name registrations are temporary and must be renewed to continue to be valid. The client will attempt to renew its registration when half (50 percent) of the time-to-live (TTL) has elapsed. If the WINS server does not respond, the client repeatedly attempts to renew its lease at ten-minute intervals for an hour. If the client still receives no response, it restarts the process with the secondary WINS server, if one is defined. The client will continue attempting to renew its lease in this manner until it receives a response from a server. At that time, the server sends a new TTL to the client and the process starts over.

Windows Internet Naming Service (WINS) proxy agent   A WINS Proxy agent is similar to a Dynamic Host Control Protocol (DHCP) Relay Agent. It listens for requests for non-WINS network clients and redirects those requests to a WINS server. A WINS proxy operates in two modes.

Windows Internet Naming Service (WINS) snap-in   With the snap-in, you can view the active WINS entries under the Active Registrations folder. In addition, you can supply static mappings for non-WINS clients on the network through the snap-in. To configure a static mapping, select the Active Registrations folder and select New Static Mapping from the Action menu. Once a static mapping is entered into the WINS database, it cannot be edited. If you need to make changes to a static mapping, you must be delete and recreate the entry.

Windows NT   The NT kernel (the core or nucleus of the operating system, which provides basic services for all other parts of the operating system) is built on a completely different architecture from consumer Windows. In fact, NT was based on the 32-bit preemptive multitasking operating system that originated as a joint project of Microsoft and IBM before their parting of the ways, OS/2. NT provided the stability and security features that the "other Windows" lacked, albeit at a price, and not only a monetary one; NT was much pickier in terms of hardware support, did not run all of the programs that ran on Windows 9x (especially DOS programs that accessed the hardware directly), and required more resources, especially memory, to run properly.

Windows32 Driver Model (WDM)   The Win32 Driver Model (WDM) provides a standard for device drivers that will work across Windows platforms (specifically Windows 98 and 2000), so that you can use the same drivers with the consumer and business versions of the Windows operating system.

WINNT.EXE program   The WINNT.EXE program is used for network installations that use an MS-DOS network client. The WINNT32.EXE program is used to customize the process for upgrading existing installations. The WINNT32.EXE program is used for installing Windows 2000 from a computer that is currently running Windows 95/98 or Windows NT.

WINS   *See* Windows Internet Naming Service.

workgroup   A workgroup is a logical grouping of resources on a network. It is generally used in peer-to-peer networks. This means that each computer is responsible for access to its resources. Each computer has its own account database and is administered separately. Security is not shared between computers, and administration is more difficult than in a centralized domain.

zones of authority   The Domain Name System (DNS) namespace is divided into zones, and each zone must have one name server that is the authority for the name mapping for the zone. Depending on the size of the namespace, a zone may be subdivided into multiple zones, each with its own authority, or there may be a single authority for the entire zone. For instance, a small company with only 200 to 300 computers could have one DNS server handle the entire namespace.